HOLLYWOOD UNKNOWNS

HOLLYWOOD UNKNOWNS

A History of Extras, Bit Players, and Stand-Ins

Anthony Slide

UNIVERSITY PRESS OF MISSISSIPPI
Jackson

www.upress.state.ms.us

Designed by Peter D. Halverson

The University Press of Mississippi is a member of the Association of American University Presses.

Manufactured in the United States of America

All illustrations are from the author's collection, unless otherwise noted.

First printing 2012
∞
Library of Congress Cataloging-in-Publication Data

Slide, Anthony.
Hollywood unknowns : a history of extras, bit players, and stand-ins / Anthony Slide.
p. cm.
Includes bibliographical references and index.
ISBN 978-1-61703-474-9 (cloth : alk. paper) —
ISBN 978-1-61703-475-6 (ebook) 1. Extras (Actors)—United States.
2. Motion pictures—United States—History—20th century. I. Title.
PN1995.9.E97S55 2012
792.02'80973—dc23 2012005306

British Library Cataloging-in-Publication Data available

THE EXTRA GIRL'S LAMENT

I wonder when he'll cease to say,
"Yes, we have no work today."
Over, and over, and then–again
He brawls this plaintive old refrain;
And smilingly, which hurts the more,
Enquires just what you're looking for.
However quick the framed reply
He'll answer back with twinkling eye,
"Sorry, my friend, nothing doing today."
The same old story in the same old way.

You get a tip from one of your pals,
The Chaplin Lot wants boys and gals.
You walk because you haven't a car
With a job in view it don't seem far.
But there he stands—the man at the gate,
And his greeting is, "Sorry, too late."

It has to break sometime, that's certain
Before the fall of the final curtain;
But if it don't and I must wait
And meet the chap at the Pearly Gate,
I won't be surprised to hear him say,
"Sorry, too late, nothing doing today."

—Anonymous

CONTENTS

Acknowledgments IX

Introduction 3

Chapter One The Extra in the Early Silent Years 18

Chapter Two The 1920s 34

Chapter Three The Hollywood Studio Club 52

Chapter Four Central Casting 62

Chapter Five The Port of Missing Girls 82

Chapter Six The Coming of Sound 98

Chapter Seven The Stand-In 117

Chapter Eight Celebrity Extras 141

Chapter Nine The Silent Star as Extra 156

Chapter Ten Ethnic Extras 187

Chapter Eleven The 1940s, Unionization, and Beyond 205

Chapter Twelve "Extras, Extras, Read All about 'Em" 224

Notes 231

Bibliography 244

Index 255

ACKNOWLEDGMENTS

The impetus for this book was a meeting in 2010 with a lady named Pauline "Polly" Wagner, who was at the time almost one hundred years old, and who was introduced to me by her friend, Steve Vilarino, as Hollywood's oldest extra. To my astonishment, not only was Polly a very personable lady, she was also incredibly intelligent, with a host of stories about her life and career. As an extra and "bit" player, Polly was one of the forgotten "names" in Hollywood. Talking with her, I began to think about the whole spectrum of Hollywood extras, their lives and their histories. And so this book was born.

Years earlier, I had the opportunity to meet with and interview a handful of other individuals, now all deceased, who could be categorized as "extras," although not necessarily throughout their careers. For their memories and their conversations, I am grateful to Paul Bradley, Lila Finn, Bess Flowers, Katherine Ann Porter, and Satini Puailoa, as well as to a handful of leading players: most notably Priscilla Bonner, Norman Lloyd, Doris Nolan, and director Robert Florey, whose reminiscences added to the story. Diana Cary ("Baby Peggy") also spoke with me, but because she plans her own, personal account of life as a Hollywood extra, she was, understandably, unwilling to answer all my questions. Fred Datig talked at length with me about his father, also named Fred Datig, a legendary casting director at Universal, Paramount, and Metro-Goldwyn-Mayer. As a resident of Los Angeles for much of my life,I have otherwise met some of the other extras or characters who people this volume, including Gertrude "Gertie" Astor and Vince Barnett.

As always, my primary resource was the Margaret Herrick Library of the Academy of Motion Picture Arts and Sciences, and I thank the staff there. At the Cinema Library of the University of Southern California, Ned Comstock was as helpful as always. If Ned should ever decide to give up his job as an archivist, he would be the best research assistant in the business. Also at USC: My thanks to Sandra Joy Lee, curator of the Warner

Bros. Archives, and to Marje Schuetze-Coburn, senior associate dean of the Doheny Memorial Library. I also made use of the holdings of the Los Angeles Central Library and the Santa Monica (California) Main Library.

Special thanks to Valerie Yaros at the Screen Actors Guild for making available to me the archives of the Screen Extras Guild.

I must also thank Robert Gitt, Patricia King Hanson, Mike Hawks at Larry Edmunds Bookstore, Marty Kearns, Bruce Long, Jeffrey Richards, Henry T. Sampson, Jr., David Stenn, Kevin Thomas, and Zareh Tjeknavorian. And thanks to Patrick Reynolds, who knows more about computers, it seems, than anyone else in the world, and who has rescued me from the abyss countless times in this horrendous computer age.

Again, I must thank Leila Salisbury, director of the University Press of Mississippi, for her support. Also at Mississippi, I would like to thank Anne Stascavage and Valerie Jones on the editorial staff, and my copy editor Lisa Paddock.

Back in 2000, when John Parris Springer's *Hollywood Fictions: The Dream Factory in American Popular Literature* was published, I described it in a dust jacket blurb as "so good and so original." As I have used it for background information on the extra in fiction, I now realize just how good it really is. My earlier comments fail to do the book justice.

All illustrations are from either the author's collection or the Academy of Motion Picture Arts and Sciences (AMPAS).

HOLLYWOOD UNKNOWNS

INTRODUCTION

"We are the mortar between the bricks," said legendary character actress Beulah Bondi, describing her work and that of her colleagues on screen.[1] If the character player is the mortar and the stars are the bricks, how then may we explain the purpose of extras, "bit" players, and stand-ins? Their performances and their contributions to the films in which they appear—or more rightly the films in which they serve—are seamless. They are the unknown performers, without whom many a project might remain unrealized, but who, with few exceptions, are irrelevant in terms of their names and qualifications. They exist neither in the credits nor (with some not always honorable exceptions) as attention seekers or celebrities. They are neither the mortar nor the bricks; instead, they provide that unknown quantity that is always part of the moviegoing experience and of the moviemaking program. The extras may constitute crowds—occasionally a face in the crowd—or they may be more accurately described as "atmosphere." To a large extent, it is the extra who adds substance to all the non-intimate scenes in a film. Extras endure and survive, and they have done so almost since the beginning of the motion picture. Yet they are both unknown to and unnoticed by their audience and generally by the players that they are hired to support directly or indirectly.

Milton Sills, one of the great dramatic actors of the silent era, came up with a sensible distinction between him and the extra: "The gulf between the 'extra' and the actor is rather wide. It is defined largely by the accolade known in the industry as 'screen credit.'"[2] What Sills ignores is that at times extras add as much, if not more realism to the scene as the actor. Above all, they provided a setting in which the lead players can demonstrate their special talents.

There was a distinct caste system in Hollywood during the silent era. At the studio, stars occupied lavishly furnished bungalows, while extras shared two rooms—one for the women and one for the men—furnished only with wooden benches, one long table, and individual lockers. Relationships among the players were described this way in 1932:

> Stars and featured players mingle freely at work and at play. There is a feeling of intimacy and friendship between them. The important free-lance actor, provided he is accepted as a good fellow, joins this group socially.
>
> Here the line tightens. The "bit" player finds himself just outside. At times he mixes with the star, due usually to a previous association in the old days of pictures or on the stage. He is not "accepted" in the full sense of the word, however.
>
> No law keeps the extra from associating with the important actors. But there is an unwritten rule governing his actions. He stays by himself or with his group on the sets and is rarely invited to social gatherings of the celebrities.[3]

The disparity between star and extra was never more evident than in salary, a disparity comparable today almost to the discrepancy between the take-home pay of workers on an assembly line and that of the CEO. For example, for the Warner Bros. 1944 production *Passage to Marseilles*, the studio hired twenty extras to play convicts. Each worked for a minimum of two weeks and took home a weekly paycheck for $82.50. In contrast, the female star, Michelle Morgan, was hired for a minimum of three weeks at a weekly salary of $3,500.00.[4]

One star of the silent era sympathetic to the plight of the extras was John Barrymore. It is reported that he walked off the set in the middle of the day, leaving a couple of hundred extras with nothing to do. He was not particularly tired, but he was aware that making a living was difficult for extras. By deserting the set, Barrymore guaranteed them another day's work.[5]

The director quickly became cognizant of the relationship between star and extra. When placed in close proximity to a star on the set, the older, more experienced extras would—once the camera began rolling—introduce little pieces of business to draw the audience's attention to themselves. At the same time, there were many kindly leading players who would watch over some of the younger extras, suggesting they keep close to the star in one shot in order to require their presence in the next. Particularly if the scene was being filmed late in the day, the extra would be called back the next day to continue the sequence of shots.

Extras learned, though, to avoid close-ups. Once an extra's face was registered in a close-up, he or she would not be wanted again in the film for fear of audience recognition. It was not for the extra to behave like a character actor, becoming a "film hog" or a "lens louse," monikers given those too cozy with the camera. As Rob Wagner explained in 1918, "Suppose, for instance, that you had appeared in a street scene in France, as a peasant; it wouldn't do to see the same face, a few minutes later, peerin' out of the Tower of London."[6] If an extra was careful, it was said, he or she might appear in every scene of a five-reel production. Extras were equally adept when it came to making an exit from a scene on camera. If one made an exit through a door while the camera was rolling, more than likely that one would be retained to make an entrance through another door in the next scene.

Some basic rules applied to extras on the set. Fred W. Beetson, then president of Central Casting, delineated these rules in 1928:

> An extra must first learn, and constantly practice until she is proficient, the art of make-up. From the moment she enters her first set, she must learn to give explicit and unquestioning obedience to orders from the director and his assistants. She must constantly observe the work of the experienced players about her, and from them learn:
>
> 1. To guard against looking into the camera unless directed to do so, or walking into the camera.
> 2. To remember her position at a given point in the production so that she can later take that same position in the event of a close-up.
> 3. To guard against walking across a scene in such a way as to cover the principals.
> 4. To know the camera range so that in doing a close-up she will not move out of the range.
> 5. To reduce the speed of action from a normal speed to a slower rate which will register in the camera.[7]

As *Photoplay* commented in 1927:

> Without the types [the extras], the majority of pictures could not be made. In the present stage of motion picture making, they are absolutely essential; yet, how little kindness and consideration and justice they receive from those who are so dependent upon them. Millions of words have been prodigally strewn before millions of eyes, describing the many phases of the stars' sugar-coated lives; but our types remain unheralded and unsung. They are mere background. And into the fabric of that background is woven stark and bitter tragedy—the tragedy of living.[8]

It was novelist Theodore Dreiser who succinctly—as succinctly as Dreiser ever could be—summed up the reality of the extra's existence. The extras knew that the majority of shots in which they appeared would never make it to the screen. The stars, the leads and the character players, would intentionally receive the most worthwhile positions in the shot. Ultimately, those who work in atmosphere are never—not even by accident—seen to advantage on the screen. As one commentator wrote in the late 1920s, extras would encounter "poverty, pathos and perversity in this fabulous paradise of prosperity, plenty and prodigality."[9]

Most commonly, extras were the mainstay of the "crowd picture," about which Vachel Lindsay wrote in 1916. According to Lindsay, at that time crowd pictures were best represented by D. W. Griffith's one-reel short, *The Battle* (1911), and by the George Beban vehicle, *The Italian* (1915), in which extras were chosen to represent Italian crowds in a recreation of Venice and then as inhabitants of a New York ghetto. And it was Lindsay who noted that the most prominent crowd picture, a film as important in the art and theory of the motion picture as in its use of extras, is *The Birth of a Nation*. It is "a Crowd Picture in a triple sense," wrote the always-perceptive Lindsay. "On the film, as in the audience, it turns the crowd into a mob that is either for or against the Reverend Thomas Dixon's poisonous hatred of the Negro."[10]

In *The Birth of a Nation*, D. W. Griffith introduces some interesting parallel casting, with leading players assigned extra roles that touch upon or correlate with their other appearances in the film. Jennie Lee, who plays the faithful Negro retainer of the Cameron family, also has a bit part early in the film as an abolitionist who is greatly moved by the plight of the Negro slaves. George Siegmann, who plays Silas Lynch, the black leader who seeks to destroy "white" Piedmont, is also the leader of the Confederate soldiers who rescue the town from an attack by a renegade Negro band. And Robert Harron, who plays Stoneman's younger son, is also, in blackface, the Negro soldier who arrests Dr. Cameron and arranges his humiliation. The casting may be nothing more than a private joke on Griffith's part, but it raises an interesting academic question as to the manner in which actors can—and obviously did— portray conflicting roles in the same production.

In later years, the crowd picture was more often than not the province of director Michael Curtiz, who was as cavalier with his extras as Cecil B. DeMille apparently was. "He just naturally loves to work with mobs," wrote producer Hal Wallis in a studio memorandum.[11] Perhaps Curtiz's most abusive, almost violent, confrontation with extras took place during the filming of *Noah's Ark* (1929) at Warner Bros. (see Chapter Two, below). Both Curtiz and DeMille, it seems, experienced a feeling of power that came from having a crowd of extras at their command. Both were autocratic when faced with a mass of anonymous extras. Brutal treatment of masses of extras on the set has become synonymous with these two directors.

Stories relating to DeMille's treatment of extras are legendary—and often, perhaps apocryphal. As illustrated in trailers for various productions, from his vantage point high above crowds of extras in one costume film or another, he would excoriate them for wearing wristwatches or for sporting modern hairstyles. Perhaps the most famous confrontation between DeMille and an extra took place on the set of *North West Mounted Police* (1940). Addressing a company of five hundred consisting largely of extras, he insisted upon absolute quiet. After a couple of minutes, he noticed that one female extra was whispering to another. He ordered the culprit to come to the platform upon which he was seated and to tell the entire company what she had said. Eventually, she revealed her comment: "I wonder what time the old baboon is going to let us go to lunch?" The assembled company howled with laughter, and DeMille responded, "Right now."[12]

It might seem a spurious argument to many, but DeMille's response may well illustrate an innate respect for his extras. As he explained during the making of *Cleopatra* in 1934, "We take 1,000 extras and break them into groups of 100, each under an assistant director. Those groups are split into tens, each under a competent actor. The scene is explained and every man and woman has a definite role to play, a definite thing to do. You may not believe it, and most audiences never notice it, but some of my finest actors are extras."[13]

DeMille always took time with his extras. In 1924 he pointed out, "The extra's only opportunity lies in his application when he is called to work. They should study closely the experienced actors' technique—instead, when not in a scene, they stroll off, talking. Even when they work, they are too often inattentive."[14] The director told of a young man with a good personality and a wonderful physique and grace, whom DeMille was considering using in bit parts. But the extra failed to pay attention to his would-be mentor and was dropped. Surprisingly, it is a tale often told about the silent era—of extras unwilling to devote themselves to their craft, who act like automatons, who in mob scenes would hide behind the scenery, knowing they would not be missed.

Working on *The Golden Bed* in 1925, DeMille attempted to inspire his extras:

> Now, ladies and gentlemen, I know it's cold and the lights hurt our eyes and it is tiresome standing around—but let's forget all that and show Keokuk a real Hollywood party. Let's have life, action, enjoyment. . . . I said *enjoyment*! I can almost see the hearse, the heads lowered, the hats off. I can hear the tum-tum- ta-tum. Enjoyment! Laughter! On the screen teeth mean laughter. I don't care how you feel—show your teeth and I'll get what I want.[15]

Pauline Wagner recalls, "Every single scene, he'd gather the cameraman, the propman. Every single person that was working for him had to come in front of him and he told them every single thing about the scene. You had to sit there, and this would take over an hour, sometimes even longer, because he went into detail."[16] Extras were nonetheless anxious to appear under DeMille's direction, so much so that in the summer of 1937, some six hundred rioted at Paramount when only half their number was selected to be interviewed for participation in *The Buccaneer* (1938).

One director who was much liked by extras was W. S. "Woody" Van Dyke, whose credits include *White Shadows in the South Seas* (1928), *The Thin Man* (1934), and *San Francisco* (1936). He was known as "one take Van Dyke," with perhaps little time for niceties. But as Minta Durfee, a silent actress turned extra recalled, "He always showed great personal concern for the extras."[17]

By the mid 1910s, extras had become proficient at understanding how individual directors behaved, knowing these men's whims, their fancies and their weaknesses. Extras noted which directors might reduce a female member of their group to tears and those who would pick upon the weaker members of the fraternity. Extras quickly determined that they had means at their disposal to obtain revenge, methods for ensuring that a scene played badly or that a star found herself suddenly out-positioned by her supporting players.

While extras, bit players, and stand-ins are here grouped together, linked by a common thread of anonymity, they must of necessity be considered as separate groups—at least during the formative years of the motion picture. First came the extras, then the bit players, and finally the stand-ins. The members of each group are strongly interconnected in that extras might become bit players, and both extras and bit players might ultimately move on to be stand-ins for the stars. All might in the fullness of time become if not stars, at least leading men and women. Even stunt persons began as extras, with the ability to perform a stunt little more than a requirement for being

Director Cecil B. DeMille demonstrates to an extra how a yoke of bricks should be carried on the set of *The Ten Commandments* (1956).

an extra, along with ability to dance or to ride a horse. But by the 1930s, these stunt persons had become screen performers in their own right.

In 1925, *Photoplay* described the elite of film extras as "Hollywood's 400." They were all relatively young, "beautiful film ornaments, haughtily graceful, well-dressed and handsome—but as superfluous to the conflict of forces in the drama as the oil paintings on the wall."[18] The "Hollywood 400," however, represented only a small percentage of the extras that the film industry might require for specific roles. They would have to be not only young—sometimes children—but often old. They might need to be bearded and to have a variety of ethnic backgrounds—"racials," they were called. They might need to be ice skaters or genuine cowboys. With the coming of sound,

Some of the 1,500 extras on location for *Gunga Din* (1939) pause for a tea break. AMPAS.

an extra might well need to have a voice—not a specific voice but one that could be part of an ensemble singing, screaming, or booing.

The number of extras actually working on a given production bore, in all probability, little connection to the number of extras that studio publicity might claim to be on the set. Extras were an inexhaustible commodity as far as studio publicists were concerned. Their number would increase in proportion to the scope and size of the production. No audience member was present to count just how many were present in a given scene, and nobody in the studio accounting office was going to provide financial figures as to the numbers actually working on a given day. When the *Los Angeles Times* reported that more than five hundred extras were at work on the George Arliss vehicle *Voltaire* (1933),[19] who could dispute the claim of a legitimate newspaper? If the studio press book claimed that one thousand extras were providing background for scenes shot in Yuma, Arizona, for *Suez* (1938), or that 1,500 men were appearing in the final battle footage of *Gunga Din*

(1939), who was there to argue with this "fact"?[20] Did the reported 350 extras watching Ingrid Berman burn at the stake in *Joan of Arc* (1948) outnumber those at the actual execution? Did two hundred extras really make the journey from Hollywood to the Mojave Desert for *Tension at Table Rock* (1956)? The heaviest use of extras in modern times was for the parade sequence in 20th Century-Fox's *Hello, Dolly!* (1969), with some sixteen units comprised of 657 persons passing amidst 3,108 extras. The only comparable sequence on the same lot was the funeral of Queen Victoria staged for *Cavalcade* (1933), which boasted three thousand extras.

Hollywood extras came from all walks of life—and many had known former (and better) careers. Among the extras appearing in George Cukor's 1933 production of *Sylvia Scarlet* are: former silent leading man Gaston Glass; the first wife of Rudolph Valentino, Jean Acker; an early flyer, Major John Farrell; Beth Taylor, the sister of actress Laurette Taylor; Russian painter Yasha Louie; and a minor former film director named Mel Forrester.

The extras are the cowboys walking around town or riding in the sheriff's posse, who, because such extras would hang out at a Hollywood drugstore rather than on the prairie, gained the soubriquet of "drugstore cowboys." These extras were generally acknowledged to be the most clannish of the group. Extras are the various types, both male and female, inhabiting the dance hall or the ballroom. They can be noble Romans or ignoble convicts. They can be well dressed or shabby. They can work six days in seven or one day in six months. Their hiring occurred initially at the whim of the casting director or the assistant director. For the women, sexual harassment was part of the hiring process. One industry commentator in 1919 wondered if extra work could be anything but "an alibi for prostitution."[21] These female extras were "movie moths—poor, fragile, lovely creatures drawn to this lamp of fortune, fluttering dizzily about it and so apt to be singed before they are through."[22] Little wonder the term "moth" quickly became synonymous with those female extras known to perform "favors."

There were what might be described as "amateur" extras, those who did it not for the money but for the "fun" of being in a movie. In the early years, this group was dominated by members of the social set, perhaps wintering in Los Angeles, a change of scene from their East Coast mansions. All a studio had to do was contact the social secretaries, and their employers would rush over to whatever set they were told to report to, all dressed up in their finest gowns and jewelry.

The attitude of commentators in fan magazines, trade papers, and the popular press, was generally positive and sympathetic towards the

Hollywood extra. One major exception was the influential critic Otis Ferguson, writing in 1941 in *The New Republic*:

> The Hollywood bureaucracy is an inhuman and absurd machine second only to that of the various bureaus in Washington, no doubt about that. But there is one problem the extras have in general. The problem is themselves. In general they constitute no class of agriculturally or industrially dispossessed; they are not victims of geographical disaster; they are not skilled workers preempted by the Machine. They have converged on the town in swarms, attracted by the smell of easy money—which some of them have enjoyed in former times and latterly fallen out of.
>
> But the main trouble with them in common is a lack of ambition, of willingness, of worth in the thing they are doing. . . . It is not pointed out that their pay when they work is three to thirty times that of unskilled labor anywhere in the world.[23]

The lives of Hollywood extras fascinated fan magazine writers to such an extent that in November 1932, *Screenland* thought it necessary to inform its readership breathlessly that extras would fake the murmur of conversation in films with the words "wah-wah-wah." However, the story of the Hollywood extra is more a story of tragedy than of elation. It might be easy to reject the hardships of life as an extra by simply acknowledging that it was self-induced suffering. Some extras had boundless enthusiasm and, at least at the beginning, a belief in themselves and their potential for success. At the same time, many went to work each day—or on those days when they had employment—because being an extra was a job, a job for life with which they were content and from which they expected no promotion.

The most sorrowful of stories relating to an extra has nothing to do with pay or treatment on the set. It involves an elderly woman who died during the filming of Thomas H. Ince's *Civilization* (1916). Her distraught husband would nightly visit the theatre where the film was being shown in the hope of seeing his wife on screen. He had no photograph of his loved one. "That is the other side of the 'extra's' life—the side we do not see on the screen; the side they are apt to forget who so readily traduce the character of those of whom they know nothing."[24] And then there is the tragedy of a particular aged couple. Only the husband was employed. On the set of *Intolerance* (1916), assistant Joseph Henabery noticed that one elderly male extra did not eat his lunch with the crowd, instead moving over to the fence that surrounded the lot. "On the outside of the fence, near the old man, was an old woman. He was sharing his food with her."[25]

Almost the only positive, enduring, and endearing look at the world of the Hollywood extra was the comic strip "Ella Cinders," written by William Conselman and drawn by Charlie Plumb, which followed the adventures of a young star-struck girl. It began syndicated publication on June 1, 1925, and was adapted as a motion picture, starring Colleen Moore, in 1926. Of the latter, Robert E. Sherwood wrote in *Life* (July 1, 1926): "There is a great need for more pictures like *Greed, The Last Laugh* and *Ella Cinders*. They serve to remind us that life is not all beer and skittles."

Among silent stars who began as extras are Evelyn Brent, Joan Crawford, Louise Fazenda, Mae Marsh, Seena Owen, Norma Shearer, Ruth Stonehouse, George Walsh, Claire Windsor, and Lois Wilson. Clark Gable was an extra and bit player in silent films (clearly recognizable, for example, as a college student in the Clara Bow vehicle, *The Plastic Age* [1925]) until he became a star with the advent of sound. Another star of the sound era, Gary Cooper, was an extra in a handful of films, including one unidentified Tom Mix production. In the 1920s, Myrna Loy made the successful transition from extra (often in Oriental roles) to supporting player, and moved on to stardom in the 1930s. Rudolph Valentino was an extra—usually appearing as a dancer—in at least five films and one serial between 1914 and 1917 before moving on to small, credited roles. Both Norma Talmadge and Florence Vidor began as extras and were spotted because of their performance in the same extra role, that of a young girl in the tumbril with the leading man on his way to the guillotine during the French Revolution in the 1911 Vitagraph and 1917 Fox production of *A Tale of Two Cities*. Ultimately, both extras were to become more famous, in retrospect, than the leading men in the films, respectively Maurice Costello and William Farnum. The most famous of stars, both silent and sound, who began as an extra was Greta Garbo, who did so in her native Sweden.

In 1928, Central Casting Corporation published a definitive listing of twenty-nine former extras who had graduated in the previous year to the ranks of screen personalities or stars. Several on the list are now totally forgotten, but among those with at least some name recognition today—primarily with film buffs—are William Bakewell, Sue Carol, Sally Eilers, Jeanette Loff, James Murray, and David Rollins.[26] During the sound era, Lana Turner was the best-known example of an extra becoming a star. And there were others, including George Hamilton, Alan Ladd, and Lee Marvin.

Rudolph Valentino is clearly recognizable as an extra looking over star Jack Pickford's shoulder in *Seventeen* (1916). AMPAS.

Unfortunately, the fact that some extras worked their way up to be stars did not guarantee a similar ladder to success for the countless young women flocking to Hollywood in the 1920s. Too many would-be stars not only lacked intelligence, but were, in all probability, mentally handicapped. As Mary Pickford explained in 1923, "Success cannot be governed by set rules or bound by conventions. While hard work will help immeasurably to achieve it, it is in no sense a guarantee."[27]

In the industry's formative years, both the American Biograph Company and the Vitagraph Company of America boasted a stock company of players who, from week to week and film to film, might be cast both as extras and as leading players. It might well be argued that the practices of early American producers such as these, with all players equal in status and pay, belie the very notion of the "extra." Financial common sense determined that producers should have stock companies, but that same financial acumen had by the 1910s determined that it was pointless to keep bit players and the like under contract. At the same time, the rise of the star system ensured that nobody of such stature was going to appear in a film supporting another star or leading player.

It was not uncommon for fan magazines to single out individual extras as potential star material, but seldom if ever did the hopes and aspirations of the players and the magazine writers become reality. Typical of such pieces is "Climbing the Mary Pickford Ladder" in the October 1922 issue of *Photoplay*; not one of the extras photographed for the feature became a "name." When a fan magazine did get it right, as in *Photoplay*'s January 1924 piece, "Extra! Extra!," it did so because some of the players under discussion had actually already been featured on screen. The extras featured here, sisters Helene and Dolores Costello, also had a famous father, Maurice Costello.

It might seem politically incorrect to refer to the female extras as "girls," but such was their description—at least through the silent era. Extras from eighteen through thirty-five were always "girls." After thirty-five, the girls became "extra women."[28]

At what point in film history did the extra or the bit player arrive? It is a difficult if not impossible to determine an exact time, as the answer lies in the year and month when the motion picture stopped consisting of just one or two players appearing in front of a camera. In 1895, the Lumière Brothers produced one of the earliest of narrative films in *L'arroseur arrosé/The Waterer Watered*, in which a young boy stands on a hose pipe preventing the flow of water. The gardener looks down the hose, the boy steps off the pipe, and the older man is drenched with water. It is a simplistic, one-scene, one-joke farce with two leading players—"stars" if you will—and no one appearing in even a secondary supporting role. But even before *L'arroseur arosé*, in 1894, Louis and August Lumière made their first film, *Workers Leaving the Lumière Factory*, in which it might be argued the entire company performs as extras. At the same time, one must question whether individuals in a film constitute extras when there are no stars for them to support.

There are at least two other Lumière films dating from 1895 that arguably incorporate extras. *L'arrivé du train en gare/The Arrival of a Train at the Station* has principal players, consisting of a little girl, her mother, and a nurse on the platform, where they are engulfed by passengers, the extras. In *Partie d'écarté/The Lonely Party*, three card players drinking beer and playing cards are the central characters, or stars, while the servant is very much an extra. One's sense of the servant's role as an extra is underscored by producer Louis Lumière's identification of the beer drinking-card playing trio as his father, father-in-law, and conjuror/employee Felicien Trewey, while the servant is simply that—a family servant without a name.[29] But it is in France during the silent era, at least in my opinion, that one finds arguably the best and, in its context, most extensive use of extras. In *L'Argent/Money* (1929), director Marcel L'Herbier gathers two thousand extras on the actual floor of the Paris stock exchange, *le bourse*, filming them in unconventional style with a camera which circles around over the group and then falls quickly down towards them.

To document the earliest American production with extras is an exercise in futility, marred by the problem of determining what is an extra and what is a genuine fictional film as opposed to one focused on reality. Intended for viewing on a kinetoscope, rather than on a screen, it may well be that *Indian War Council* (aka *War Council*), produced by Thomas Edison at his West Orange, New Jersey, plant in September 1894 is the first American film employing extras. Here, in a subject that consists of a mere fifty feet of film, Buffalo Bill stars, surrounded by a group of extras comprising Sioux Indian warriors and white men. While not actually produced by Edison, but rather licensed by him, the *Passion Play of Oberammergau*, filmed between December 1897 and January 1898 and three reels in long, is in all probability the first full-length American (it was shot in New York, not Oberammergau) production to incorporate extras. Frank Russell as Christ is the star, and the extras are considerable in number. The earliest Edison-produced film using extras is (again arguably) *Cripple Creek Bar-Room Scene*, shot in March and April of 1899. The principal players in the fifty-foot long subject are a barmaid and a "rough miner," while three card players in the background are extras.

It would be impossible not to discuss Edison's *The Great Train Robbery*, produced in November 1903. The one-reel subject boasts a large number of star players, including the head bandit, the murdered passenger (played by Max Aronson, later to become George M. "Broncho Billy" Anderson), and the sheriff. The film even has a number of what might be described as supporting players, such as the signal operator, the train conductor, the fireman, the telegraph operator, and his daughter (one of America's first child performers). The extras here are passengers on the train that is being robbed, bandits, and the sheriff's posse.

The extras in *The Great Train Robbery* come from the ranks of Edison's employees. Within a few short years, extras were more than likely to be recruited from the theatre. And just as the motion picture borrowed many of its earliest players from the legitimate stage, so did it appropriate the term "extra," which had been used in the theatrical community since the 1880s, if not earlier. While an "extra" in newspaper argot refers to a special edition, something of importance, an "extra" on stage or screen is someone who is extraneous or irrelevant to the production. As far as can be ascertained, in theatrical circles the term "extra" was first used not on the legitimate stage but in vaudeville, denoting a part not requiring a voice and played by someone who was not a regular member of the vaudeville company.

At least as far back as the 1940s, Hollywood Extra was the name given to a cleansing cold cream, more properly called "Hollywood Extra Theatrical Cold Cream," a product popular with everyone in the theatrical and motion picture acting profession, including extras. By 1929, the term "extra" had taken on another meaning, that of dull or boring, as it was used in A. A. Milne's 1931 play, *Two People*. To a large extent, dull or boring might also be used to summarize life on the set for most extras. The glamor and excitement of Hollywood was something that eluded them. "The reason why they are called 'extra' girls," quipped *Photoplay* in 1920, "is because of the extra amount of work that one had to do. The only thing that isn't extra is the pay."[30]

Chapter One

THE EXTRA IN THE EARLY SILENT YEARS

The extras on screen have their antecedents in the extras on the stage, the "supernumeraries" or "supers," as they were commonly known. In the 1800s, these supers earned fifty cents a performance.[1] Supernumerary has a meaning of surplus, in excess of the number needed (here to put on a play). These were "types"—anything from a Roman citizen to a member of high society—hired locally by touring companies specifically and only for the roles they were assigned. The screen extra, however, is in many ways not comparable to stage supers. On the New York stage or as members of the companies of major regional theatres, the latter were definitely a part of the theatrical family, actors on the way up or on the way down. They might have been treated with little respect by their colleagues with speaking roles, but they were, nonetheless, members of the theatrical profession. The first screen extras, in contrast, had no background in film, no experience as actors. Rather, they were individuals transfixed by the glamor of the movies and the possibility of not only being part of a scene but, more importantly, of being spotted and offered a real role.

As one early commentator put it, the studios attracted "the aged and the infant, the educated and the illiterate, the professional and the amateur." All might have earned a better living picking lemons or selling newspapers.[2] One widow, who at the age of twenty-six decided to try for work in the movies, commented that in the 1910s extras—at least those in the New York area—might be divided into four leading types:

> One of these is the chorus girl or man who wants to make a little money on the side. The second is the actor or actress of the legitimate stage waiting for an engagement. Next comes the woman who is bored with life. And last is the wife or daughter of the small-salaried man, who uses the screen as the magic to bring her the gold-mesh bag, the ostrich plume, or any of the little frivolities that Home Sweet Home will not provide.[3]

Harry Carr, a prominent writer both for the fan magazines and with the *Los Angeles Times*, placed extras in various other categories. There were the daughters of once well-to-do stockbrokers, whose fathers' financial empires had suddenly collapsed. Such women automatically owned the correct wardrobe for scenes involving society types and, even better, knew how to behave in society as depicted on screen. Some extras were genuine members of European royalty, whose regimes had ended along with World War One. It was reported that financially strapped members of the British nobility—among them individuals identified as Sir and Lady Poppem Young and Lady Sackville West—would pretend to be appearing on screen as a novelty or a "lark," but in reality such work provided their only source of income. Having once been a footman to the Duke of Connaught furnished John Holmes Howell with his impressive knowledge of how the aristocracy behaved—and this experience provided him with a Hollywood career as an extra and as an adviser for some films.

More unusual extras included: a boy, who was employed because he could roll his eyes upwards until the pupils entirely disappeared, suggesting that he was blind; a Dr. J. S. Garthwait, who had been a physician with the Grand Central Railroad and worked as an extra because he wanted

Male extras enter their dressing room at the Fox Studios in Hollywood, circa 1917.

something to do in retirement; and novelist Gertrude Atherton's niece, Jane Atherton. A successful extra named Jack Odin was supposedly in a former life a well known opera star. One ex-cowboy was renowned for looking like Jesus Christ—or at least like Americans believed Jesus looked. Another extra was a well-educated, church-going San Francisco society girl who would only play prostitutes. One gentlemen from Texas, who was much in demand as a type, told producer Thomas H. Ince's casting director Horace Williams that he was looking for a new outlet in the movies, "because, seh, Ahm tired of shooting up niggers."[4]

In 1920, Louis M. Goodstadt, casting director with Famous Players-Lasky, noted the number of French and British military officers, injured during World War One and now working extra at the studio. Other notables included: a former valet to General Lord Kitchener; defrocked preachers; a former Tammany Hall leader; a seventy-year-old former US consul general to Peru, a former Texas Ranger; a six-feet-nine-inch tall, 350-pound former US naval officer; Oxford University graduates; and numerous former members of the Royal Northwest Mounted Police. Goodstadt also described "Two daughters of a New York banker who was overwhelmed by adversity . . . . They were later joined by their mother. Now, altho their father has regained his footing, they enjoy the game too well to quit." He continued: "When a lady of the aggressive business type is required a former woman president of an Illinois bank is called on. Shot at in a quarrel by her cashier, she was so upset that she pulled up stakes and came to California. She has made good as an extra, as she did as a business woman."[5]

Indulgent eating scenes required the presence of "Appetite Bill," who boasted that he could eat nine pies in one sitting. He was also capable of "leaning on air," planting his feet firmly on the ground while moving his body in a circular motion. V. Higgins, a young man in his twenties who looked to be in his forties, was noted for his full beard and specialized in portraying "Rough Men of the Great Outdoors." A former beachcomber named "Beach Pete" found sufficient work as an extra in that category. "Old Pop" Purdy was in demand to play judges, and because he wore false teeth and was willing to take them out as required, he was often cast in what was described as "Si Perkins stuff," in which a group of garrulous and toothless old men would sit around shooting the breeze. One extra, identified to history merely as "Mary" (probably Mary McConnell), was considered the best scrub-lady of the 1920s.[6]

It was not unusual for entire families to appear as extras, often working together at the same studio. Some even argued that the employment of

In the early years of the twentieth century, S. S. Simon was the head of several oil companies and worth many millions of dollars. By 1937, his fortune had gone, and he was working as an extra in Paramount's *Souls at Sea*.

an entire family by a producer made for stability and harmony. As a result, members of the same family might work together but in different capacities: "Your wardrobe mistress may be the wife of your leading-man, whose sons may be anything from an artist to a property boy, or an assistant director to a camera-man, of even the exalted and exclusive scenario writer."[7] What was true in the 1910s was also the norm in the 1920s. At MGM, extras would report to the casting office, where the window was manned by Billy Joy, described as "unfailingly polite." Joy's sister was leading lady/star Leatrice Joy.

One very active extra was Mrs. Trebaol, whose thirteen children worked as extras, too. She might also have drawn her husband into studio service had he not disappeared some years earlier. "She issued a challenge to

Some of the Trebaol children, supporting Will Rogers and Mary Alden in *Honest Hutch* (1920).

the studios, 'What is Your Picture Without a Trebaol?' and with her offspring fairly oozing from the battered old family automobile, she started the rounds of the studios."[8] There were at least five documented Trebaol children: Edouard/Edward (?–1944), Francois (1910–96), Yves (1906–74), Jeanette, and Marie. Edouard, Yves, and Jeanette appear together as siblings in the 1920 Will Rogers vehicle *Honest Hutch*. A similar family, the Weidlers, was busy in the 1930s. The youngest, Virginia (1927–68), was fairly well known, with prominent roles in *Mrs. Wiggs of the Cabbage Patch* (1934), *The Women* (1939), and *The Great Man Votes* (1939). Working in a minor capacity on screen were her siblings George (born 1926), Walt (born 1924), Warner (born 1923), Verena (born 1921), and Sylvia (born 1919).

Many mothers in Hollywood exploited their children as extras, much as many mothers today appear to exploit their heavily made-up, glamorized, and ludicrously-costumed children in so-called talent contents. Indeed, one writer criticized movie mothers of the 1910s for the manner in which their children were paraded "and dressed up to resemble bisque dolls."[9] In all probability, many of the children working at Hollywood studios were better cared for and protected than they would have been had they been kept at home.

Producer Thomas H. Ince, who relied upon stock players as often as he hired extras, was obsessed with what he described as the "type" actor. For ballroom scenes, for example, the players had to know how to wear good clothes and display an understanding of polite society. Elderly actors were generally preferred to sport whiskers and white hair. But these same actors need not apply to play "old soldier types." Such characters were hired by Ince from the Soldiers' Home in Sawtelle (now the Sawtelle Veterans Hospital) in the Westwood area of Los Angeles. "The old soldiers get a lot of fun out of their work in the pictures, besides the money that we pay them," Ince noted. "These old soldiers are the real article. They require no make-up, their uniforms are correct in every detail, and they bring an 'atmosphere' to the picture that we could not get with professional actors."[10]

The residents in Sawtelle were also useful if a Civil War drama was being filmed, in that many of them had actually seen active duty in the war and could provide technical assistance. There is a story about one veteran who timidly approached a director to make a suggestion. He was curtly dismissed. If the director had listened he would have avoided a costly retake and learned that privates in the Civil War did not salute their officers in the same fashion as prevailed in the 1910s.[11] One veteran from the Civil War, Tim Gullivan, was en route to the Soldiers Home when he came across a film crew on location. He was asked if he would like to work in a scene. He did, and he never made it to the retirement facility, instead working on screen until his demise.

Ince declared that female extras were in greatest demand for society scenes. "As a rule these women types average forty-five to sixty-five years, and the whiter the hair and the more aristocratic their appearance, the more favored they are in the matter of engagements and renumeration."[12] Ince paid his extras five dollars a day. He recalled one extra in the William S. Hart feature, *The Silent Man* (1917), who demanded ten dollars a day at the end of an evening's filming. Why, asked Ince. Because I am one of the fellows who walked into the saloon, replied the man. Sarcastically, Ince asked if the extra expected twenty dollars to walk out of the saloon. "Anyway you want to look at it suits me," replied the extra. "But if you don't pay me ten dollars a day I won't report for duty tomorrow morning—and, remember, I am one of the fellows who walked into the saloon!"[13]

At least through 1918, Ince actually kept a card index of all the various "types" of extras. Here he recorded all manner of extras, short, fat, and lean—as well as those with special features, such as crossed eyes, missing front teeth, and even humpbacked men, who, he explained, were difficult to find because generally they were sensitive to their deformity and did not wish to capitalize upon it.[14]

In the early 1910s, not all studios hired extras directly. A gentleman by the name of "General" Ted Breton operated a business in New York providing extras for most of the local studios. He would hire individuals at $1.25 a day and then transport them, en masse, to the appropriate producer—a process that often included ferrying extras from New York across the Hudson River to Fort Lee or the New Jersey Palisades.[15] The initial notion of maintaining a stock company began to fade by the late 1910s, as producers realized that it was cheaper to hire extras by the day than retain them under contract by the week, month, or year. This was not always a reliable decision in that stock players knew how to act in front of the camera, but many extras, applying for work for the first time, did not. A stock company player could afford the luxury of tram fare to the studio, but the extra might make the trip on foot, walking for miles and arriving physically exhausted. And an extra without a steady source of income might very well resort to dishonesty on the studio lot, stealing from the producers or from his fellow extras.

An article from 1915 in *Motion Picture Magazine* identifies a number of extras working at the Essanay Studios in Chicago: Eva Campbell, Agnes Henkel, Madge Kearns, Alice McChessey, and Marie MacDonald. The piece does not mention two prominent and very different literary figures who enjoyed early careers at Essanay: gossip columnist Louella Parsons, who worked there as a story editor at the beginning of her career, and novelist Katherine Anne Porter (1890–1980). In the early 1970s, Ms. Porter recalled for me that she was a reporter at the *Chicago Tribune* when she visited the Essanay Studios, "just an awful-looking place," in search of a story. Finding two rows of people lined up before a large door, she pushed into one of the lines and moved along with it. Finally, the studio manager called her out of line and directed her to a dressing room, where planks served as benches and make-up tables and a pile of clothing lay in the middle of the center of the room. "You should have been as green as I was," commented Porter. "I had been elected to be an extra." She watched as the girl next to her (whom she later identified as Gloria Swanson) made up, and then began to use the other girl's lipstick. Politely but firmly, she was told to give it back and bring her own tomorrow. The assembled extras were called on stage to appear in a courtroom scene, and each received five dollars.

"I forgot all about having the job at the newspaper until five or six days later," said Porter. When she did return, she was fired, but Essanay kept her on as an extra for six months. She was nicknamed "Little Blue Boy," because she was one of the few girls there with short hair. As she recalled, "The company raised me little by little, and by the time I was ready to go, I was making twelve dollars a day." Her movie career ended when she declined the opportunity to go with the company to the West Coast. Hollywood "was just what I thought," she told me. "I was right to stay away. There wasn't one thing I saw there that was good for me."[16]

One identifiable male extra and bit player at Essanay in the mid 1910s was George Sherwood, who was later a theatrical producer and the husband of silent screen star Pauline Starke.

In the 1910s, the salaries paid to extras were relatively uniform from one studio to another, although there were always studios dubbed "cheap sets" where the pay was poor. If the extra was expected to work through the night, he or she would be lucky to receive an additional dollar and a basic meal. In 1915, *Motion Picture Magazine* put the salaries paid to extras at between only one dollar and $2.50 a day.[17] "Day checks," indicating the extra was hired by the day and not by the film, were the norm. Extras working for D. W. Griffith on *The Birth of a Nation* in 1914 were paid $1.10 a day. For *Intolerance*, a year later, Griffith paid $1.25, plus lunch. The latter film provided employment for between 2,500 and 3,000 extras.

As might be imagined, it was difficult to manage the large number of extras working on the massive *Intolerance* set, so much so that some forty Babylonian warriors were able to leave the set during the shoot to play cards and smoke cigarettes on the walls of Babylon, even as the Persians were banging on the gates to the city. "No wonder they got in," joked Rob Wagner.[18] Griffith's assistant on the film, Joseph Henabery, was less sympathetic. He blamed the problem on the IWW (International Workers of the World or The Wobblies) and threw the organization out of the studio.[19]

The IWW was behind the formation of the short-lived International Union of Photoplayers of America in the spring of 1916. The organization advocated strikes at both at the Griffith lot and at Universal, where extras had unsuccessfully attempted a strike the previous year. The impetus for the strike at Griffith was not Henabery's abrupt dismissal of a group of extras, but rather a claim that male extras had been ordered to strip nude and work in the hot sun for one dollar a day.[20] Whether such male nudity was demanded is a mystery, as the only nudity in *Intolerance* is limited to harem scenes, in which it is believed that prostitutes rather than typical extras were used. Of course, the use of the word "nude" does not necessarily imply being naked, as it would today, but could suggest that the men were instead relatively unattired. Certainly, while extras portraying the armies of Babylon or the Persians in *Intolerance* are somewhat scantily clothed—as soldiers of the period would have been—they are far from nude. The extras at Universal

Robert E. McIntyre mans the door to the casting office at Metro-Goldwyn-Mayer after leaving Samuel Goldwyn, and is faced with a typical line-up of extras. The gentleman behind the dog looks suspiciously like publicist Peter Smith, who probably thought up this stunt. AMPAS.

who similarly engaged in strike action must, one can only surmise, have been required to play Native Americans, and, again, would not have been naked. Strike action was doomed to failure simply because for every extra refusing to work, there were many more happy for the chance of employment.

According to *Photoplay*, the US Census Bureau reported there were 23,456,112 young women living within the United States. The fan magazine joked that that same number was qualified for, and desirous of, a screen career.[21] Certainly it sometimes seemed that most made the journey to Hollywood, aiming to start out as an extra and often ending up with the YWCA providing them with funds to return home. There was no point in sending a written application or a photograph. Only a personal visit to a studio would suffice.

The offices of studio casting directors were mobbed, not just early in the morning but throughout the day, with the familiar phrase of "Anything In?" issuing from the mouth of one extra after another. The most accessible of studios for the extras was the Jesse L. Lasky Feature Play Company, which released through Paramount. Its casting director, Louis M. Goodstadt, was often willing to give a new applicant the opportunity to work. However, in the first five years of its existence, only three extras—Marcia Manon, Edna Mae Cooper, and Julia Faye—progressed from extra to stock company player.

Goodstadt's opposite number at the Fine Arts Studios of D. W. Griffith in the mid 1910s was Lucille Brown, the mother of cinematographer Karl Brown, who also served as the company's wardrobe mistress.[22] As Karl Brown recalled, "She was the official chaperone of the lot and she had a regular police badge to prove it. The badge, which designated her as City Mother No. 1, was strictly honorary and carried no power of arrest or anything else."[23] As *Photoplay* (April 1917) noted, "She's not one of your hard-eyes policemen of the properties, but a real human being with an ear for every woe, a competent and discriminating eye, and an understanding heart." Brown would receive applications from up to two hundred girls, and on average ten would be selected for regular studio employment. At least three of Lucille Brown's extras went on to become leading ladies: Jewel Carmen, Pauline Starke, and Winifred Westover. Brown herself appears as an actress, one of the Uplifters, in the "Modern Story" of D. W. Griffith's *Intolerance* (1916). In later years, she also worked as an extra in films such as Cecil B. DeMille's *King of Kings* (1927).

Contemporary sources indicate Brown was a strict employer:

> The moral character of the majority of my girls is very commendable, despite idle rumors to the contrary.
>
> Before encouraging any of the girls who show possibilities, a complete investigation is made of the girl's character, her home and environment.
>
> Any number of my applicants are impossible types for picture work, and these we discourage immediately.[24]

Mrs. Brown's appointment at Fine Arts led other producers to consider the appointment of "studio mothers," who would replace casting directors and whose presence would improve the environment in which extras were employed and worked. It was not so much the children working as extras who needed mothering, but the young women, facing moral dangers that the studios might well represent. At Paramount, one of the studio's former leading ladies, Anita King, was appointed as "mother." King (1889–1963), who was sometimes identified as "The Paramount Girl," was an adventurous type who in the fall of 1915 made what was described as "a daring cross-country trip" from Los Angeles to New York by automobile, accompanied only by her English bulldog. She was also active in the 1910s delivering positive lectures on the film industry across the United States. According to commentator Rob Wagner, the studio mother "becomes very alert in sorting out the frivolous, romantic youngsters from the girls of real talent and serious ambition. After they are employed they are chaperoned from morning until night, and must constantly report when off-duty. If a director wants extra girls, he sends to the studio mother and she assigns the best one available."[25]

Goldwyn casting director Robert E. McIntyre[26] insisted that there should be no suggestion of any improprieties with the extra girls at his studio. "The Goldwyn studio is the safest and sanest place in the world. Healthy morally, mentally and physically," he proclaimed. "A place every mother should be content to have her daughter be. . . . There is no reason why a motion picture studio should not be the cleanest place under the sun." To this end, McIntyre favored the kind of extra who came from a good, wholesome home, "the kind of girl you'd like to know."[27] It was reported New Yorkers stood little chance of employment at Goldwyn. Into the late 1930s, if not beyond, Samuel Goldwyn was the only major producer who did not hire extras through Central Casting. The same logic applied then as it did early in Goldwyn's producing career, in large part because Robert E. McIntyre was still there; Goldwyn could find a better class of person if individuals were selected outside the system.

The casting department at Metro was headed by an excitable young man named Clifford Robertson. He would come out of his office screaming, "Get out. There's nothing doing. . . . What are you waiting for? Get out, get out."[28] The extras generally paid no attention and stood their ground, silent and expressionless. Robertson met his match in 1918, when a young ingénue named Priscilla Bonner arrived at the studio, properly chaperoned and anxious to become a star:

> I went out to Metro, and there was a casting director there. I was very nicely dressed as a very young girl would be, with my hair hanging down my back. He said, "What experience do you have?" I said, "Oh, I haven't any experience, but I expect you to give me some." He leaned back in his chair and said, "Jesus Christ!" Of course I wasn't used to such language, and I was shocked, but the end of the thing was he gave me some extra work and I didn't know I was to be paid. So I worked four or five days and I never collected any money.

Bonner quickly found work elsewhere as a leading lady to Charles Ray and Will Rogers. "When I got through, I went out to Metro and the casting director said, 'Hello, how are you? What have you been doing?' I said, 'I just finished playing a lead with Mr. Charles Ray.' He leaned back in his chair and again said, 'Jesus Christ!'"[29]

It was either Roberston or his predecessor who came up with a novel solution to the paucity of male extras during World War One. Female extras working on the 1918 May Allison vehicle, *The Testing of Mildred Vane*, were encouraged to bring their fathers or their uncles to the studio to act as their partners in a ballroom sequence. The general manager at the F.B.O. Studios, B. P. Fineman, had an original solution to the extra problem. He would select fifty and guarantee them twelve days of work per month. His notion was that the extras he chose would be experienced at working in front of the camera, assuring fewer problems on the set. It would discourage novice extras, who "unused to work before the camera . . . often spoil expensive scenes, which have to be discarded."[30]

At least one studio, that of comedy producer Al Christie, published a list of rules for women seeking work on a regular basis:

1. Must be between 5 feet and five feet eight in height.
2. Weigh not less than 100 or more than 130 pounds.
3. On days when not called for pictures, must report for dancing training or scene rehearsals at 10 a.m.
4. Must not alter color of hair or cut same without permission.
5. Must be at the studio every working day at 8.30 a.m.
6. Must be able to pass tests for riding, swimming, dancing and social etiquette.
7. Must not smoke cigarettes in studio nor in public places.
8. Must not chew gum.
9. Required to participate in annual girls' hike and other athletic activities.
10. Must possess at least one—evening dress, sport suit, street suit, afternoon dress; one pair of—dancing shoes, walking shoes, street slippers and hats for same.
11. Must not attend cafes or other public places at late hours except on Saturday night, or when not called for work next day.[31]

No such information was provided for male extras, because, in all probability, there was no call for any such extras at Christie, where attractive young ladies were in the majority in whatever part of the action was not dominated by comedians.

Another comedy producer, Mack Sennett, opined that "a girl cannot screen well unless she has even well formed teeth; that wrinkles down the sides of her lips from the outer rim of the nostrils are fatal, that large animated eyes are essential; that a face should be round and soft of contour."[32]

Fred Datig at Famous Players-Lasky in the mid 1920s, interviewing two extras and "bit" players, Valentina Zimina and Maris Jannes. Zimina had a few screen credits in the 1920s.

Of course, the problem, as Sennett so succinctly put it, was that a horse with three legs is not likely to win the derby—but then the possession of four legs does not necessarily denote a winner.

Samuel F. Kingston, casting director at Fox's New York studios, had a simple rule, "Forget yourself."

> Most of the applicants who come in here to see me—and I interview everyone who asks to see me—are either painfully self-conscious, or just plain conceited. The girls will fuss with their hair and hats. The men will twirl their canes or assume a frightful mask of egotism. They under-estimate ability and over-rate self-confidence. When anyone comes in and simply tells me, quietly and sincerely, what he wishes to do, how many parts he has played, and why he thinks he can play a particular part I am casting for, I listen—and more often than not, engage.[33]

Kingston pointed out what might seem obvious, something many young people throughout the United States—if not the world—could not understand. There was no point in writing or sending photographs. Extras could only be hired in person. All were welcome, from ten to five hundred at a time, on the one floor open to the public at the Leavitt Building of the William Fox Film Corporation on West 46th Street.

At its East Coast studio, Fox maintained an organization headed by fifteen regular directors, each of whom presided over a company consisting of an assistant, a cameraman, a general utility boy, a carpenter, a property man, and an accountant. There was no stock company of players, and it was the policy of William Fox not to use the same supporting actors and actresses with the same stars repeatedly. As Kingston explained, "We go even further than this with extra people. We try not to give the same director extra people he has used before."[34] All extras were card indexed, with their photographs filed under general type headings. If a director or William Fox himself asked for a specific, unidentified extra from one film to be used in another, the request presented no problem for Kingston. He kept a record, photograph by photograph, of every player in every film.

One of the most prominent of casting directors from the 1910s onwards was Fred Datig (1891–1951), who began at Universal in 1912, before it moved to Universal City, and who, in all probability, created the casting profession. He was "as kind-hearted and comprehensible a man as there is on earth," wrote one contemporary commentator.[35] By the 1920s, Datig was called "The Man Who Never Forgot a Face," and supposedly could identify twenty-five thousand people working in the film industry. As his son, also named Fred Datig, recalled of his father's work at Universal:

> If they needed extra people, they got them off the street or locally. Because they were doing so many Westerns, my father basically rounded up horses and cowboys, people to put in those Westerns. One time he had to drive all the way to Arizona to find enough horses and riders to fill up a scene. Most of the stars and the bigger players, the featured players, were picked by the directors. But when it came to the director having too much to do, they turned it over to my father. It evolved. If somebody came along and said we want to put somebody in there, he'd say either that's great or I don't agree with that. Other times, they would come and ask his opinion. He didn't have a choice when it came to the star, unless he was asked.[36]

Sam Kingston had much the same response to would-be extras:

> Persons are constantly coming to Hollywood without any more chance to enter the picture business than they have to become president. Oftentimes, they haven't the slightest talent, but many times they have a most exaggerated idea of their own ability. They have gotten this idea back home and while their intentions are good, their avocation for the picture business is not good. Search yourself. Be natural. Be human. Get a reasonably good

> wardrobe. Ask someone about yourself who is unbiased. Your friends will always tell you you are wonderful. Then you will be prepared to walk the path to success in this difficult business.[37]

Paul Bradley recalled coming out of the army at Fort Bliss, Texas, and coming to Hollywood in 1922, determined to get into movies:

> My first experience was at Universal. People used to stand outside the studio and the casting director would come out in the afternoon, and they would pick people. The casting director would say, "Hey feller, can you ride a horse?" I said, "Yes I can," because I'd been discharged from the 62nd Field Artillery. The next morning, I was there at seven o'clock, and the bus picked us up and took us to location, which was at Calabasas Hills. When we got there, I went over and I got a horse from the wrangler. And he bucked all over the hillside. Then I rode the hell out of him. I rode back to the wrangler and I said, "You trying to hurt me or something?" They didn't like extras riding the horses. He said, "You ride good. You won't have any problems."[38]

Bradley, who appeared in silent films under his real name, Anthony Poliseno, did not remember the title of his first film, which starred Hoot Gibson. But it was the first of more than two hundred he appeared in before he retired in 1972.[39]

Extras would do most anything to get attention. One male extra from the mid 1910s, named Roland Blake, was an expert at stunts. When a particular director came into the studio in the morning, Blake would be there performing handsprings. When the director went to the beach, Blake would be in the ocean performing diving stunts. Eventually, the director hired Blake to jump off a cliff, and then cut the poor man's scene from the film, substituting a subtitle in its place. When Blake asked why he had performed a stunt that was not used, the director explained it was to lend realism to the subtitle.[40] Perhaps Blake should have paid attention to the manner in which some of his male contemporaries obtained employment. Instead of spending money on clothing or special skills, they would purchase automobiles. If a studio wanted an automobile like one owned by an aspiring extra, then the studio would have to hire the car's driver.

The majority of the first group of extras in Hollywood may have been dominated by individuals who came from the legitimate stage. The ranks of younger male members of that contingent were decimated by World War I.

Novelist Cedric Belfrage claimed that in order to prove their commitment to the war effort, the stars joined the Lasky Home Guard,[41] while the extras—the slackers—were shipped off to Europe. "A police round-up among the extras was arranged. On one day the patrol wagon made three trips to Hollywood and back from downtown. The slackers were held in the city jail until the army could call for them."[42]

The end of World War I brought in a second group of extras, the majority was female, but a considerable number of former members of the military sought both a new career and a new life in Hollywood. A similar influx into Los Angeles took place after World War II, but this new generation of soldiers, sailors, and airmen were less interested in film industry work than in the potential that the city offered for reasonably priced accommodation and employment in general.

The Lasky Home Guard, comprised primarily of extras, parading outside the studio on Vine Street.

Chapter Two

THE 1920s

It would be nice to think that as the motion picture developed and came to be regarded as something of an art form, the industry began to treat its lowly employees somewhat better. Sadly, this is far from an accurate assessment. If anything, the 1920s saw a diminution in respect for extras. There were simply too many of them, with more arriving by the bus- and trainload. They were as much a glut for the movie market as an over-harvest of apples might be for supermarket chains. America became movie crazy, with some twenty thousand theatres showing the best that Hollywood could offer. And a large minority of Americans—primarily female—went plain crazy believing there was a career for them acting in Hollywood.

As the *Hollywood Citizen News* (February 15, 1924) reported, "'Between pictures,' the extra[s] flit from one casting office to another. A few indulge in selling real estate, some peddle silverware, some wash dishes in restaurants—while awaiting the great opportunity they hope will come some time." The situation in Hollywood was becoming close to desperate, with more and more would-be screen players arriving from across the United States. They congregated in Hollywood, perhaps ignorant of the fact that the only major studio within the confines of the Los Angeles suburb was Paramount, perhaps unaware of the distances between studios and of the time involved in traveling from one to another. According to the Hollywood Chamber of Commerce, as many as ten thousand "movie-mad men and women"[1] were arriving on a monthly basis. On December 3, 1923, in an unprecedented action, Mary Pickford spoke to a crowd of twenty thousand gathered in Pershing Square in downtown Los Angeles. She explained that she did not want to keep young people away from Hollywood, because the "movies always need new blood,"[2] but she urged that they have sufficient funds to live on for at least five years, and that young women always be accompanied by their mothers.

Few would-be Hollywood stars took Pickford's advice, and in the spring of 1927, concerned at the continued migration of young girls to Hollywood, the Motion Picture Producers and Distributors of America hired writer Thomson Burtis[3] to collect relevant information and arrange for its publication in magazines and newspapers. Burtis interviewed not only the women themselves, but also social workers and probation officers.

Just like the studios themselves, in the 1910s the city of Los Angeles had some ten "mothers" on its payroll, with Aletha Gilbert serving as director of the program. These city mothers would chaperone all types of activities within the city, where young, immature girls might be found—from dances to juvenile court appearances. At least one "mother" was assigned responsibility for young women coming to Los Angeles in search of employment in the film industry. She would find them appropriate jobs outside the industry, and also contact local authorities at the women's hometowns, arranging for the exiles' return.

Amidst all the negativity, in 1922 and 1923 the fan magazine *Picture-Play* published a series of articles explaining what would be required of any woman—or man—who wished to have a career as an extra. The fan magazine dismissed the jealousy that extras might feel towards their movie star superiors, pointing out that jealousy occurred in any profession, except that "[i]n an office, the clerks see very little of the comforts and pleasures of the executives."[4] *Picture-Play* also documented facial characteristics that were desirable in the female extra:

> The nose should be flat at the bridge. Many saucy-little beauty has been discarded because her tiptilted nose looked Irish-American off the screen, and Oriental-Ethiopian on. A turned-down nose may be helped somewhat by red used on the tip, which photographs a deep shadow.
>
> Teeth may have many fillings, but should be even and straight. If this is the one drawback to a girl's face, and if she is under twenty, it would be wise to have them straightened before attempting movie work.
>
> A receding chin is a decided handicap, but an aging chin need not be an absolute disqualification. By smearing red on the neck the hanging, or puffy appearance, is often done away with.[5]

While good hair was not a necessity, with wigs available both to extras and stars, those women with a "deformity" such as bowlegs or overlarge feet were advised to move to the country, where there were no movie houses.

The wardrobe of an extra was carefully considered, with anything artistic or faddish quickly rejected. The stars' "weird" costumes were to be avoided. The article pointed out that the average assistant director employing an extra would know little about appropriate clothes, but he would know if the effect was correct. Among the costumes that female extras should have in their wardrobes were: evening gowns and wraps; an afternoon gown which might also serve as a dinner frock; a riding habit and other appropriate outdoor costumes; a one-piece bathing suit; hats to go with any costume; shoes which were neat rather than elaborate; a parasol; and a good-looking fur. The male extra would need a wardrobe that included: a conservative business or street suit; evening clothes and dinner jacket; a riding habit; sports clothes with white flannel trousers; appropriate hats; and well-shined shoes. Tweeds should be worn only if they were well made and had the effect of making the wearer look "racy." Male jewelry should be limited to a large signet ring and a scarf pin. "Diamonds are not good form and even a second-rate director knows this."[6]

Many would-be extras failed to follow *Picture-Play*'s advice, no matter how sensible it might seem. It was noted that the soda counter of a Hollywood drugstore would be peopled by young women wearing too much clanking jewelry, their faces too white and their lips too red. In contrast, buying magazines in a corner of the store would be a quiet, well-dressed young lady, garnering no attention—unless she was recognized as Norma Talmadge or Leatrice Joy or Betty Compson.[7]

Just as a fan magazine like *Picture-Play* might have a hidden agenda in promoting extras in a positive light (it has to sell copies, and the purchasers are often those with a Hollywood dream), the *Los Angeles Times* succumbed to the desire to ignore negative aspects of life in the city. Beginning on February 16, 1919, longtime *Los Angeles Times* entertainment reporter Grace Kingsley wrote a series titled "Ella, the Extra Girl." While Ella is realistic about the hardships of life as an extra, she is always upbeat, emphasizing the glamor of studio life and her ability to balance her career as an extra with her duties as a housewife promoting her husband's transition from delivery man to actor.

One long-time Hollywood agent specializing in extras and bit players was Harry St. Albans, who had opened his Screen Service Bureau in August 1917. He noted the inability of many extras to recognize that their individuality was an irrelevancy:

> Being but one of a mob has a certain psychological effect upon them. Perhaps they are too much together. They come here because they have

> been called "the prettiest girl" or "the handsomest fellow" in the home town. At first, they have individuality, personal pride in their appearance. But after a little while they seem weighed down by the realization that they will never progress. When that spark goes, they are hopeless, and all we can do is to send them out as atmosphere.[8]

"The casting office looks for style rather than breeding," noted *Picture Play*,[9] acknowledging the growing importance of the casting director. And nowhere is this more apparent that in the career of Fred Datig, whose work involved not only stars and supporting players, but also extras. According to the *New York Times* (January 13, 1924), by the middle of the Roaring Twenties, as many as one hundred thousand were registered with various casting agencies across the city. After establishing the title of casting director at Universal, Fred Datig left in 1925 to join Famous Players-Lasky/Paramount, where he was to remain until 1937. That year, he moved on to MGM, where he stayed until his death in 1951. One of his favorite habits at Universal was to sneak onto a set and hide in the shadows, carefully watching all that was going on. By such means he not only learned every new motion picture technique, but also how good or bad a specific actor or actress was. While at Universal, Irving Thalberg was hired by studio boss Carl Laemmle, and Thalberg began studying production in much the same manner as Datig. The two men did not care for on another, and after leaving Paramount, Datig worked briefly as an independent agent before joining MGM—after Thalberg's death.

Aside from the honorable exceptions of D. W. Griffith's *The Birth of a Nation* and *Intolerance* a decade earlier, it may be argued that the 1920s saw the introduction of the spectacular into American film production, with appropriately large crowd scenes that provided employment for hundreds of extras. It was Fred Datig who oversaw the casting of the first two such films, both starring Lon Chaney: *The Hunchback of Notre Dame* (1923) and *The Phantom of the Opera* (1925). For the ballroom scene in the former, Datig employed some one hundred extras to provide "atmosphere." Included in the number was Malcolm Waite (1892–1949), known as "the millionaire extra," whose local residence was the Ambassador Hotel, and who was a member of the social elite (or so it was reported) in New York, London, and Paris. Waite was also an amateur heavyweight boxer, often cast in parts suitable to his build. He received credit as a bit player in a number of films—including *The Gold Rush* (1925), Eddie Cantor's first feature film, *Kid Boots* (1926), and *Noah's Ark* (1928), in which he has a dual role—into the early 1940s. On *Noah's Ark*, Waite was certainly far more than an extra, garnering a salary of $450 a week. One of the film's stars, Noah Beery, received $3,000 a week, while Nigel De Brulier, who was later to become little more than an extra in sound films, was paid $750 a week.

Also present in the ballroom scene was Marion Gray, whose marriage to Robert E. McIntyre, casting director at Goldwyn and later MGM, gave her somewhat of an advantage. Other extras in the scene include artist's model Eric Mack; Brigadier General Robert Wahlberg, a former member of the Austrian Army; and Max Garnetz, who had escaped the Russian Revolution with nothing to show for his daily trade paper or the four theatres he had owned in Moscow and elsewhere. It was reported that only one-quarter of the players in the ballroom sequence were actually extras, with the others consisting of minor supporting players, juveniles, stage actors, musicians, and dancers—all of whose names would have meant nothing to the moviegoing public then or now.

Sidney Olcott, who had been active in the film industry since before the 1910s, had been an actor and an extra prior to graduating to direction with the Kalem Company, where he was responsible for the first *Ben-Hur* and the early feature-length *From the Manger to the Cross*. He explained that directing mob scenes, which required a minimum of thirty extras to be so described, was no routine matter:

> Nothing can be more disturbing in a picture than the "shots" of a mob that moves with puppetlike precision. To be effective it must be spontaneous. The whole idea of the mob is expressed in the word "uprising"—a throng beyond control giving vent to their emotions. A proper mob scene should show expression of body and mind gone wild.
>
> If this is the situation, then the plan for the director is to see that there is individualism in his crowd—a mosaic of men, women and children, each unit with its own part, just as well acted as a leading role. Then all of this blended into a surging, infuriated, frantic mass of humanity. Think of notes of music, blending when played, into a stormy symphony.
>
> One of my first experiences as an "extra" was the thought that before the camera I ought to do my best. It might be noticed. I understood why I was protesting so wildly, and I imbibed a full conception of the anger of the mob. I found this self-direction invaluable. I became a leader of the group of which I was a unit.
>
> My experience has taught me to get together a hand-picked mob. I can see at a glance just what types I want most.[10]

Generally, extras enjoyed appearing in mob scenes—particularly those shot out-of-doors—because often they could get away with "not-appearing." They would show up on the set, and then slink off to the side, out of camera range and the director's sight, for a smoke or a snooze. In the 1910s, such characters were known as "squirrels," for reasons that now seem unclear. However, it may be relevant that squirrels eat nuts, and only "nuts" would work as extras. If these extras were caught, they would be "cut off the list," dismissed for cause, and find themselves unemployable in the industry.

As late as the 1940s, similar problems occurred with what may have been only a small group of extras or a hard-core number of aggrieved ones. Film critic Otis Ferguson wrote:

> They are complacent in bungling, often sullen, sometimes vicious. The idea seems to be that the world owes them a living, and furniture to scratch their matches on.
>
> Their eternal soldiering, remember, never works out against the Oppressors. The willfulness or incompetence of seven or eight in the morning for a company of more than a hundred weary people, simply to push the production into overtime checks for themselves. They will be rehearsed one by one until the whole scene is foolproof, and then on the final take fall to muddling and muttering when they should be still, passing in lockstep when they should be a subway crowd, never alert to anything save a request made on them could be called an imposition by the book, and charged for as such.[11]

Two Cecil B. DeMille productions of the 1920s made extensive use of extras, including many of the Jewish faith. On location in the sand dunes of Santa Maria, California, where much of *The Ten Commandments* (1923) was shot, more than two hundred Orthodox Jews added verisimilitude to the portrayal of Israeli slaves. *King of Kings* (1927) employed a large, undisclosed number of Jewish men, supporting a cast that included prominent Jewish actors, Rudolph Schildkraut as Caiaphas and Joseph Schildkraut as Judas, who were father and son. Their presence was of no account when the film garnered a storm of controversy from the Jewish community over its presentation of events immediately preceding the Crucifixion, strongly implying that Jews murdered Christ. More than ten years earlier, D. W. Griffith had faced the same criticism with regard to his filming of the same sequences in *Intolerance* (1916). And like DeMille, Griffith had hired "all the

Extras enjoy a box lunch while working on Cecil B. DeMille's *The Ten Commandments* (1923). AMPAS.

orthodox Hebrews with long whiskers that he could secure"[12] to appear as extras in the lead up to the Crucifixion. Griffith supposedly burnt that portion of the negative showing Jews crucifying Christ and refilmed the scenes with Roman soldiers nailing Christ to the cross.

Without question, the most daunting experience for extras was working on the Warner Bros. production of *Noah's Ark*, directed by Michael Curtiz and released in November 1928. While the number is in all probability heavily exaggerated, the studio claimed that some five thousand extras were hired for the film, with the casting department interviewing at least six thousand. Wardrobe, dressing, and makeup tents were pitched on the studio lot, which contemporary reports compared to an army camp.

Military service was probably far less unpleasant than time at Warner Bros. Because the extras were light-skinned, they did not adequately resemble the dark-skinned tribes of the Middle East. As a result, the extras were ordered to strip, marshaled into line, and marched to enclosures, where some eighty makeup men and women sprayed them with a quick-drying, liquid brown solution. Once suitably darkened, the extras were ordered to costume themselves in robes, wigs, and beards. What followed was a carefully coordinated march to the Temple of Jaghut set. "There could be no loss of time or waste of effort allowed," explained the studio, "an hour's delay

meant 5,000 hours of lost time that must be paid for and efficiency is the main-spring of motion picture production necessary to such a tremendous undertaking as *Noah's Ark*."[13] Extras were classified as to type, directed to the appropriate tents, and once made-up and costumed, given a group number indicating where on the set they were to congregate. Each area of the set featured a stand-card with a corresponding number.

Based on what little documentation there is about the production, it would seem that the extras were not told from day to day what was planned. It might be "a scene of splendor" or it might be a flood of water. Just how much water was used for the flood cannot be determined. A pressbook for the edited, Robert Youngson reissue claims fourteen thousand tons of water was used. Jack L. Warner wrote of one million gallons "under terrific pressure," and then contradicted himself by describing "[t]hree immense tanks with a combined capacity of four million gallons."[14] Whatever the amount, it was an extreme shock for the unsuspecting extras. Warner Bros. noted:

Some of the extras on *Noah's Ark* (1928) with appropriately dyed skin, unsuspecting of what director Michael Curtis has in store.

> The possibilities of sudden illness or injuries were anticipated through the establishment of temporary hospitalization facilities. Completely equipped with every modern necessity, with competent nurses in attendance and skilled physicians on hand the hospital functioned with perfect efficiency. Happily there was little need for the services of the hospital staff—but it was there in competent working order, had there been need for its ministrations.[15]

While some decades later the studio would refer to a "miraculously low rate of injury," there is no question that many extras were severely hurt during the filming of the flood sequence. It is generally believed that there was at least one fatality. When cinematographer Hal Mohr pointed out the danger of unleashing tons of water over the ill-prepared extras during the climactic deluge sequences, the director supposedly responded: "They're just going to have to take their chances." Mohr walked off the film in disgust and was replaced by Barney McGill.[16] The Warner Bros. archives are silent as to what took place, and the studio carefully prevented any reports about the filming of the flood from appearing in the Los Angeles press.

Depending on the site, extras might find location shooting pleasurable or harsh. For those extras and others, a company of 225, working on the Corinne Griffith vehicle, *The Divine Lady* (1929), on location on Catalina Island, filming could hardly be described as an unpleasant experience despite the hours. Tent houses were provided for the extras, who were expected to rise at 6:00 a.m. for a breakfast of ham and eggs. They were encouraged to take advantage of the ocean and enjoy a morning swim prior to work. Some half-dozen boats transported the extras to three warships in the bay, representing the French fleet and that of Lord Nelson. Once the lunch break was called, period costumes were removed, revealing bathing suits beneath, and more swimming ensued, followed by a return to the island. With sunlight insufficient for filming after 4:00 p.m., the extras were able to enjoy additional swimming, followed by dinner and various activities in the recreation hall. No noise was allowed in the tents after 9:00 p.m. If nothing else, location shooting even for a day meant a good meal. As early as 1915, one extra noted that a typical lunchbox would include a pint bottle of milk, three sandwiches, a piece of pie or cake, a small potato salad, a peach, a plum, and a pickle.[17]

In January 1929, an intrepid *New York Times* reporter wrote of the trials and tribulations of working as a male extra on location for the 1929 Clarence Brown-directed feature, *The Trail of '98*, starring Ralph Forbes. The crowd racket, he called it:

> In a big marquee tent I had changed from my clothes into those of a gold digger in the time of '98. I had been given my costume—a woolen hat of sorts, a thick coat, breeches and a pair of boots which the camera would eventually show to be heavy, serviceable footwear. . . .
>
> During a night of marching and remarching from one spot to another, with packs upon our backs supposedly filled with mining implements and foods, but really containing seventy-pound loads of sand, I met some interesting people.

Among these was the brother of a British admiral, who usually played butler roles, a cousin of actor Cyril Maude, a Belgian who could speak few words of English, and a young Irishman with a large vocabulary of swear words.

Many of the extras played cards, gambling away their seven-dollar paychecks even before they were received. The report continues:

> At 3:30 A.M. a whistle blew for food. Three hundred extras surged toward the vans where dishes and cups were being brought out. The meal was not only adequate but excellent. Meat with two kinds of vegetables, canned peaches, cookies, tea or coffee were given out with generosity. It was a better meal than a number of the extra players had had for many a day, and there were second helpings for all those who wanted more.
>
> When dawn came all of us were cold and tired. . . . We had been marching, waiting about and remarching from six the night before until now.
>
> The fifth time we tramped up a hill Ralph Forbes, who was leading player in the film we were making, appeared before the camera without his hat, although the temperature was supposed to have been "forty degrees below."
>
> And so we had to do it again.
>
> Nobody was very pleased. The flaring torches some of us carried made us cough and our eyes water. The shoulder straps, weighed down with their sandy loads, hurt our shoulders, for some of us were new to the game and didn't know what clothes to bring.[18]

Also in 1929, director Raoul Walsh shot the most ambitious sound film to date, a historical Western epic titled *The Big Trail*, starring John Wayne, in the desert near Yuma, Arizona. Business manager Arch Buchanan and assistant director Sid Bowman hand-picked the extras: "There were champion bronc peelers, ex-Texas rangers, ex-marshalls, prize fighters, wrestlers, ex-marines, English sailors, two ex-gunmen from Chicago, famous stars and two ex-big league baseball layers, aviators and ex-flyers also. . . . All told,

those extra men were as interesting a group as I ever met. Anyone who believes that the Hollywood cowboy is a joke should have seen that crew perform," commented the film's co-writer, novelist Hal G. Evarts[19] Female extras ranged from teenagers to women in their sixties. One extra, Pete Morrison, is credited with saving three of those women from death by stopping the six oxen pulling the wagon in which they were seated from going over into a canyon. It was reported that four hundred Indians were gathered from Idaho, Wyoming, and Montana—and separately housed, of course, in an Indian village. Represented tribes included members of the Arapaho, Crow, Bannock, and Northern Cheyenne nations.

While most newspaper and fan magazine space at the time was devoted to the hardships faced by female extras—and these cannot be under-estimated—there can be little doubt that life was far from easy for their male counterparts. Handsome young men were as available as beautiful young women—and as little in demand.

A half-hearted chorus line of extras in the 1926 production of *The Boob.*

In 1923, it was estimated that two-thirds of the seventy-five newcomers arriving in Hollywood on a daily basis were male. Lured by the success of

William S. Hart, Charlie Chaplin, Harold Lloyd, and most of all Rudolph Valentino, they faced an additional difficulty in that social workers concentrated on newly-arrived young women, ignoring the male newcomers.[20]

Male extras congregated on Sunset Boulevard, in an area a block or so east of Vine Street. Extra Morris Raphael was named the honorary mayor of Poverty Row, while Aileen Dee was given the title Corinne Griffith of Poverty Row, in honor of a major dramatic star of the period. Their lives centered around Dad Kelly's Corned Beef Parlor, the Christie Studios, Al Marsh's Poolroom, and Raphael's Drug Store. The last provided a "Mourner's Bench" outside for the use of weary-footed extras. In February 1927, two extras, Jimmy True and Roy Caylor, founded a club for their fellow extras, which they named the Struggler's and located on Gower Street. The setting was a "not very decorative" house,[21] owned by Isaac Chadwick, who operated a small independent studio nearby. The club sponsored baseball, swimming, rowing, and football teams. It also hosted an annual "rumpus," titled the Struggler's Ball, which first took place at the Chadwick Studios in 1928. Also in 1928, the club held a dance at the Hollywood Roof Ballroom, where extra Leona Leigh was selected as Miss Struggler of 1928.

There were apparently two publications associated with the club, *The Extra* and *The Poverty Row Bugler*, neither of which appears to have been archived in any library. Members were defensive about their position within the industry, arguing: "The extra is not the isolated creature 'the human interest stories' so often reveal him to be. The very traits which make him desire to act for the world, make of him also a special person. His life after working hours is if anything more alluring than the star's because his leisure is his own, to do with as he pleases."[22]

Older male extras and their female counterparts might be found at the Troupers, a club founded in 1925 and housed in a former church on El Centro in Hollywood. It was open only to extras and others from the screen or the stage with at least thirty years of service. Its dues were one dollar a month, payable only if a member could afford it.

The studio set itself was also, of course, a popular social gathering place—if for no other reason than the necessity for extras to stay there for long periods of time. Some sets were more exclusive than others. No mere casting director selected the extras for the 1924 Rudolph Valentino vehicle, *Monsieur Beaucaire*. The star's wife, Natacha Rambova, who reportedly had an exacting eye, performed this duty. Extras were contracted for at least one week's work, with compensation paid for dress rehearsals. They were encouraged to read appropriate books, and the language on the set was not rough or crude, but French, Russian, German, and Spanish. It was reported that "one handsome beau in powdered wig and golden-embroidered coat is a Swede who speaks nine languages—including the Scandinavian and Hebrew—and who fences every morning with the lithe and graceful Rudolph."[23]

The more plebeian extras spent their time on more plebeian sets having their palms read. The most popular individuals at the studio, the fortune-tellers, did not charge extras for their time. Extras tried to avoid discussing their personal lives, did not argue, did not give advice, and would never make suggestions, however appropriate they might be. Most important to the extras was protecting their personal belongings. The large rooms, known as "bull pens," in which the extras dressed, segregated only by sex, offered no privacy and little security. Clothes were always placed in lockers or locked suitcases. Furs were taken to the set, regardless of whether they were to be used. Even a personal makeup case was carried onto the set, where it was kept out of camera range but within eyesight. Extras carried only a minimal amount of money on their persons, just enough to pay for lunch and car fare home.

These plebeian extras might take heart from a 1925 article in *Photoplay*, in which the fan magazine recognized what it claimed to be Hollywood's "Four Hundred," extras who through breeding or "prudent observation" had taught themselves to attain the manner of rank and elegance. Already graduated from this group of superior extras were: Mary Philbin, under long-term contract to Universal and Lon Chaney's leading lady; Laura La Plante, also a Universal leading lady; and Betty Bronson, who had achieved stardom with her performance in the title role of *Peter Pan*. Others were destined for stardom, but never actually to make it, appearing uncredited in 1924 releases: Marjorie Whitus in the Anna Q. Nilsson vehicle, *Inez from Hollywood*; Christina Montt (supposedly directly related to four Chilean presidents) and Stella de Lanti in the Corinne Griffith vehicle, *Love's Wilderness*; and Virginia Adair in the Aileen Pringle and John Gilbert vehicle, *His Hour*. Others named—and quickly forgotten—were Fronzi Gunn, with her saucer-like eyes, Clara Morris, Frances Dare, Gene Barham, and Betty Mulligan, spotted by a casting director at Fox. Charles Farrell would become a star within a few years. Another male extra, Gene Cameron, had the right characteristics to be spotted in a crowd scene by director Robert Z. Leonard and cast as modiste "Madame" Ducelle in the Mae Murray vehicle, *Circe the Enchantress* (1924).

For some Hollywood players in the 1920s, no hard work was involved in being signed to a contract. It was just a matter of being in the right place at

Extras in period costume for the 1925 production of *Not So Long Ago.*

the right time. Pauline Wagner recalls that students at Santa Monica High School in the late 1920s would congregate on the beach outside the home of Marion Davies:

> We were down there for two years on the beach, swimming, playing volley ball, baseball. We were never told we couldn't do that. I remember Joel McCrea. He didn't go to Santa Monica High School. He'd come down, and he'd have his special-made hat and special-made shorts and a towel that matched everything. He'd shake his towel and put it in front of the wall between the mansion and the sand. And he'd sit there, posed all day long on that towel. He'd never speak to us. Anyway, one day, the maid came out from Marion Davies' house, and said, "Hey, would you kids like to work in the movies?" So immediately Joel gets up and walks over. "Go to MGM and report down there." So we did. Out of the group, they took Fay Webb. Then they took me. They took Joel McCrea. They took twelve of us.
>
> They signed me up on a contract—$75.00 a week. You had to take dancing lessons. You had to take drama lessons. I had a slight Oklahoma accent, so they said you have to go to school and get rid of that accent. We had to go to makeup. We had to do our hair over. They plucked all my eyebrows out—and they never did come back. They wanted to file off two teeth because they were longer, and I said, "Nobody's touching my teeth."[24]

Pauline Wagner's first role was in the 1929 production of *So This Is College*. With no other work at MGM forthcoming, Wagner went to Universal, where she appeared in Westerns. When she returned to MGM, she discovered a batch of checks waiting for her. The studio was unaware that she had gone over to Universal on her own, and it was still paying her under the original contract. Wagner took the checks. Pauline Wagner continued to appear on screen as a bit player, extra, and stand-in until World War II.

One director who seems genuinely to have cared about Hollywood extras is French-born Robert Florey (1900–79). His film, *Hollywood Boulevard*, honors many former silent players now reduced to bit or extra work in the 1930s. The first of four avant-garde short films that he made between 1927 and 1929, *Hollywood Boulevard* is a tribute to the Hollywood extra. Florey had been directing Hollywood features since 1926, and he was responsible for such major feature films as the first Marx Brothers film, *The Cocoanuts* (1929), *Murders in the Rue Morgue* (1932), *The Desert Song* (1943), *God Is My Co-Pilot* (1945), and *The Beast with Five Fingers* (1945), as well as countless television productions.

While listening to a concert performance of George Gershwin's "Rhapsody in Blue," Florey conceived a short subject that would portray the life and death of a Hollywood director in synchronization with the Gershwin music. (Neither the original musical score nor the film in its entirety has survived.) To help realize the project, Florey enlisted the aid of cinematographer Paul Ivano and Slavko Vorkapich, who has subsequently gained fame for his montage sequences in countless Hollywood films. The title role is played by Jules Raucourt, an extra who had once been a leading man, the female lead by Adriane Marsh, herself an extra, and the "star" by Voya George, a friend of Vorkapich.

The twelve-hundred-foot film took three weeks to prepare and film and cost just over ninety-seven dollars. When it was finished, Florey showed it to his friend, Charlie Chaplin. The comedian was most impressed and invited many of his Hollywood-celebrity friends to a screening. Joseph Schenck arranged for a premiere at the United Artists Theatre in Hollywood and for its release by FBO. The Los Angeles-based *Film Mercury* (July 27, 1928) commented, "If this production had been made in Europe and heralded as a hit, it would . . . have been called a masterpiece."

The Life and Death of 9413—a Hollywood Extra is a simple, satirical fantasy, whose hero, Mr. Jones, bears a letter of recommendation, addressed to Mr. Almighty, a Hollywood casting director. Once an individual, Mr. Jones is changed to a number, 9413, which is written upon his forehead, and he begins to talk in the gibberish of Hollywood, using slight variations upon "bah-bah-bah-bah-bah." Meanwhile, handsome number 15, formerly Mr. Blank, is screen tested and enthusiastically approved by executives proclaiming "bah-bahs." At the premiere of his new film, number 15 becomes a great success, with a star painted on his forehead and "bah-bah-bah-bahs" that are now haughty and assertive.

Number 9413 does not enjoy success and is received with cries of "nbah-nbah-nbah-nbah," meaning no casting today. The nonsense phrase dominates his dreams, until they shrink to the level of "Pork and Beans—15 cents." Holding a telephone from which the "nbahs" of the casting director issue, number 9413 falls to the floor and dies of starvation. But all Hollywood movies must have a happy ending, and number 9413 ascends to heaven, where an angel wipes the number from his forehead and he becomes once again a human being.

The film is an amalgam of miniature sets made up of paper and metal, newsreel-like shots of Hollywood, and close-ups with the actual actors, all held together through distortion and superimposition. Florey said at the time, "It is not much. Just about a man who is a fine actor in Iowa or somewhere and who comes to Hollywood and expects to conquer it overnight.... The would-be idol goes to the studios.... The casting director—he is merely a hand that rejects or selects.... And the rest just tells how he loses out all around."[25]

The short opened at New York's Cameo Theatre on June 17, 1928, when it was viewed, by a critic from *Variety* (June 20, 1928), who commented:

> Many little twists of photography that look like an assembly of clips from many of the German made [German productions]. Interesting enough for 12 minutes for the sure seaters or among those audiences with members having had their own picture heroing dreams. Could fit in anywhere, if that $97.50 bunk is worth something outside a theatre.
>
> If so it should be ballyhooed to teach the community that some picture actors or extras must work for nothing, that celluloid isn't charged for by Eastman [Kodak], and that the high cost of picture making must be the hooey, for here's 12 minutes of something with three actors or extras costing $97.50.Consequently 60 minutes of the same thing couldn't cost over $177.50.
>
> Page Mr. [Louis B.] Mayer!

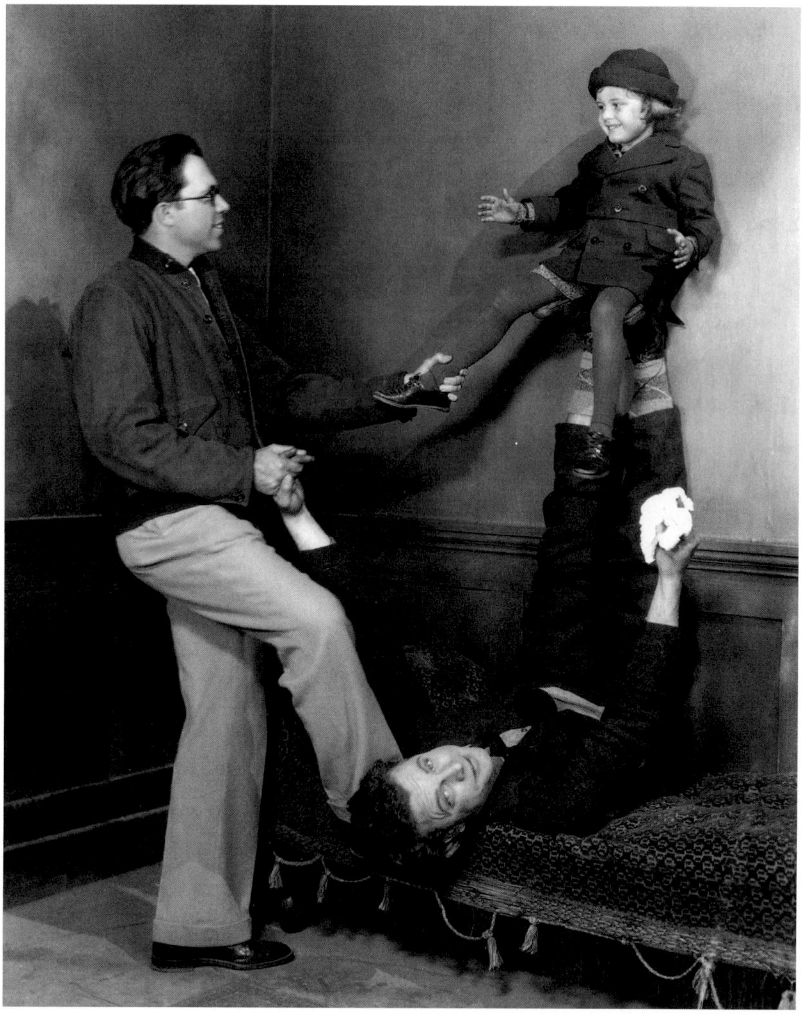

The Crowd (1928), with director King Vidor (standing), leading man James Murray, and Alice Mildred Puter, who plays Murray's daughter.

In late 1927, director King Vidor produced a classic of the silent screen titled *The Crowd*. It is a simple story of a young couple that meets, marries, has two children, and experiences a series of life's tragedies. The couple is typical of many hard-working Americans of the decade. The film's leading man, James Murray, is also typical of a small group of actors who suddenly emerge into stardom only to find that fame is fleeting. Born in the Bronx on February 9, 1901, Murray had worked as an actor in one of the historical dramas, *The Pilgrims*, produced on the East Coast by Yale University in its Chronicles of America series in 1924. He came to Hollywood, worked as an extra, and had the good fortune to be spotted by King Vidor, who was looking for an unknown to appear in *The Crowd*. In 1928, the same year in which the film was released, Murray married extra Lucille McNarre. With the coming of sound, his career slowly declined and he became an alcoholic and a bit player, appearing in six films between 1933 and 1935. On July 11, 1936, Murray fell or jumped into the Hudson River and drowned.

James Murray was a male victim of Hollywood, one of perhaps a relatively small number of men who fell afoul of the system. Compared to the female extras of the 1920s, these men probably fared relatively well. "No one will ever know how many girls journeyed there [Los Angeles] in the ten years beginning in 1919, nor what became of most of them," wrote Benjamin B. Hampton in his pioneering 1931 work, *A History of the Movies*. Hampton continues:

> Perhaps 20,000, perhaps 50,000—the latter figure is most likely to be correct—were drawn to the city by movie ambition and the hope of romance . . . but by 1922–23, when the oil and reality booms had lost their initial force, there were so many applicants for every job that any sort of work became hard to get, and the matrons at the police stations had to find lodgings and food for many young women whose visions of stardom had faded into a harsh reality.[26]

It might well be argued that the only good to come out of the 1920s for extras—at least the female ones—were a revamped Hollywood Studio Club, offering limited accommodation, and Central Casting, providing jobs with—at least in theory—no strings attached.

Chapter Three

THE HOLLYWOOD STUDIO CLUB

The exploitation of young women in Hollywood, particularly those seeking work as extras, was a regular and familiar topic with fan magazine writers and others. The Young Women's Christian Association (YWCA) had been founded in 1866 to provide accommodation and assistance for single women in major industrial centers. With the influx into Hollywood of so many determined to be future movie stars, the film community might well be considered such a hub, and in 1916, the YWCA, with the help of local businessmen, was able to acquire a building at 6129 Carlos Avenue, which could house some twenty women. The Hollywood Business Men's Club took care of the first year of the lease of the property from owner E. W. Twist. The catalyst for the creation of what was named the Hollywood Studio Club was a local librarian named Mrs. Eleanor Jones, who had become aware of the number of young hopefuls who would congregate at her library to read plays, and who were obviously in need of a stable environment in which to live and continue their educational activities.

The facility, a large house of salmon-colored stucco, surrounded by pepper trees, which contemporary commentators noted might have belonged to a Hollywood star, also offered a library and a clubroom. "There are great possibilities in the house," reported the *Los Angeles Times* (July 23, 1916), "which has an attic large enough for amateur theatricals, and a basement where shower baths can be located when funds for the outdoor gymnasium are secured." Various prominent females within the industry, including opera singer turned silent star Geraldine Farrar and director Lois Weber, as well as the wives of producers William C. de Mille and Jesse L. Lasky, hosted weekly teas at the house. Among the leading ladies mentioned as helping out are Lila Lee, Carmel Myers, and Constance Talmadge.[1] Anne Bauchens, head of the stenographic department at the Lasky Studios was the first president, followed by actress Louise Huff. Gertrude Griffith, the first "house mother,"

The dining room at the original Hollywood Studio Club, circa 1920. ZaSu Pitts is clearly recognizable in the front row, fourth from right. AMPAS.

was succeeded by Edna Harris, a social worker who had graduated from the Chicago School of Civics and Philosophy and had practical work experience with Hull House. Among her charges were at least four leading ladies of the 1920s—Marjorie Daw, Helen Jerome Eddy, Julanne Johnston, and ZaSu Pitts—as well as the future prolific fan magazine writer, Myrtle Gebhart, and screenwriter Sarah Y. Mason. Betty Bronson lived at the club prior to gaining the title role in the first screen adaptation of *Peter Pan* (1924).

One of the first public presentations—if not the first—residents put on was an allegorical play in pantomime, titled *Youth*, performed as part of a YWCA gala night on January 30, 1917. In the cast was Mildred Harris, who within a year was to become Mrs. Charlie Chaplin, and who was to end her acting career as an extra.

Residents of the club, who never were threatened with eviction if they could not pay their bills, were encouraged to sign a "friendship book," on the first page of which appeared a quotation from Oliver Wendell Holmes:

There is no friend like an old one,
Who has shared our morning days.

As Edna Harris explained:

> Girls have come to Los Angeles with just enough money to make the trip. They are usually the most difficult to convince that they are not fitted for the screen and inevitably we must obtain positions for them in other lines or get them back to their homes. The employment directors of the various studios are splendid and are always willing to help us with the girls who are badly in need of work but they are in a highly organized business and not in philanthropic work. It is a hard game even for the girl who comes prepared for a long and arduous artistic siege.[2]

Initially, Hollywood personalities made donations of clothing and other items to the club's residents. But they balked at this "charity," and actress Alla Nazimova worked out an arrangement whereby residents might purchase the clothing at a fraction of its original cost. As Myrtle Gebhart recalled:

> A gorgeous sequin evening gown that had cost several hundred dollars was bought for ten or fifteen, or whatever a hastily dumped-out purse would yield. Exquisite lingerie was exchanged for a few coins. Nazimova, smiling over the girls' fierce young pride, solemnly collected the money—and gave it to a local charity.[3]

Publicity relating to the Hollywood Studio Club has always emphasized the camaraderie between the residents and their willingness to help each other. In reality, there was substantial competition for work. When *Photoplay* writer Ruth Waterbury, on assignment in disguise as a would-be extra, approached one of the residents for help, she noted, "That was when I first glimpsed the Hollywood fear and distrust. . . . I could see her figuring desperately how to get rid of me."[4] It also seems obvious from all the stories published about the Hollywood Studio Club that its occupants were highly respectable women, probably all from decent homes and many subsidized by their parents. The extras residing at the Hollywood Studio Club were not on a par with the extra eking out an existence in order to pay the rent for a room at a cheap Hollywood hotel.

When the club outgrew its original premises, leading members of the Hollywood acting community were invited to pay for the building and furnishing of individual rooms in a new building. Among those contributing between $150 and $200 each were Mary Pickford, Douglas Fairbanks, Cecil B. DeMille, Jackie Coogan, Harold Lloyd, Gloria Swanson, and Alec B. Francis. Over two thousand players offered money, including Louise Dresser, Jetta Goudal, Ruth Roland, and Florence Vidor. Eventually, Norma

Talmadge agreed to donate $5,000 to complete the building fund in February 1925.

The YWCA was joined in its work by Will Hays, head of the Motion Picture Producers and Distributors of America, who headed a committee that had initially sought to expand the Carlos Avenue building. Eventually, however, the committee determined that it made more sense to find a new location. As Mrs. Edward M. Townsend of the National Board of the YWCA noted:

> And so the roads to Hollywood are lined with movie-mad children, walking to save fare, sublimely confident that a pretty face, a slight gift for amateur theatricals, or in some cases nothing further than a blind adoration for some popular screen star will be sufficient to open the doors of the great motion picture studios.
>
> Once there they must be cared for. Hollywood is a place of residences with few available hotels. Opportunities for work outside of the studios are negligible, and dreams are a poor substitute for three meals a day and a place to sleep.[5]

The new clubhouse opened on May 8, 1926, at a reported cost of $250,000. The dedication was attended by some 2,500 individuals, beginning at 4:30 in the afternoon and ending with dancing at midnight. The three-story building at 1215 Lodi Place, just south of Sunset Boulevard in Hollywood, was designed by Julia Morgan, who is best known for her design of the William Randolph Hearst estate, San Simeon. Julia Morgan was also responsible for the design of the YWCA national board's Asilomar conference center near Monterey, California, which opened in 1913. The director of the new establishment was Marjorie Williams, who had held a similar position at the Carlos Avenue building. The new Hollywood Studio Club could be widely touted as an example of the accuracy of the film community's moral compass, of its concern for its workers and its distance from the various scandals that had plagued the industry in the early 1920s. The rape-murder of starlet Virginia Rappe, in which Roscoe "Fatty" Arbuckle was implicated, was still very much discussed throughout the United States. In the *California Graphic*, Nellie Barnard Parker wrote, "This beautiful and spacious building is but one more jewel in the crown of Achieved Results which this progressive and cultural little city is wearing so proudly and shows its ever increasing desire to give unstinted moral and financial support to every progressive endeavor."[6]

The new clubhouse could accommodate eighty women, not only would-be actresses, but also secretaries, studio telephone operators, scenario writers, script girls, and designers. Each paid ten dollars a week for a room shared with two others, or fifteen dollars per week for a room shared with one other resident. Rent included two meals a day. By the 1940s, the price had risen to either eight or fifteen dollars a week, still an incredible bargain. Throughout its history, the Hollywood Studio Club welcomed residents as young as eighteen, but none older than thirty. None of the residents was permitted to stay more than three years. Non-residents were also welcome, paying a minimum of three dollars a year for access to the tennis court, a communal room, or a meal

Aside from a room and board, the Hollywood Studio Club guaranteed respectability and an unimpeachable address for any potential employer. The women offered each other moral support, and each was protected by that support, which residency guaranteed. The club had a relaxed, democratic atmosphere. No effort was made to enforce any religious beliefs. As *Photoplay* stressed, the Hollywood Studio Club was "not a gospel home or rescue mission."[7] Residents could smoke in their rooms, and by the 1930s, they could entertain male visitors in the library and the lounges until as late as 1:00 a.m. In the 1910s, the YWCA permitted informal parties on Sundays. Dancing was prohibited on the Sabbath, but not on Friday, a day when Los Angeles hotels were forbidden by law to permit such fun. Alcohol was banned, but there was no formal rule against it. "The Motion Picture Business is essentially a business of Youth," it was explained, "and Youth must play—especially if it works hard every day and several evenings."[8] As director Marjorie Williams, who was described as having "a broad smile and a broader mind,"[9] explained it to the *New York Times* in 1926:

> The Studio Club is unique among such organizations because rules ordinarily observed cannot apply there. Because of the unusual hours of the motion picture actress in pursuing her work it is not feasible to have closing hours at which the girls must be home. And, too, actresses look upon smoking as a necessity. Therefore, Miss Williams says, these problems have to be handled differently. The honor system has been pressed into service most successfully, she says, and only a few general rules are required.[10]

The annual budget for the Hollywood Studio Club was reported in 1935 as $50,000, which came primarily from income. A small deficit was made up by the national board of the YWCA.

The club remained an integral part of the Hollywood community, a permanent residence with accommodation for ninety-four female extras, bit players, and occasional non-acting talent for many decades. A Western Union clerk from San Francisco, it is said, checked into the Los Angeles Biltmore Hotel as Princess Beatriz de Ortega y Braganza, a cousin to both King Alfonso of Spain and Manuel, the former king of Portugal. In a community obsessed with royal titles, she was welcomed with enthusiasm until she was revealed to be a fraud. Friendless, she was taken under the wing of actor Antonio Moreno's wife and became a resident at the Hollywood Studio Club. Nobody there was aware of her former fake identity.[11] Contestants coming to Hollywood in the 1930s to appear on producer Jesse L. Lasky's radio talent show, *Gateway to Hollywood*, were always housed at the club. Later residents there included Janet Blair, Linda Darnell, Barbara Hale, and Evelyn Keyes (who noted in later years that pregnancies among the residents "could be troublesome"[12]), Dorothy Malone, Kim Novak, Donna Reed, Gale Storm, and Marie Windsor. Perhaps the most famous resident was Marilyn Monroe, who moved into room 307 on June 3, 1948, sharing with Clarice Evans, and later had a room of her own, number 334.

Marilyn Monroe may have been the most famous tragic Hollywood figure associated with the Hollywood Studio Club, but she was not the only one. In the 1930s, director Marjorie Williams commented, "Oh we have our tragedies, little and big . . . Two deaths—accidental, and not on the premises; and a suicide . . . a girl named Julia Graham, a former choir singer of 22 [who shot herself at the home of a cameraman friend on July 15, 1935]."[13] In the early 1930s, the Hollywood Studio Club housed many residents who had no income. As Marjorie Williams noted:

> Since the depression we have had to carry a larger number of girls who could not pay, and although the majority try to pay their accounts when they do secure employment, we have found it necessary to write off a larger amount each year for uncollectable and doubtful accounts. We consider this a legitimate charge and a service for which we exist.[14]

The Hollywood Studio Cub played an uncredited role in the creation of one prominent Hollywood film of the 1930s, Gregory La Cava's *Stage Door*, released in October 1937. The film was supposedly based on a 1936 play by Edna Ferber and George S. Kaufman, with a storyline set in a New York theatrical boarding house inhabited by a group of young women in search of stage careers (played on screen by Katharine Hepburn, Ginger Rogers, Gail

Eve Arden, Katharine Hepburn, and Ginger Rogers in *Stage Door* (1937).

Patrick, Lucille Ball, and others). The screen adaptation of *Stage Door* finds a new plotline and dialogue based on the lives and gossip of the residents of the Hollywood Studio Club.

Director Gregory La Cava had his mistress, actress Doris Nolan, and his continuity girl, Winfrid Thackrey, hung out at the club, listening in on the stories the women there had to tell. According to Thackrey, La Cava told her:

> You'll be paid $100 a week, which will include expenses at a place called the Studio Club. I'm told it's the Hollywood version of New York's Footlights Club. Mrs. Cecil B. DeMille is head nun. Move in. Find me some dialogue that's alive—get some case histories. Who are these kids? Why do they want to be in pictures? Where do they come from? What was their home life? Small town? Why did they leave home to come here? Are they having any success? Have they been to the "casting couch"? Was it worth it? . . . I want it *in their own language.*[15]

Thackrey would visit with the residents at the dinner table, talking with forgotten extras like Jane Cavitt (who became an interior designer) and Laurie Douglas. Doris Nolan recalls spending time elsewhere: "He [La Cava] asked Winnie and me to sit around in the powder room. We'd sit by the hour, taking down all the dialogue for him."[16] After the success of *Stage Door*, Warner Bros. announced in 1938 that it was going to produce a similar film, one

1946 Paramount starlet Mary Edwards tests the water of the swimming pool at the Hollywood Studio Club.

actually set at the Hollywood Studio Club. Edmund Goulding was to direct, with Anita Louise and Olivia De Havilland starring, but nothing came of the project.

The Hollywood Studio Club also served as a convenient backdrop for studio publicists promoting a new starlet. For example, in 1946 Paramount released a series of photographs showing newly signed Mary Edwards at the club pool, playing ping-pong, listening to music in the lounge, and even enjoying a cup of tea. Mary Edwards's only credit is in a 1947 Paramount film, *Variety Girl*, in which she plays herself. While promoting the charitable Variety Clubs International, the movie does contain scenes filmed at what is obviously the Hollywood Studio Club, here renamed the Hollywood Girls Club.

Ayn Rand.

To celebrate the club's fortieth anniversary in May 1956, by which time over seven thousand guests had checked in, residents put on a revue titled *HOLLYWOOD 5-3166*. By the 1950s, guests had the choice of a single (for $14.50) or double (for $19.50) room, with breakfast and dinner included. Marjorie Williams, who had retired in 1946, was replaced first by Marion H. Weed (who had at one time been a resident), and subsequently by Florence Williams, who left in 1965 to become dean of women at Whittier College. She was succeeded by Agatha Campbell, formerly director of Christian education at the First Methodist Church of Pasadena, who was to reign over the club's gradual demise.

As early as June 1959, the Hollywood Studio Club had resorted to advertising vacancies. In October 1968, the club decided to merge with the

Hollywood YWCA Center, which had served as an employment service for women since 1930 and also offered educational courses. The club's new name was the Hollywood YWCA Studio Club. As the notion of women living in a residential club lost its appeal, the Studio Club reported significant operating losses. On February 23, 1971, a secret decision was made by the YWCA board of directors to close the club. Four years later, this decision became a reality, and the Hollywood Studio Club closed its doors in February 1975, "a victim of changing times and new fire codes."[17]

One surprising guest at the Hollywood Studio Club was Ayn Rand, who stayed there while writing the play *Night of January 16th*. For three months, Rand had worked as an extra for Cecil B. DeMille in his 1933 production of *Cleopatra*. In 1936, she wrote:

> The Studio Club is the only organization I know of personally that carries on, quietly and modestly, this great work which is needed so badly—help for young talent. It not only provides human, decent living accommodations which a poor beginner could not afford elsewhere, but it provides that other great necessity of life: Understanding. It makes a beginner feel that he is not, after all, an intruder with all the world laughing at him and rejecting him at every step, but that there are people who consider it worthwhile to dedicate their work to helping and encouraging him.[18]

Chapter Four

CENTRAL CASTING

In October 1925, the *Los Angeles Record* reported that the forty producers active in Hollywood had available to them some forty thousand extras. Of the latter, only four thousand could be guaranteed regular work. As Murray Ross has written, "This enormous oversupply of both professionals and amateurs who were determined to 'break into the movies' presented a social, moral and economic hazard."[1]

Two organizations were concerned about the situation, one part of California state government and the other very much a representative of the film industry. When the Motion Picture Producers and Distributors of America (MPPDA) was formed in 1922, with former postmaster general Will Hays as its head, its primary function was to clean up the film industry in the wake of a number of widely-publicized scandals, and to fight off any attempt at federal censorship of motion pictures. A related—and praiseworthy—effort, emphasized by Will Hays, was to change public perception of the industry, in part by getting rid of the obvious implication that women and children, working as extras, could easily be exploited, both financially and sexually.

In 1919, the studios had established an informal employment agency, known as the Service Bureau, for extras.[2] It operated out of a Victorian house, which was described in 1923 by Hays's Hollywood representative, Thomas Patten, as "a disreputable looking shack [that] has been permitted to run down to such an extent that its physical condition presents an appearance of utmost squalor and decay."[3] This was not a situation Hays could condone. He appointed Mary Van Kleek of the Russell Sage Foundation to study social and employment conditions in Hollywood. While her report, completed in 1923, was surprisingly positive, it did criticize employment problems within the community, and the manner in which extras were often forced to use high-priced casting agencies in order to gain employment.

At the same time, the California Department of Industrial Relations was receiving a large number of complaints about Hollywood's violations of the state's labor laws. The California Industrial Welfare Commission investigated unfavorable working conditions for women and children within the industry and reported that female extras were required to work overtime without pay. They were called to the studio at 7:00 a.m., and they would have to wait around until 10:00 a.m. or even noon, without pay, before being taken to the set. Both women and children were working ten- to twelve-hour days.

It was not only the studios that were at fault, but also many of the casting agencies that had sprung up all over Hollywood and did little but exploit low-paid extras and bit players. Some players would negotiate directly with a studio regardless of whether they were under contract to an agency, and often they would be offered salaries in excess of those the casting agencies had been able to obtain. One casting director offered a character actress to a producer at $250 a week. She went directly to the producer and was offered $500 per week. When the agent discovered what the actress had done, he told the producer that the salary was now $750. The actress turned around and signed a studio contract at $500 a week. The girl would be punished, *Variety* reported (July 15, 1925).

One 1923 incident, under-reported except by *Variety*, involved a mob of extras rushing an agency to obtain a return of commissions. The agency had hired a guard, who fired on the extras, several of whom were shot. Subsequently, the guard had to be rescued by police from extras who were threatening to lynch him.[4]

In November 1925, a meeting was attended by the California Industrial Welfare Commission, the Motion Picture Producers and Distributors Association of America, and representative of extras. The commission and the producers were reported to be in agreement that the maximum working day for female extras would be eight hours, and that in general these actors' lot would be made easier.[5]

In January 1926, the California Industrial Welfare Commission reportedly issued a set of orders regulating the employment of women and minors as extra talent in the film industry. (The studios voluntarily extended this set of orders to include men.) An "extra" was defined as a woman or a minor employed on a daily basis at a wage of fifteen dollars or less. After eight hours, extra women were to be paid overtime at no less than one-quarter of the daily wage up to ten hours. From ten to twelve hours, overtime was to be not less than one-half of the daily wage. From twelve to

Will Hays, second from right, with, from left to right, director E. Mason Hopper, Fred Beetson, first president of Central Casting, and Chief Scott of the Los Angeles Fire Department. AMPAS.

fourteen hours, overtime was to be three-quarters of the daily wage. And after fourteen hours, it was to be not less than double. Wardrobe fittings and related activities were to be paid for at the daily rate, regardless of whether an extra was finally employed. Extra women working at night had to be dismissed in time to return home by public transportation, or the studio had to provide transportation. Extra women working in excess of the standard day after 11:30 p.m. were to be provided with meals and hot drinks. "Proper sanitary conditions" were to be provided on location. Carfare was to be paid on "weather permitting" calls. Extras were to be paid in cash or "negotiable paper" at the end of each day's work.[6]

Concurrent with the release of the set of order from the California Industrial Welfare Commission, Will Hays announced the creation of the Central Casting Corporation. As reported by Murray Ross, Central Casting Corporation was to be the employment office for all members of the Motion Picture Producers and Distributors of America—in essence, for all producers active in Hollywood, aside from a small group of minor independent filmmakers.

The Division of Labor Statistics and Law Enforcement of the Department of Industrial Relations of the State of California provided four basic rationales for the establishment of Central Casting as of June 30, 1926:

1. To do away with the high fees charged by private employment agencies to extras in the motion picture industry
2. To eliminate the violations of law arising out of methods of paying off extras
3. To discourage the constantly increasing influx of persons as extras in the industry, and
4. To develop a residue of efficient extras who would be called upon frequently and would be able to derive a decent living from their employment as extras[7]

Central Casting was officially established on December 4, 1925, and formally opened its doors on January 26, 1926. Will Hays pontificated, "Good moral character and ability to act will be the primary references necessary to listing.... The 30,000 aspirants here for extra work will be classified, investigated and segregated."[8] Further, Hays noted, "It will do away with the evils of the employment bureaus which have extracted more than $500,000 a year from extras. It will cause the elimination of all make-up and screen acting schools."[9] To one trade paper, because of Central Casting "[t]he motion picture industry has given the lie to the scoffers and cynics who claim that it is nothing but a money-grabbing institution. It produces concrete evidence that it possesses a heart and a soul. Both of them well developed and functioning every day of the week."[10] On a more mundane level, as was noted, Central Casting would substantially reduce the cost—in 1925 claimed to total some three million dollars—to the studios of hiring extras.

Curiously, Central Casting was soon embroiled in a morals scandal of its own when a seventeen-year-old girl, Rose Marie Dolan, accused the corporation's manager, David "Dave" Allen, of making improper advances. But the scandal was actually a conspiracy thought up by Dolan's mother and her partner, Frank O'Neil. Working with the police, Allen pretended to agree to pay $500 to Dolan's mother in order to hush up the non-incident, and the trio was arrested in August 1926. Journalist Adela Rogers St. Johns used the story as the plotline for one of her "The Port of Missing Girls" pieces the following year in *Photoplay*, changing Allen into a director.[11]

David Allen's tenure as head of Central Casting was to end as a result of another, similar accusation. Twenty-four-year-old June De Long (real name Ann Snyder) was an extra noted for her shapely hands, which had doubled for many a star's in a close-ups. She claimed that on April 26, 1934, Allen and another extra named Gloria Marsh, age twenty-six, had visited her apartment, where they engaged in a "wild party" involving sexual activity. De

Long and Allen were seen in a compromising position by a witness. David Allen and Gloria Marsh were indicted by a grand jury, and on July 9, 1934, their trial began. It was by all accounts a circus, with five hundred spectators fighting for admission. Noted criminal defense attorney Jerry Giesler (whose later celebrity clients were to include Errol Flynn, Robert Mitchum, Charlie Chaplin, and Bugsy Siegel) represented Allen. There were accusations that not only was the charge a "frame-up," with prosecution witnesses taken from the ranks of the Motion Picture Extras and Supporting Players, then involved in a dispute with Central Casting, but also that the charge had anti-Semitic undertones, in that the accused was Jewish. To add to the excitement, after giving evidence June De Long vanished, leaving a suicide note. Then one day after her disappearance, she was found alive and well. A jury of eight men and four women was unable to reach a verdict, with eight favoring conviction. Allen was never retried, but he was forced to resign from Central Casting that same month. Allen moved to Columbia Pictures, where he remained for nineteen years. He died in Los Angeles on January 3, 1955, at the age of sixty-eight.

Succeeding Allen was British-born Campbell MacCulloch, who was hired on September 11, 1934, and who had previously been heavily involved with the California division of the National Recovery Administration (NRA). MacCulloch remained with Central Casting until April 1940; he died in March 1941 at the age of sixty-seven. Following MacCullogh, Howard R. Philbrick became general manager. Philbrick had formerly been a Justice Department agent and was currently director of the State Department of Motor Vehicles. Philbrick's service to the state ended in scandal when a dictagraph, which he had planted, was discovered hidden in the hotel room of Speaker Gordon Garland. Philbrick's appointment was subject to approval by the Screen Actors Guild, whose members were increasingly complaining of "pay-offs, favoritism, nepotism and other irregularities"[12] at Central Casting, charges which dated back to 1939. One of the first items in Philbrick's order of business was to lay off two casting directors, Frank Roderick and Al Smith, while at the same time denying the suspensions had anything to do with complaints from extras. Philbrick died of leukemia at the early age of forty-five in October 1951 and was succeeded by Arthur S. Bronson.

The main office of Central Casting was located in the Guarantee Building at the corner of Hollywood Boulevard and Western Avenue. The building is still extant and was owned for many years by Louis B. Mayer. Fred Beetson, secretary of the Motion Picture Producers and Distributors of America, was

The entrance to the Central Casting Bureau on Hollywood Boulevard. AMPAS.

named the first president of Central Casting, with O. C. Wyman tapped as the organization's first general manager. Dave Allen initially held the position of casting director. In 1929, Central Casting organized the Call Bureau, subsequently renamed the Actors Agency Directory, to maintain lists of agency affiliations and later to compile cast lists of major studio productions. Players with screen credits, no matter how ancient the credit, could register with the Call Bureau for "bit" as opposed to extra work.[13]

A downtown office for Central Casting was also maintained at the California Free Employment Bureau, located at 307 West 1st Street. It was, as one reporter commented, "close to the downtown parks and missions and cheap lodging houses, where aging and unemployed men congregate, [and] it is a window of hope to the jobless."[14] This office appears to have operated on a less formal level than did the Hollywood office. Groups of unemployed men would gather outside, watching a bay window—"the most closely watched window in the world"[15]—at which stood C. B. Collins. If Collins raised his hand to his chin, it would signify there were openings for bearded men. Or he might simply point at one of the men in the crowd.

From the start, Central Casting emphasized that extra work was nothing more than "casual employment," which should never be depended upon for a livelihood. Its registration forms always contained the warning, "The great variation of types of pictures made, requiring all races and nationalities, etc., makes extra employment most casual. It may be months before a picture will be made requiring YOUR services." The warning was followed by a waiver aspiring extras were obliged to sign: "I have read the above statement carefully and in making my application I understand that there is no guaranty of work."

The first task of Central Casting was to register all available extras, 60 percent of which reportedly consisted of women. To check if they had work, extras were required to telephone Central Casting, sometimes as often as every fifteen minutes. The switchboard was open from 6:00 a.m. and often stayed open until as late as midnight. Initially, there was one telephone number, GARfield 3981, but as of 1944, the organization had two numbers: GARfield 3621 for male extras, and GARfield 3711 for women. In the beginning, three operators handled an average of 1,271 incoming calls and five hundred outgoing ones every hour.[16] In more recent years, eight telephone lines were dedicated to male extras and six to females. With evolving tastes, the content of movies and television programs changed to such an extent that by the 1980s, there was far greater demand for male than female extras. "There's . . . more calls for cops, cowboys, military personnel," explained Central Casting's vice-president Carl Joy in the early 1980s.[17] Both to check on potentially discriminatory practices by switchboard operators, and also to speed up call processing, anyone within the Central Casting organization could, with the flick of a switch, listen in to all incoming calls.

In response to suggestions that casting be made only by out-going calls, it was pointed out that such a change would mean extras would be forced to remain close to the telephone all day. Others noted that if one extra received a call for a certain type of player, Central Casting would almost immediately receive calls from other extras of the same type as the word was passed from the one to another. "[W]ithin a very few minutes of the first call the whole

Paramount assistant casting director Holly Morse studies a file of photographs and information on extras registered with Central Casting, while fellow casting director Scotty Groves looks on. AMPAS.

board will be covered with calls from the players of a certain class. This is the famous Hollywood grapevine."[18]

By 1944, extras were blatantly abusing the policy regarding calls to the switchboard. Rather than phoning every fifteen minutes, some extras were telephoning every sixty seconds, and Central Casting reported that calls had jumped from two thousand to four thousand per hour. Extras had discovered the potential to tie up the lines and thus prevent others from getting through. *Daily Variety* (May 18, 1944) reported that, "Central call board was lighted up like a Christmas tree yesterday as calls poured in and extra help had to be assigned to handle the calls. Continuous dialing delayed efforts of Central to fill the calls and made it difficult for other players seeking jobs to get through."

When Central Casting telephoned an extra with employment information, conversation was kept to a minimum. In the 1930s, an extra might receive an abrupt early evening call along these lines: "Hello. Central calling. This Mabel Jones? Berkeley company. Warners. Be there at 8 tomorrow. Street clothes." A click followed, as the call was ended.[19] Eventually, Central Casting telephone operators adopted a form of abbreviated speech. A caller would identify himself or herself by name, and the response would be "Tra-lay," meaning "try later." More depressing would be the one syllable response,

"Nerk," signifying "no work." It was not long before "Nerk" became common on the set, with extras asking, "Did you get nerked today?"

In 1927, *Photoplay* profiled one of the switchboard operators, whom it dubbed "The Mother Confessor of Hollywood." Any emotional calls were passed from the regular operators to her. She would deflect angry calls from extras who claimed to have been discriminated against. She would advise would-be extras to find other employment. She would even find employment elsewhere for women on the verge of starvation. "In cruelly ambitious Hollywood where fate is as impersonal as death and contentment unknown, there was somebody who listened kindly," commented *Photoplay.*[20] In the mid 1930s, Central Casting reported more than one hundred telephone calls a day appealing for work to solve personal or financial problems. The organization acknowledged sympathy with the calls, but refused to do anything to help other than recommend the applicants seek employment elsewhere.

Requests for extras were sent by teletype, with studio casting directors providing specific information as to the type of extras needed. The Central Casting staff was incredibly knowledgeable about many of the extras calling in for work. Staff members could immediately determine if an extra fitted a studio's specific request.

Central Casting moved into the machine age in the fall of 1935, under the guidance of Campbell MacCulloch. From the accounting world, he introduced multi-punched cards for each of the extras. Each card, which was similar in appearance to those used by utility companies to document their customers' bills, was three inches wide by seven inches long. These cards could store as many as 540 pieces of information, including height, size, appearance, hair color, physical characteristics, clothing available, experience, ability to sing, dance, play musical instruments, sports abilities, languages spoken, and ethnic background (with forty-two nationalities acknowledged). Fritz Lang's *Metropolis* had come to Hollywood, with extras reduced to the level of automatons, granted neither a name nor individuality.

The *New York Times* published information from the card of a preferred male, extra No. 105:

> Class A, 27 years old, 6 feet tall, weight 190 pounds and in appearance is an athlete, good looking, with a good figure. He has large blue eyes, is clean shaven and his head has the rating of "artist." Good-looking feet, dark brown hair, medium-sized, good-looking and well-kept hands, and medium-sized, straight legs mark him. His skin is light Nordic.[21]

The card identified No. 105 as having a wardrobe that included a tuxedo, business and sports suits, a riding habit, and knickers, and added that his appearance might identify him as an aristocrat, a city dweller, a Northerner, or a cowboy. He was an accomplished adagio, ballroom, classical, soft-shoe, and tap dancer. He was an acrobat, a gymnast, a human fly, and a juggler. He could sing tenor. Sporting abilities included those associated with archery, badminton, baseball, bowling, mountain climbing, deck tennis, diving, swimming, high jumping, riding, ping pong, roller skating, rowing, surfboarding, soccer, squash, and all types of athletic competition. He could speak Belgian, Dutch, English, and French, and play the piano. "It is a lot of man to buy for from $7.50 to $15.00 a day," commented the *New York Times*.[22]

By the 1940s, it was reported that Central Casting had such unusual breakdowns as "Arabians able to handle camels," "Hindus able to handle elephants," "Girls—sweet looking," "strong men," "rough characters," and "drivers capable of handling from one to six-team rigs."[23] Later, Central Casting would install a teletype connection to Western Costume, allowing the company to have immediate knowledge of which films were using extras and the types of costumes that would be required.

Through the 1920s, interviews with potential extras were conducted between 1:00 a.m. and 3:00 a.m. by Marian L. Mel, director of the women's division and former assistant secretary of the California Industrial Welfare Commission, and by Colonel O. C. Wyman, who headed the men's division. Their recommendations were passed to casting head David Allen for approval. Marian L. Mel was polite, kind, and efficient. To would-be extras, she would say, "Think over your life and recall the thing you do best. Then go home and do it. Hollywood doesn't need or want you. Go home. If you stay here, you will only suffer and possibly starve." When begged for help, she would respond, "I can't, and for your own sake, I won't."[24] According to the *Film Daily*, Mel assured that

> the proper type of women is registered. They must meet certain well defined tests as to character and intelligence as well as screen adaptability. Thus that important factor of maintaining a proper moral standard is assured, in addition to a more commercial aspect of building up a work force that will meet all the innumerable demands of the various productions.[25]

Prior to registration, minors were required to provide a certificate of health and a record of their school attendance. Interviews with children were conducted only before or after school hours, with mothers, of course, in attendance.

Unfortunately, casting directors and production staff at the studios still had the right to ask for specific extras for specific productions. Sadly, this meant that Central Casting could do nothing about the proprietary interest of certain studio personnel in certain female extras. Reportedly, when a call came in from a studio, it might well be that seventy-five of the eighty requested female extras were already on call at that studio. In 1938, casting of some 59 percent of all extras cast resulted from direct placement by the studios.[26] "And behind each of those demanded names there is always a story of personal influence," commented Ruth Waterbury. "Central protects itself by marking the girl's pay check 'requested.' Then if such a girl is unsatisfactory to the studio for any reason, the blame cannot fall on the agency."[27]

Undoubtedly, the Central Casting staff was sympathetic to the extras. One staff member, Burt Hampton, actually organized a softball team comprised of female extras, and it played for charity under the name Burt Hampton's Movie Girls. Hampton resigned as casting chief in May 1940 under circumstances suggesting impropriety. As early as October 1934, Central Casting had created a complaint bureau under the supervision of Allan MacDonald. During its first two hours of operation on the first day of the month, some fifty protests were filed, most being nothing more than appeals for work. In its first month, the bureau was able to provide hospital treatment for ten extras and placed sixty more in steady employment outside the industry.

A description of the casting room at Central Casting was provided in a 1939 radio broadcast by its then general manager, Campbell MacCulloch. In all probability, the arrangement had not changed since the 1920s:

> A big, well-lighted room. On one wall, an illuminated directory board with hundreds of names, and facing it, four desks. At each desk sits a casting director and an assistant. There is a loudspeaker on each which transmits the names of the extras from the telephone girls to the casting desks. Then, there are special electric looking devices and switching keys which give instant communication with the switchboards so the casting directors can have any caller turned over to them in one second. I might say nearly everything was designed and built especially for us. Behind the casting desks is the call desk, mostly outgoing and routine calls. Five girls sit on that, sending about 1500 calls a day. Sometimes we want people of a particular type who haven't called in. So we call them. After a particular call has

This photograph is captioned "Rush Hour at Central Casting." AMPAS.

> been filled, it is necessary that every extra must have an individual voucher made out for him, and there must be eight copies of each call sheet or list of names for each particular call. . . . As soon as the vouchers and call sheets are completed, they are sent by special messenger to the studio in readiness for the next day. The office stays open until its work is finished which might be two o'clock in the morning.[28]

In the past, it was reported, extras had been paid with vouchers that could only be cashed at specific locations, leading to exploitation by scalpers offering to perform that service in return for a consideration. Under Central Casting rules, extras were paid with studio checks that could be cashed at any bank.

In July 1926, it was noted that in its first six months of operation, Central Casting placed 113,837 extras (629 a day), who received total remuneration of $863,804.65. The average daily wage of the extra was a mere $8.84.[29] The good news was that the salary reduction demanded of all employees by studios in the summer of 1927 did not affect extras; it affected only those earning more than fifty dollars a week.

A committee appointed by the Academy of Motion Picture Arts and Sciences made recommendations to the National Recovery Administration (NRA) in September 1933, following an investigation of the conditions among the "extra players" of Hollywood. The committee urged "[t]hat there be a thorough re-registration of genuine 'extra players.' That employing producers immediately restore rate of pay for 'extras' to level existing prior to 1931." The committee pointed out:

> Pay of extras has been radically cut, in the past few years those in the brackets between $7.50 a day to $15, getting an average cut of 20%. While in 1930, there were no $2 and $1.50 extras, yet these small salaries were paid in 1933 . . . many former well known names were among those called for $3 jobs. Average per call in 1930 was $9 but in 1932 it had been reduced to $7.48. Only 69 persons averaged as much as two days a week in the first half of 1933, and no one averaged three days.[30]
>
> That no-one shall be employed as an "extra player" or as an "atmosphere worker" who is a member of the immediate family of any regular employee of a motion picture company; and that no one shall be employed as an "extra" on account of personal favoritism.[31]

Three extras, Allan Garcia, Ted Oliver, and Fred Williams, had been co-opted to the committee, whose recommendations were honorable if not exactly likely to be accepted by the studios.

A publication titled *Motion Picture Code Provisions Governing Extras* was published by Central Casting in November 1934 (although it was dated January 30, 1931), in collaboration with the National Recovery Administration and the Industrial Welfare Commission of the State of California. The publication provides detailed information on working conditions for extras and identifies minimum wages and requirements for various types:

> REQUIREMENTS FOR $10.00 EXTRAS
> Character Women
> Extras required to furnish wardrobe which will be maintained for picture purposes only, for example:
> Spinsters.
> Small town teachers.
> Period wardrobe, et cetera.
> Outstanding individual types who qualify for the following:
> Police matrons.
> Landlady.
> Hag beggars.
> Waitresses
> Social type.
> Professional dancers for musicals or showgirls.

REQUIREMENTS FOR $10.00 EXTRAS

Character Men

Extras required to furnish wardrobe which is maintained for picture purposes only, for example:

Ministers.

Small town judges.

Period wardrobe, et cetera.

Outstanding individual types who qualify for the following:

Detectives.

Gangsters.

Roman Guards.

Eccentric people.

Waiters.

Butlers.

Social types.

Professional dancers for musicals.

REQUIREMENTS FOR $15.00 EXTRAS

Women

Evening gowns, complete—Requiring suitable wraps, fur or otherwise—no shawls or mufflers.

Dinner gowns, complete—Requiring suitable wraps, fur or otherwise—no shawls or mufflers.

Formal afternoon clothes, complete—Requiring furs or fur coats.

Suitable street clothes—All types requiring furs or fur coats.

Note: For this type of work wardrobe must be "acceptable modern" wardrobe.

REQUIREMENTS FOR $15.00 EXTRAS

Male

Full dress complete.

Tuxedo complete.

Cutaway complete.

Boulevard complete.

Riding Habit complete.

Note: The above to include topcoat, silk hat muffler, cane, gloves, etcetera. For this type of work wardrobe must be an "acceptable modern" wardrobe.

REQUIREMENTS FOR $10.00 EXTRAS

Women

Smart clothes. In addition to good physical qualifications these people will be required to maintain a wardrobe suitable for motion picture purposes such as:

Light and dark street clothes.

Light and dark coats.

Bathing suits, including robe, slippers, etc.

Lounging pajamas, robes, slippers, etc.

Palm Beach or light suits.

Sport clothes.

Note: For this type of work, clothes must be strictly up to date.

REQUIREMENTS FOR $10.00 EXTRAs

Male

Smart clothes. In addition to good physical qualifications these people will be required to maintain a wardrobe suitable for motion picture purposes, such as:

Light and dark business suits.

Light and dark overcoats.

Bathing suits, including robes, slippers, etc.

Lounging pajamas, robes, slippers, etc.

Palm Beach suits.

Flannels.

Note: For this type of work, clothes must be strictly up to date.

REQUIREMENTS FOR $7.50 EXTRAS

Women

Costume furnished. This to include all sets where costumes are furnished, for example:

Maids.

Nurses.

Peasants.

Period sets, etc.

Ordinary street clothes: This is to include clothes that would represent ordinary wardrobe owned by the average individual outside of pictures, such as:

Street clothes—light—dark.

Sports clothes.

Bathing suit.
Coat—light—dark.

REQUIREMENTS FOR $7.50 EXTRAS
Men
Costume furnished: This to include all sets where costumes are furnished, for example:
Period sets.
Soldiers.
Sailors.
Policemen and firemen with this minimum graded upward according to the character and type of performance.
Ordinary street clothes: This to include clothes that would represent ordinary wardrobe owned by the average individual outside of pictures, such as:
Street clothes—light—dark.
Flannels.
Bathing suit.
Overcoats—light—dark.

REQUIREMENTS FOR $5.00 EXTRAS
Men and Women
Any group of miscellaneous people where no costume fitting or interviews are involved, but if costume fitting is required the costume shall be fitted the same day the person works.

In addition, the booklet includes seven pages of rules and regulations governing the employment of extras. Included here are promises of full pay for costume fittings; partial pay when shooting is called off because of weather conditions or cancelled; and partial pay for travel time on one-day locations. Meal breaks are defined, as are hours of labor and overtime. Producers are responsible for injuries due to night work, "wet" work or dangerous work, and extras have the option of refusing such work. Female extras are provided suitable seats. Dressing rooms and locker rooms are to be private and adjacent to sets. On location, there is to be at least one toilet seat for every twenty women, screened and with washing facilities and toilet paper provided and sanitary napkins obtainable. It is an impressive document.

While the Motion Picture Code might formalize the identification of various types of extras, those within the profession had devised their own, more entertaining descriptions. The lowest classification of extras was "vags." Extras working for three dollars a day were "three-dollar stiffs," while those also receiving meals were identified as "cannibals." Extras who could handle rough assignments were "bumpers." Extras with formal attire were "stuffed dummies," "the soup and fish," or, in the 1920s, "bronze boys". The latter preferred to be described as "number 1 boys," although there is nothing very boyish about them. Gentlemen of a certain age with bushy beards were appropriately identified as "beards." "Front line barnacles" were those to be found hanging around casting offices on a regular basis. Young female extras were "pinkies," and females of any age working tediously on a large production were known as "weary Annes." Those working in courtroom scenes and routinely photographed through railings were called—inexplicably from a modern perspective—"tripe." To play in a mob scene was identified as "mobbing." The cancellation of a call for extras was a "death knell." By the late 1920s, Central Casting was known among its users simply as "CC."

As of 1934, the total number of extras registered with Central Casting remained pretty much unchanged from previous years at 17,541. (In 1929, oddly, the same number of extras was registered.) The problem of the constantly high number of registered extras stemmed from the number of individuals arriving in Hollywood, victims of the Depression who believed that the film industry offered both glamor and work. It could provide neither. Studios were producing fewer spectacular productions that needed large numbers of extras, instead concentrating more on intimate dramas employing few if any extras. The situation was so dire that a small group of extras actually built themselves a shantytown near Universal City. At least two female extras were sharing a tent. Male extras were reportedly living five or six to a room, sharing clothes when a job came up. "The others sit around pantless, coatless, shoeless, till their pal returns with their clothes and a few dollars."[32]

It was the professional extras, those who were the mainstay of the extra community within the industry, who came up with a solution: Central Casting should cut its list of available extras to a mere 1,500 individuals. A committee, consisting of men and women from outside of the film industry, was formed and given responsibility for whittling down the list. The committee solicited advice from casting directors at each of the studios; the more casting directors recommended a specific extra, the more likely she or he was to make the list. When Campbell MacCullogh was named head of Central Casting, he tried to persuade many of the registered extras to enter other fields of employment. Eventually, 350 agreed to seek other occupations, but most eventually returned to the only job they had really known.

Central Casting was becoming increasingly aware that many so-called "dress" extras were not particularly well dressed. Some males wore suits that had changed from black to green with age. Some of the more elderly women wore long out-of-date attire more appropriate to the silent era or to comedies. In the winter of 1934, Central Casting asked extras to display their clothing available for on-set use. Reportedly, purchases and rentals of evening attire surged to previously unknown heights, with extras collectively spending an estimated $50,000 in a desperate attempt to gain Central Casting approval. Extras loaned clothing to each other, and desirable items were immediately passed on to the next extra waiting to appear before the judges. The *New York Times* reported that a male dress extra earning $2,800 a year might spend as much as $700 per year for upkeep and replacement of his clothes. "Hollywood is a place where 50 cents is more important when spent to have a suit pressed than it is for a dinner."[33] A year later, in April 1935, Central Casting decided to eliminate the category of dress extra, claiming it caused jealousy and dissent and prevented younger "faces" from obtaining employment. Elimination of the dress extra category was, in all probability, only in force for a limited amount of time.

In February 1935, Central Casting announced that it was registering no new extras. The only exceptions were special types, who would be placed on a special list and called only if and when there was a need for that type. Interviews were discontinued. Those extras who were registered earned little. In 1936, only 533 earned more than $500 in a six-month period. In other words, only thirty-five extras earned as much as nineteen dollars a week.

In the summer of 1938, Central Casting agreed to open its interview department, with casting directors available to interview extras every three months. The Screen Actors Guild reported: "Members will be given an opportunity to apply for more desirable calls, place any complaints directly before proper persons, and to discuss personal problems with the men who do the casting for all studios."[34] Matters were getting somewhat out of control with the influx of new, would-be extras, and in September 1942, Central Casting suspended interviews for a month, noting that in August the agency had interviewed some thousand persons, and that organizing the data received was taking longer than anticipated.

When many technical workers and laborers in the industry received a 10 percent pay increase in November 1939, extras agitated for a 15 percent increase in their daily rate. The studios ignored these demands. And little wonder, as in May 1940, Central Casting reported that it had nine hundred extra jobs available each day, with some seven thousand registered extras available and eager for work at any salary level. By 1946, perhaps through attrition of male extras involved in the military, 5,500 extras were registered, of which 2,500 were minors under eighteen years of age. All were required to be members of the Screen Extras Guild, and just as in the late 1930s one requirement for registration was membership in the so-called Junior Screen Actors Guild. Effectively, Central Casting was operating a closed shop.

Rules and regulations still did not deter persistent would-be extras. In the lower hallway of the Central Casting building women, who apparently had nothing else to do or who lived nearby, congregated—as did cowboys in Western attire and mothers carrying babies in their arms. All hoped to be spotted by one of the casting directors as he made his way to the elevator and the safety of the third floor offices.

One major issue with which Central Casting had to deal from the time of its inception involved juvenile extras. As early as 1927, Will Hays had commented, "Children and pretty girls are a drug on the market. . . . Only twelve children a day, on an average, are employed through the casting bureau."[35] In the late 1930s, one drunken mother arrived at reception and offered to sell her baby to Central Casting for $500. A woman in Detroit put her two daughters, aged eight and ten, on a bus to Hollywood with a note to Central Casting to "put [the girls] in pictures." The Travelers Aid Society helped return the children to Detroit, but a short time later, the mother contacted Central Casting again, announcing that her daughters were improved and she would be sending them back. During the same period, Central Casting helped an indigent male extra and his pregnant wife get into a local hospital in time for the birth. A week later, Paramount needed a newborn baby, sent an ambulance to the hospital, and hired the baby for seventy-five dollars a day. The director of the film was not ready to shoot the scene involving the baby, and for sixteen days, mother, baby, and a nurse were transported back and forth from the studio to the hospital. As a result, the baby earned $1,200 for its parents in the first three weeks of its life.[36]

According to Murray Ross, writing in 1941, Central Casting placed only twenty-four children in 1926. In 1940, it placed thirty-three children. The lowest number placed was nineteen in 1930 and the highest forty-eight in 1939. The Los Angeles educational authorities reported 1,268 children working on screen in the years 1929–30, and 2,093 in the years 1939–40. The reported numbers do not, of course, indicate how many children were actually used, but rather how many child extras had appeared on screen, some multiple times.[37]

As of 1950, Central Casting had a standing register of one thousand juveniles, ranging in age from two weeks to fourteen years. The previous year, the average pay for a juvenile had been one hundred dollars, with the minimum for a speaking part being fifty-five dollars. The pay scale for children actually shrank as they aged. Those between two weeks and one month old (who could actually work only fifteen minutes per day under state law) received seventy-five dollars a day. At two months, the pay went down to fifty dollars. Those children from two to six months were paid twenty-five dollars a day. After six months, there was a massive reduction to $15.56 a day. Babies might earn far more than their parents working as extras. In the mid 1930s, Mrs. Bernice Saunders, who was in charge of calls to Central Casting for young babies, would receive telephone calls two or three times a day from expectant mothers advising her of their probable delivery dates. Apart from Central Casting, a number of agencies specialized in children. Also, MGM casting director Mel Ballerino would set aside Saturdays for interviews with children (and, of course, their doting mothers).

On March 1, 1961, Central Casting became the extras' employer, paying their salaries directly. It was now a moneymaking institution rather than simply a service organization. It was not surprising, therefore, that, in June 1976, Central Casting was sold to Production Payments, Inc., the West Coast subsidiary of Talent & Residuals. Also that same month, Universal established its own casting unit, in effect turning the clock back to the 1910s. The new unit was headed by a former extra, Karl Brindle, who noted that the previous year Universal had employed a total of 45,744 extras.

As of 1962, it was reported that the total wages of extras working in the industry amounted to more than $3,300,000, with dress extras taking home $33.54 a day and other extras pulling in $25.47.[38] This compensation compares more than favorably with that of the first decade of the Central Casting's existence, when there was little change in the total annual wages of extras between 1926 ($2,195,395.65) and 1940 ($2,529,766.10). Ultimately, thanks to Central Casting, the lot of the extra was improved, in part, it must be noted, by a drop in the numbers of naïve females and equally naïve males who flocked to Hollywood. Some have even argued, erroneously I believe, that Central Casting was "the first formal organizing of any members of the Hollywood labor force."[39] A more accurate description from a labor perspective might be company union.

Chapter Five

THE PORT OF MISSING GIRLS

In the March 1927 issue of *Photoplay*, Adela Rogers St. Johns published the first of six short stories bearing the overall title "The Port of Missing Girls."[1] Each story features a different girl with a dream of a Hollywood career, to which all are attracted "like flies drawn to a honey pot."[2] The first, Greta, is a farm girl who comes to Hollywood, becomes pregnant by a married man, and loses the child at its birth. The weight she gains during pregnancy makes it difficult to obtain work as an extra, but she is hired as a member of a poverty row company filming in Tulare. There she meets a local farmer, and, inevitably, falls in love with him, realizing that life on the farm is better than life in Hollywood. "And then she turned suddenly to kiss him. It was Greta's first kiss. Oh, she had been kissed before. She had lain acquiescent before love. But it was the first time she had ever kissed a man."[3] Great literature it is not, but the author assures the reader—perhaps in apology for the melodramatics of the storyline—that "The only thing untrue about this story is the girl's name."[4]

In addition to the Adela Rogers St. Johns series, there were others stories about Hollywood dreams, most notably Margaret E. Sangster's "The Stars That Never Were," published in *Photoplay* from August through December 1928. In Sangster's tales, the leading characters are both female and male. (In reality, calls for male extras in the 1920s and beyond generally outnumbered calls for women by two or three to one.) In general, fictional works concerning Hollywood extras adhered to a theme enunciated by John Parris Springer: "For the extra, as for the star, the drive to work in films and to pursue a career in Hollywood had to be punished."[5] To a large extent, writings such as these advanced the notion that women should be made to suffer for pursuing independence rather than the respectability and controlled environment that marriage would bring. The naivety of the innocent, foolish, and even narcissistic women coming to Hollywood to pursue a career they hoped would begin with a life as an extra and end in the fabled glamor of

Adela Rogers St. Johns.

stardom was caught by Norman Rockwell in an illustration that appeared in the July 1930 edition of *Ladies Home Journal*. Titled "Hollywood Dreams," the painting shows a young innocent girl seated beside an elderly couple outside a casting office bearing a sign that announces: "Closed."

In the 1929 novel *Extra-Girl*, Stella G. S. Perry's heroine, Odile Vaure, is a beauty contest winner from Louisiana who comes to Hollywood in search of a career. Her experience of Hollywood involves one of her friends being raped, while another moves in with a male extra and becomes pregnant, and yet another becomes a drug addict and commits suicide. The reality of the Hollywood extra's desperation is vividly portrayed by a young mother, who takes her sick child with her rather than miss a casting call. Eventually, the heroine, like so many in the fiction of the day, rejects Hollywood and what it represents, instead settling down to a life of domesticity as a happy wife and mother. She will live in "the other Hollywood . . . where the real houses are. And the little real hopes. And the little real people." As John Parris Springer notes, "The book's culturally conservative admonition was for young women to stay home, get married, and have children rather than pursue an ideal image of themselves as rich, glamorous, and beautiful—an image that was shaped by fan magazines and movies and by powerful but illusory cultural myths about Hollywood."[6]

Reckless Hollywood, published in 1932, is credited to Haynes Lubou, the pseudonym of an unidentified female writer. Its central character, Petty Love, is introduced on the set of a film directed by the dictatorial and abusive R. B. De Lacey, a thinly veiled version of Cecil B. DeMille. Her next day's work is contingent upon her sleeping with the assistant director (presumably not modeled on DeMille's real-life assistant, Cullen Tate, who was responsible for much of the extra casting). The novel concludes with Love sleeping with him, thus assuring that she can work tomorrow.

There are, of course, many other Hollywood novels of this period with a similar theme, but in them the central characters are generally not extras but players with contracts—which does not by any means place relieve them of the burden of providing sexual favors, but does mean they are outside the purview of this book.[7] Hollywood studios boasted about the morality clauses in their contracts, but such contracts were written for stars and leading or supporting players. The poor extra girls had no contracts and no morality clauses to protect them.

Probably the earliest and most entertaining short story concerning a would-be female extra in Hollywood is Frank Condon's appropriately titled "Hollywood," published by *Photoplay* in 1923. Here a small town Ohio beauty announces to her retired businessman father that she intends to go to Hollywood to seek employment and fame. The father warns her, "The motion picture is a fiery dragon, sinking its ruthless claws into the innocent young womanhood of America." When his daughter remains adamant, he decides to accompany her. While she sets up a home for them in Hollywood, he makes friends easily and is persuaded to work as an extra appropriate to his appearance. He explains to the daughter: "I'm just doing bits of extra work. I am also making valuable friends. Any time you say so, I'll take you along and introduce you. Of course, Angela, you must remember there are shoals of pretty girls looking for a chance to get in. What the movies want is *types*. I happen to be a type—that's all there is to it." The outraged daughter, rejected by the film industry, persuades her two spinster aunts to come to Hollywood to try to extricate her father from the industry. The aunts arrive and are promptly persuaded, thanks to their appearance, to work as extras. Eventually, it is the daughter who returns home to small town married life.

There are novels and short stories in which the principal character is a male extra. The most notable, of course, is Harry Leon Wilson's *Merton of the Movies*, first published in 1922.[8] Also of interest is Paul Alexander's 1941 self-published work, *The Hollywood Bug*, which is nothing more than a series of short stories about a young European, who works as an extra in Hollywood and beds the wife of the studio head, only to have the latter sexually harass his girlfriend.

Unlike their female counterparts, male extras are not depicted as subjects of sexual harassment. Yet, in more recent years there have certainly been casting directors who demanded sexual favors from the young, good-looking men seeking work at their studios. And there have been some notorious Hollywood agents who expected payment of a sexual nature for whatever work they were able to offer. In that male sexual harassment is an accepted, if illegal, aspect of life within the Hollywood community today, it seems unlikely that it was not present decades earlier—even if it went undocumented.

The casting couch is almost synonymous with the history of Hollywood would-be actresses and, to a certain extent, actors. Reportedly in the 1950s a well-known Culver City producer had a plaque on the ceiling above the office couch reading, "Don't forget, darling, tomorrow you're going to be a star."[9]

Almost concurrently with "The Port of Missing Girls" series, *Photoplay* published three lengthy essays, titled "The Truth about Breaking into the Movies," by Ruth Waterbury. The premise of the series is that *Photoplay* editor James Quirk had bet Waterbury $500 that without revealing her credentials she would be unable to break into the movies as an extra. Waterbury arrives in Hollywood, checks into the Hollywood Studio Club, and quickly discovers that Quirk is correct. Waterbury finds that Central Casting is taking no more registrations, and visits to individual studios are immediately met with rejection.

She learns the extra's routine: Never purchase a round-trip ticket on the bus line, because you hope you can pick up a ride coming back. "It's risky, but it saves you twenty cents."[10] A studio carpenter stops and offers a ride in his automobile to United Artists. He explains that he is married, "But I've got her so trained that she doesn't say a word if I'm missing a couple of nights . . . How about our having dinner together tonight?"[11] When Waterbury rejects his advances, she is told to get out of the car. At MGM, she witnesses extras fighting over rolls of mints that one of the male extras passes around. Despite it all, "You know why girls stay there and starve. You know why boys rob to remain. It takes so much and so little to get in. Success is an accident. Failure is an accident. The mirage occurs. You sniff the gold dust and your sense of values is destroyed."[12]

Only after Ruth Waterbury has identified herself to casting director Dan Kelly at First National is she offered work as an extra: a prostitute in the Colleen Moore vehicle *Twinkletoes*. Waterbury arrives at the studio, as requested, at 7:30 p.m. After her two-and-a-half-hour wait on the set, director Charles Brabin appears. Waterbury and another girl are told to walk out of a store and down the street. After three takes, she is told to wait again. At 12:30 a.m., she and the other extras are dismissed to check in their wardrobe, collect their pay and, if necessary, catch a studio bus back to Hollywood. Ruth Waterbury arrives back in Hollywood at 1:30 a.m., and by 8:10 a.m., she is back on a bus to First National in Burbank. That day, she is a member of a theatre audience. At 6:00 p.m., the company goes into overtime, and there is a rush to finish. Waterbury works on until midnight. She has worked a straight twenty-four of the last thirty hours, and she receives $6.25 for the day, with overtime and $5.00 for the evening. If she were a genuine extra, it would be good news when Dave Kelly promises to telephone Central Casting and get her registered.

As a finale for the series, Waterbury contributed an essay bearing the simple warning, "Don't Go to Hollywood!" Here, she explains that she had left the Hollywood Studio Club and moved into a cheap Hollywood hotel. The room clerk there introduced her to an assistant director, who also lived at the hotel and who would perhaps be able to help her. The introduction made, the assistant director tells her, "Say, a friend of mine's got a house in Laurel Canyon. He's away and I've got the key. Let's go up there for the evening. I can help you a lot and I bet we'll find we're on the same mental plane."[13] Waterbury ate dinner alone.

Novelist Theodore Dreiser had a highly personal reason for addressing the morality of Hollywood's relationship with the extra in a series of four articles he wrote for the fan magazine *Shadowland*, which published them between November 1921 and February 1922. In November 1921, Dreiser had met Helen Richardson, a bit player and extra who usually appeared in comedies. She had previously been married to a minor actor named Frank Richardson. In his diary, Dreiser described his mistress as "the Sweetest, Prettiest, Grossest Girl I ever knew," with the last adjective referring to her sexual performance. Richardson and Dreiser remained together for many years, although the novelist was too promiscuous to settle down with one woman. The couple did not marry until 1944, and the marriage lasted until Dreiser's death a year later. It is obvious that Richardson supplied the novelist with the anecdotes that he uses in his articles. He begins with the same dreary picture of the would-be aspirant arriving in Hollywood, carrying her high school diploma. Eventually, she will return home, having "snapped a picture" of the boarding house or room or street where she has lived. Dreiser paints the type of picture that will never make it to the screen, because it does not end happily.

The young extra will be spotted by a casting director who knows the requirements of a certain director on the lot. The young lady will be flattered, particularly when at the close of day she is offered a ride home in the director's car. Those that are not subjected to sexual harassment will endure day after day without pay. Everyone else connected with the industry is paid, from the carpenters to the electricians, all of who have unions that can call strikes. The extras will be stalled by casting directors or assistant directors, told to wait around until tomorrow or the next day. "Ordinary trade decency might suggest, you would think, some limited form of reward in such cases. But not in the moving picture world. Aren't there high-salaried directors and stars and stockholders and bankers to be paid? And don't they always come first? They do. Besides it is easy to get away with this type of graft in the case of the 'artist,' and so it continues to be done."[14]

In 1924, Marilynn Conners self-published a curious paperback volume, *What Chance Have I in Hollywood: The Mystery of the Movies*, which is at times incredibly dull and lifeless, but which also sizzles with sex, as she warns of "procurers from Tia Juana [*sic*], in search of hapless female extras."[15] She also writes about "Mexicali Red" from Kaukauna, Wisconsin, a poor extra "enticed to Mexicali upon promise of employment in a cabaret [and] was drugged, assaulted, and found herself in a brothel without any recollection of how she got there. She now leads a life of shame."[16]

In his 1923 novel, *The Girl from Hollywood*, Tarzan creator Edgar Rice Burroughs's heroine, freshly arrived in Hollywood from the Midwest, is persuaded by a minor actor and director to pose nude for a screen test. Later, pregnant and rejected, the girl dies.

A few years later, Jack Lait began publishing a series in *Variety*, the second episode of which was concerned with "Extra Girls." Acknowledging that some of these girls were made of sound moral fiber, Lait concludes that "most of them are unconventional in one sense or another, or they wouldn't

THE MAIL ORDER NEWS 45

This Book Reveals the Secrets of the Motion Picture Studios and the Great Hollywood Lure

"IT TELLS ALL"

What Chance Have I in Hollywood?

A remarkable volume of vital information concerning the movie capital of the world, issued as a direct answer to more than 250,000 letters of inquiry from movie fans.

Written at Hollywood by

MARILYNN CONNERS

Author of many famous screen successes.

MYSTERY OF THE MOVIES REVEALED

WOULD you like to go to Hollywood? Do you want to know whether the life there is clean or evil? Are you wondering what chances you have there for success in the movie field? If you are seeking intimate knowledge concerning the magic screen city, its studios, directors, and stars,—if you want to learn about the vicious Tia Juana trap, by all means read this remarkable book. It reveals true conditions and vividly explains actual facts. No other work of this character shows so much intimate knowledge of this famous movie colony as is given in this volume by Marilynn Conners, who has written this book right at Hollywood, where she has lived all her life.

Hordes of Girls Fall an Easy Prey to the Hollywood Lure and the Notorious Tia Juana Trap. Protect Them. Place This Remarkable Expose Into Their Hands

Just Glance Over This Condensed Description of Contents:

The Slums of Hollywood in Tia Juana and Mexicali.—An expose of the small town just beyond the border, a short distance from Hollywood—a town known as Tia Juana, a dirty blot on the map, one of the lowest and most disorderly resorts on the earth's surface. Mamie Swemp and hundreds of other girls seeking fame at Hollywood were lured to this despicable trap, by men posing as motion picture directors. More than FIVE THOUSAND girls disappear annually through the mysterious gateway of missing persons in Hollywood. They are swallowed up in the border towns, of which Mexicali is just another one of the centers of vice and illicit traffic.

Words of Advice by Norma Talmadge.—This famous movie star offers words of caution and tells movie aspirants not to go to Hollywood unless they have means, ability and determination.

That Fascinating Hollywood.—An intimate description of this wonderful movie capital of the world. Details about stars, studios and general attractions of the magic city.

Studio Life.—Interesting information concerning studio life, narrating particulars of all the organizations, their "lots," the great "sets," and the wonderful pictures produced there.

Getting Acquainted with Stars and Stories.—It is amazing how much people talk and how little people know about the movies. This chapter will explain much that is not generally known concerning stars, directors, and "types." Even the schedule of picture is described, explaining the preparation, the filming or "shooting," the cutting, the titling and the release.

Your Chance in Hollywood to Act.—To remedy certain exaggerated ideas that are afloat regarding the easy methods of obtaining employment in the cinema field, the author has written this vital chapter. It tells much which you should know. You have heard about Hollywood's wild parties, about stars addicted to drink, about bribery and temptations. This chapter will reveal many things that have hitherto remained untold.

How Much Money Must I Have Before Venturing to Hollywood?—The minimum amount is mentioned in this chapter. And if you have the requisite funds, the author tells exactly where to go, how to live within reason, what the charges are for rooms in private families, the rental cost of bungalows, how to get acquainted with studios and stars, etc.

Your Chance in Hollywood to Write.—This important chapter should prove of interest to the thousands who feel capable of writing continuities, better known as "scenarios" or screen scripts. There is no established scale of prices for the stories, so study this chapter.

Those Who Take a Chance.—The concluding chapter cautions against a trip to Hollywood, unless, after carefully studying this book of revelations, you feel that you can well afford to take that chance. But, by all means, read this book first. It is better to be safe than sorry.

Learn The Truth:- *Protect yourself or your dear ones.* ***Send for this book now.***
You will find it intensely interesting.

PRICE POSTPAID $1.00

HERE YOUR IMPRINT

NOTICE TO THE TRADE.—The above is a fac-simile of a 6x9 circular supplied to dealers under their imprint at $5 for one thousand. Orders for the Hollywood books filled at 50c postpaid to your customers under your label. Order the circulars NOW.

MAIL ORDER SERVICE CORPORATION, 500 Fifth Ave., N. Y.

Promotional flyer for *What Chance Have I in Hollywood?*

be there in the first place." Many signed with agents, "little more than call-system girl-providers for almost any demand." At private parties, the girls meet Hollywood producers and directors. "The beneficent paternal arm of organized filmdom doesn't and can't protect all these girls or any appreciable part of them. . . . The women's clubs of Los Angeles hold solemn meetings and sit on the grave and puzzling problem. . . . They think something should be done about it. Then they adjourn."[17]

It was an accurate, distasteful account of reality, and it deeply offended the Hollywood establishment. The next week, on January 19, 1927, *Variety* reported that producers Marcus Loew and Joseph M. Schenck demanded the series be discontinued; it was "Aimed at sensationalism." It was evident that exploitation of women would continue unabated in Hollywood.

The response of Hollywood executives to the article leads to an understanding of why Max Knepper in his 1935 volume, *Sodom and Gomorrah: The Story of Hollywood*, compared them to the much-maligned (because of his anti-Semitism) Henry Ford. As Knepper points out, "Henry Ford may be a calloused, narrow man, but his private life, as far as morality is concerned, is irreproachable." The same cannot be said of Hollywood executives and their treatment of extras and others.

The power of the casting director and the assistant director over female extras remained strong into the 1930s. As one extra told Gladys Hall in 1939, "The assistant director rules the extras." A couple of these assistant directors had actually said to her, "If you go out with me tonight. I'll see that you work tomorrow."[18] As already noted, accusations of questionable activities at Central Casting had been around as long as the bureau itself. In 1934, new head Campbell MacCulloch appointed an advisory committee to supervise the bureau's casting. The committee consisted of all the Hollywood clergy, the chairman of the community chest, a policewoman, a former grand jury foreman, a former president of the American Federation of Woman's Clubs, and an economics professor. Every time a complaint was made, the committee investigated.

Of two major novels dealing with the Hollywood extra, one, *Promised Land* by Cedric Belfrage, is relatively unknown, while the other, *The Shoot Horses, Don't They?* by Horace McCoy, remains in print and has been adapted for the screen.[19] First published in 1935, *They Shoot Horses, Don't They?* is a short novel, little more than a novella, about two young extras, Robert Syverten and Gloria Beatty, who meet outside Paramount Studios on Melrose Avenue and decide to enter a dance marathon in Santa Monica. The story concerns not their lives as extras but rather the drama they and others encounter at the marathon, which serves as an existential metaphor. Syverten is a sympathetic hero, who at one point (almost the only time the film industry is shown to have any relevance to the principal protagonists) talks about his chances for a career with director Frank Borzage, a celebrity visiting the dance marathon. The novel ends with Syverten's shooting Beatty with a gun she gives him, because "She asked me to."[20] There are some readers, including this one, who cannot help but think that it would have been better had Syverten shot the constantly irritating Beatty a lot earlier. Perhaps what makes the storyline intriguing is its modernity, with casual talk of abortion and use of obvious but censored four-letter words. The novel does make the point that the exploited dancers are well fed even as they compete in the marathon. Similarly, it has been pointed out that extras who were actually working were provided with decent meals, which were undoubtedly more substantial than what they could afford outside of the studio.

Around 1950, actor-director Norman Lloyd and Charlie Chaplin purchased the screen rights to the novel. The idea was that Chaplin would write and produce, Norman Lloyd would direct, and the project would be perfect as a vehicle for Chaplin's son, Sydney. As Norman Lloyd recalls, the intention was to cast Evelyn Keyes, "who was going with Sydney—a nice way to put it," opposite Sydney. Lloyd saw the Gloria Beatty character as lumpen, and, after meeting a young starlet named Marilyn Monroe in the casting office at Goldwyn, he decided she would be ideal for the role.[21] Sadly, because of Chaplin's problems with US Immigration, nothing came of the film, and the rights were eventually sold to others.

Eventually, *They Shoot Horses, Don't They?* was filmed in 1969 with Jane Fonda and Michael Sarrazin in the leading roles, under the direction of Sydney Pollack. But as Joseph Morgenstern wrote in *Newsweek* (December 22, 1969), the film failed to understand that the ballroom is a metaphor "where all the losers and drifters and failed apple sellers of the world are put through the tortures of the damned, physically and spiritually." Interestingly, a principal character in the novel, Mrs. Layden, an elderly lady who is an enthusiastic and sympathetic member of the audience for the marathon, is played on screen by Madge Kennedy (1891–1987). A major stage star of the 1910s and 1920s, Kennedy was also a Goldwyn film star of the 1910s. She retired from the screen, but returned in 1951 as a character actress in George Cukor's *The Marrying Kind*. She was never considered an extra, but in *The Shoot Horses, Don't They?*, she gets no credit and might just as well have been an extra as far as the producers were concerned.

Michael Sarrazin and Jane Fonda, center, in *They Shoot Horses, Don't They?* (1969).

They Shoot Horses, Don't They? received nine Academy Award nominations for Best Actress, Best Actress in a Supporting Role (Susannah York), Best Actor in a Supporting Role (Gig Young as the master of ceremonies), Best Art Direction, Best Costume Design, Best Directing, Best Film Editing, Best Music Score, and Best Writing. Gig Young was the only winner.

Three years after publication of *They Shoot Horses, Don't They?*, a second McCoy novel, *I Should Have Stayed Home*, appeared. In some respects, it is more Hollywood-oriented and more relevant to the lives of screen extras than McCoy's earlier novel in that its principal character, Ralph Carston, comes from Georgia to Hollywood, lured by the promise of a screen test (much like Horace McCoy himself). Carston shares a bungalow court apartment with another hopeful, Mona Matthews, and befriends a neighbor, Dorothy Trotter, who kills herself after escaping from prison, where she had been sent on a shoplifting charge. The novel provides a highly realistic portrait of Hollywood in the mid- to late-1930s, with Ralph and Mona clinging to their decency. When photographers want a shot of Dorothy's corpse, Mona puts a handful of fan magazines into her hands, telling them, "That's what really killed her . . . Go ahead—show the world an authentic picture of Hollywood."

Cedric Belfrage's *Promised Land: Notes for a History* was published in the United Kingdom in 1938 by Victor Gollancz and the New Left Book Club. Not surprisingly, in view of its publishers' identities, the novel depicts the life of a Hollywood family from the mid 1800s (prior to arriving in California) through 1936, with a distinctly left-wing view of society there. In fact, the novel concludes with what is little more than a frantic dissertation on how society in general and Hollywood in particular will improve with the acceptance of socialism. Through it all, the matriarch of the family tries to hold on to her Hollywood real estate with a greedy zeal, matched only by her religious fervor and pro-prohibition stance. Her family does not fare well, with her son, Clark Laurie, working as a Hollywood extra: "To-day he was a pair of feet that had got photographed and to-morrow he might be earning the income of two hundred coal miners, if luck should spin the camera round in such a way that it came to rest focused on his face."[22]

Clark's girlfriend (subsequently his wife), Ellen, is also a Hollywood extra. She is called for nightwork at the X.Y.Z. studios, put on a bus along with other female extras, and driven to a ranch in the desert. It is a salesman's convention, and she and the others are there to entertain the convention goers. "If they refuse the assignment—and God alone knows how they're going to get home if they do—there'll be no more calls from X.Y.Z. studios."[23]

Ellen's clothes are torn from her by a drunken salesman, but she escapes rape and eventually gets a ride back to the city. Unlike her sister extras, Ellen will not forget what has happened. She hires a lawyer and sues X.Y.Z. Of course, the studio looks into her past, her former association with a Hollywood madam is exposed at trial, and those who knew what had taken place are reluctant to give evidence. The jury fails to reach a verdict. "[T]he papers left the mass of the public with the idea that Ellen had torn her own clothes off, blacked her own eye, and gone for a country walk so she could blackmail the salesman, who was a respectable married man with three kids."[24]

The story of Ellen so closely parallels real life that Cedric Belfrage must have based it on what happened in 1937 to a twenty-year-old dancer and extra named Patricia Douglas. If Cedric Belfrage was the first writer to tell Douglas's story (albeit in fictional form), then David Stenn is the one who brought it to prominence, and his account, published in *Vanity Fair*, is vivid and horrifying. Like so many before her, Kansas-born Patricia Douglas had come to Hollywood with her mother. The latter wanted to be a dress designer for the stars, but instead ended up creating costumes for high-priced prostitutes. Patricia worked in various films, including *Gold Diggers of 1933*.

On May 2, 1937, she received a casting call from MGM, which was hosting a salesmen's convention that was slated to climax on Wednesday, May 5, 1937, with a Wild West-themed stag party at the Hal Roach Studios ranch. At 4:00 p.m., 120 young female dancers reported at the Culver City Studios of Hal Roach (who released his productions through MGM). They were provided with appropriate if somewhat skimpy Western attire and bused to what was described as "Rancho Roachero."

The subsequent party was wild and uninhibited. One extra named Ginger Wyatt was actually rescued by MGM star Wallace Beery, who supposedly punched a couple of salesmen who were trying to molest her. Patricia Douglas was accosted by David Ross, described as a "roly poly 36-year-old Catholic bachelor from the Chicago sales office," forcibly fed scotch and champagne, dragged out to Ross's car, and raped. The young woman was helped by a parking attendant and taken to Culver City Community Hospital, where she collapsed. Despite Douglas's being accompanied to the hospital by a motorcycle cop, no crime report was filed, and at the hospital, the doctor who treated Douglas (and who had close ties to MGM) refused to confirm that intercourse had taken place.

What Patricia Douglas had suffered was obviously nothing new to the sorority of extras, but unlike others in the same situation, she decided to fight back, swearing out a complaint at the Los Angeles County District Attorney's office. Her story was published in appropriate tabloid format by William Randolph Hearst's *Los Angeles Examiner*. MGM responded, deliberately smearing Douglas's reputation and producing witnesses from the party who denied its depravity. One parking attendant who witnessed Douglas's attack was given a job for life at MGM. A grand jury investigation failed to indict David Ross. Patricia Douglas did not give up, filing suit in Los Angeles County Superior Court against Ross, Hal Roach, executive Eddie Mannix, MGM casting assistant Vincent Conniff (who had hired the women to entertain), and others. On February 9, 1938, a superior court judge dismissed the case. MGM had won, and for her own preservation, Douglas was forced to leave Hollywood forever.

Quite amazingly, David Stenn rediscovered her, at eighty-six years of age, in Las Vegas. "The lion raped," he reported, "but Patricia Douglas was—and still is—the mouse that roared. Her heroic cry was once cruelly silenced; 66 years later, the last word is hers."[25] And the last word was not limited to a *Vanity Fair* article, but also appeared in a documentary—*Girl 27*, released in July 2007—Stenn created, in which he stars along with Douglas. It was a story that might have been lifted from the pages of a fan magazine, the type

Virginia Rappe, an extra who gained fame not for her life and how she led it, but for the manner of her death.

of drama that dominated the magazines' fiction. But, of course, no fan magazine could and would publish such a story. The power of the Hollywood studios—particularly MGM—was simply too strong.

MGM's attempts to control its image were not limited to the legal system. It has been suggested that Mabel E. Kinney, in the 1930s head of the California Industrial Welfare Division, which looked into extras' complaints, obtained her job through the efforts of Louis B. Mayer. As in Patricia Douglas's case, the California Industrial Welfare Division "naturally interprets cases of abuse in a way which puts the victim on the spot rather than the producer."[26]

One of the worst reported cases of physical abuse of extras took place on the set of MGM's *Riffraff* in October 1935. As reported in *New Theatre*, an admittedly left-wing publication:

> Forty women were called to the MGM set at 5:30 P.M. . . . In the rain scene, they were soaked and hurled down by the full force of water from three fire hoses, backed by wind machines. Driven water, cold and sharp as icicles, blinded them and flung them about. Many were skinned from ankles to thighs. One woman was knocked unconscious. Another was paralyzed for hours. No drying equipment was provided; no towels until a few appeared at 3:30 A.M. For working from 5:30 P.M. To 5:30 A.M. under these conditions, each woman got $11.25. The union obtained an adjustment for them and additional payments for their treatment and injuries. The film itself, blurred by so much water, had to be retaken, but the few women who returned next night said that because of the organized protest, conditions were vastly improved.[27]

Despite what the Patricia Douglas incident might suggest, Fred Datig, casting director at MGM from 1937 through 1951, was in many ways Victorian in his attitudes, strict and straight-laced. He was a studio employee who was virtually unknown to the outside community, a man who would not even permit his name to appear on his office door. He would actually fire employees who took advantage of their positions in the casting department. Unfortunately, he had no control over what went on above him. As his son recalled, "His big boss at MGM, Benjamin Thaw, that's all he did. My father just had to keep signing these cute girls and put them in his office every hour. Thaw was an animal, a sex maniac. He was in charge of all talent. He was a friend of Louis B's [Mayer]."[28]

Typical of the many young women who came to Hollywood in search of a career on screen in the 1910s is Virginia Rappe, who had a few minor roles in comedy shorts and features. By all accounts, she was free with her sexual favors. Possibly a prostitute, she had at least five abortions and was infected with gonorrhea when she died. It was the manner of her death in San Francisco on September 9, 1921, that made her a "star"—at least in the tabloid press of the day. She was supposedly raped with a Coca-Cola bottle and murdered by comedian Roscoe "Fatty" Arbuckle. Despite enduring multiple trials, Arbuckle was never found guilty except in the court of public opinion. That same court found Rappe guilty of being "cheap, wanton, and in the parlance of the day, thoroughly stained."[29] While supporters of Arbuckle can find nothing good to say about his "victim" (and she was a victim no matter the circumstances), nobody has made a concerted effort to uncover the "truth" about Rappe, whose victimization in many ways typifies how the

American public and the American media viewed female extras and their lifestyles.

Undoubtedly, many younger women in Hollywood were easily seduced by what its predatory denizens suggested was on offer for them. Others were less easily beguiled and listened to those who warned of the dangers. Pauline Wagner recalls going to a party at Wallace Beery's home. "I was just shocked. I had never seen anything like it before. They were drinking and carousing. Gloria Swanson was out under a tree making out with some guy, and Wally Beery was saying, 'Gloria, for Christ's sake, if you're going to do that we've got fifty bedrooms upstairs.' This was on a weekend." On Monday, Wagner went to the studio and spoke with director Sam Wood about what she had witnessed:

> He looked at me and he said, "I'm going to give you some advice. Don't go to any parties. Don't socialize with anybody in the picture business. You may not ever be a star. But I'm going to tell you, you'll never be without a job." I went home and told my father and mother what he said. And I never socialized with anybody in the picture business. Except Andy Devine, because I thought he was funny.[30]

For those female extras interested in making some money on the side with a little prostitution, there was always "Frenchie." He operated as a pimp out of the Hollywood Roosevelt Hotel. Extras would approach him, and he would pair them with various of his industry clients. "Frenchie" was himself an extra. Franco Corsaro, born in 1900, was active on screen from 1930 into the 1980s. He was generally cast as a French or Hispanic character, and his films include *Jezebel* (1938), *Down Argentine Way* (1940), *The Mark of Zorro* (1940), *The Razor's Edge* (1946), *Arch of Triumph* (1948), and *Pay or Die* (1960). He may be glimpsed in *Casablanca* (1943) as a French police officer.

The amount of coverage of the negative treatment of female extras certainly diminishes—it might be more accurate to say it largely vanishes—after World War II. This development may well have occurred because by the late 1930s there was a steady decline in the number of women being placed as extras. The fewer female extras, the fewer accusations of sexual harassment or worse. It is believed that the number of female extras was at its peak in the Depression years, when these workers were supplementing the family income. With World War II and the rise in prosperity, fewer women may have felt the need to grapple with the industry.[31]

There might have been a large amount space in the fan magazines devoted to warning female readers of the dangers the Hollywood community represented, but not all of the articles were negative. One of the more ridiculous series, published from January through October 1925 in the pages of *Picture-Play*, concerned author Margaret Reid's education about the delights of being an extra. She gushes that for the extra, "Hollywood and all that therein lies has its solid platinum, diamond-studded center in the 'Lasky Lot' [Paramount]."[32] As she explains, it is the only studio that provides all the clothes that an extra needs, many of which were apparently previously worn by such Paramount stars as Lois Wilson, Betty Compson, or Pola Negri. An extra not only had the privilege of working for directors such as James Cruze or Paul Bern, but also might casually wander around to watch other directors at work before receiving the ultimate call to be a Russian peasant in a Pola Negri film being directed by Ernst Lubitsch. What a glamorous life those Hollywood extras enjoyed in *Picture-Play*—even if ultimately they would be sexually abused in *Photoplay*.[33]

Despite the lack of positive commentary coming out of Hollywood, few would-be movie stars heeded the advice that an anonymous extra girl, who had begun her career in the Greta Garbo vehicle *Romance* (1930), had to offer: "No girls, take a tip from me. Don't come to Hollywood. For the extra's life is heartbreaking and bitter. Instead of buying that ticket, stay at home with your dreams!"[34]

Chapter Six

THE COMING OF SOUND

The sound era is generally defined as beginning with *The Jazz Singer* in 1927, despite this not being the first sound film or even the first sound feature-length production. Because of its star, Al Jolson, and because of interest in the film, producer Warner Bros. had little difficulty in finding extras for some of the sequences. The studio brought one hundred from Hollywood for the filming of scenes at New York's Winter Garden Theatre on June 26, 1927, during which Jolson was to exit the stage door. However, between 7:30 p.m. and 11:00 p.m., several thousand New Yorkers assembled on Broadway between 50th and 51st Street, happy to appear, without payment, on camera, and rendering the extras shipped in by the studio superfluous.

The situation vis-à-vis the producer and the unpaid crowd as extra was an anomaly, but a new era was dawning not only for the film industry, but also for the extra. As Murray Ross has pointed out, the coming of sound "created a sharp division between those with speaking parts and those without. This division did not exist in the silent-picture days, when a number of prominent screen stars rose from the ranks of the extras."[1] Now, producers looked not to the extras for potential new talent, but to the legitimate stage.

"The extra girl is gone," announced *Photoplay* in 1929. With the coming of sound, "[a] new era has dawned. It is heralded with sound effects. And the new extra girl is a pair of dancing feet, a lithe, hardy body and a throat that can sing 'Mammy.'"[2] With the coming of sound came the advent and overabundance of the musical, with its demand for chorus girls. Some five hundred were used by Warner Bros. for *The Show of Shows* (1929). Such chorus girls came not from the ranks of the extras of the silent era, but rather from local dancing schools and the choruses of theatrical musicals playing across the United States. It was no longer a matter of looking French, German, or Greek, but a question of whether an extra could actually speak French, German, or Greek. Marian L. Mel, in charge of female talent at Central Casting, noted:

> It isn't beauty that counts half as much as the ability to sing and dance and make noises.
>
> We have all sorts of strange registrations. One man can make a noise like a wolf's howl. Now the company could get a real wolf, but it's better to have a man because he will howl when he's told. Wolves are not so accommodating.[3]

Photoplay listed the requirements of the 1929 extra as:

1. A pretty face
2. A pretty figure
3. Ability to dance
4. A voice
5. Youth
6. Personality
7. Excellent health[4]

The ideal movie "chorine" was identified by First National as Maxine Cantway, with a thirty-two and one-half inch bust, a twenty-three inch waist, thirty-four inch hips, twelve-and-a-half inch calves, and seven-and-a-half inch ankles.[5]

Chorus lines on the Broadway stage would be no more than thirty-six in number, whereas a typical Hollywood musical of the late 1920s and early 1930s could need between 120 and 250 members. Because of the numbers involved, it was reported, "Individuals lose their identity."[6] As Larry Ceballos, who emphasized effect and few dance steps, explained it:

> On the stage, you remember, the eye focuses on one girl or one group. That corresponds to the camera close-ups. But the stage audience may choose its point of interest, whereas the camera does the choosing. The eye concentrating on a figure keeps it still a part of a moving unit. A careless close-up jerks one out of a scene and separates the eye from the rest of the action. I try to have my ensemble or my group look like one figure, each a part of the other.[7]

The camera had always made players appear older than they actually were. Now, suddenly, extras had to look young and be young. Reportedly, the chorus line in *Fox Movietone Follies of 1929* (1929) consisted entirely of dancers sixteen years of age or younger. This requirement meant that local

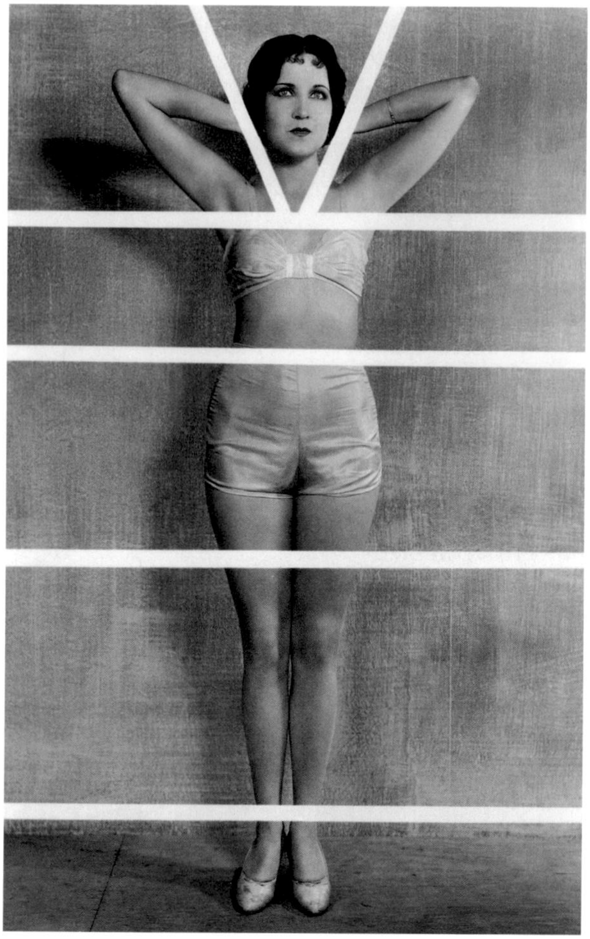

In the early 1930s, MGM used a composite of six extras to create the ideal screen figure. AMPAS.

talent had a better opportunity for employment than did chorus girls from Broadway, who were often too old, too set in their routine, and too hard-boiled. "There are no women in pictures past twenty-five," reported one fan magazine writer.[8] Extras for the chorus also had to be small, perhaps because quite a few of the leading men lacked stature. Statuesque showgirls were definitely not wanted in the typical chorus line. "The chorus girls one sees at First National, Warners, Paramount, and Radio Pictures are pretty much the same type—small, active and pretty," reported *Photoplay*.[9]

One 1929 sound production that did not require a glamorous line of chorus girls was *Applause*, with its story of burlesque life. Over a three-week period, director Rouben Mamoulian interviewed some two thousand individuals from the world of burlesque. It took three calls for extras before Mamoulian was able to cast a chorus of fifty-two. He told the *New York*

Times, "Some of the oldtimers insisted that they could dance just as well now as they did twenty years ago, but when they were put to the test it was soon seen that time had relegated them to the ranks of has-beens. Some were, however, surprisingly spry and won parts."[10]

The chorus girls did not have to gain the approval of casting directors, but rather of dance directors, such as the aforementioned Larry Ceballos, Sammy Lee, Pearl Eaton, Earl Lindsay, Seymour Felix, and others. The most prominent of female dance directors—and the one most noted for her discipline—was Madame Albertina Rasch at MGM, whose routines were often more strenuous than those of others and required chorus girls with strength and larger bodies.

The best known of dance directors is, of course, Busby Berkeley. For *Gold Diggers of 1933*, he used 180 chorus girls, some forty-one of which were kept on by the studio, Warner Bros., to work in other chorus lines, including that of *Gold Diggers of 1935*. A handful from the original 1933 chorus line returned to the New York stage, while twenty remained in Hollywood, working as dress extras. The most famous of chorines at Warner Bros. was Toby

The chorus line on stage for *The Great Gabbo* (1929).

For *Music in the Air* (1934), Fox hired extras who, it was claimed, were proficient at Bavarian folk dancing.

Wing, whose saucy looks became familiar to film buffs if not to the average moviegoer.

"The screen has widened its scope so that extra players have a chance to do a hundred more colorful things than swarm around in mob scenes," commented Paramount casting director Fred Datig in the *Los Angeles Record* (February 8, 1929). However, in contradiction to Central Casting's Marian L. Mel, he did warn animal imitators to stay away from Hollywood: "Those who have hopes of providing proxy voices for dogs, cats and other animals are cautioned that Hollywood will not employ synthetic animal sounds because of the many trained animals already available for this purpose."

The influx of chorus girls was a further reminder that the film industry also had a more limited need for models, statuesque women who could look good in all manner of attire on screen, could pose without faltering, and could attract the audience without actually distracting attention from the star. As one fan magazine writer put it:

> The chorus girl is lost in a crowd of fifty or seventy-five girls kicking their legs, but when a girl wears an expensive gown or costume, she is photographed along with the dress she is displaying, and gets a chance to show her individual charm. Modeling cannot be depended upon for a steady income, but it's an excellent means for earning some extra money and making the battle of gate-crashing much easier in this heartless town on the shores of the blue Pacific.[11]

For *Vogues of 1938*, producer Walter Wanger hired fourteen models from New York, but Hollywood had more than its share of models. By 1938, it was reported that there were some four hundred available to the film industry. These women also worked for artists and sculptors and took on more mundane tasks such as stenography. One model, nineteen-year-old Violet Ownby, worked in the fan mail department at MGM more than she worked at her chosen profession. Another, Elissa Bohnen, could be found manning a cash register at a Los Angeles department store. Of course, as the *New York Times* commented, "There are probably more pretty stenographers, salesgirls and waitresses in Hollywood than anywhere else in the world as, as disappointed movie stars, they are excellent behind their typewriters, counters and trays."[12]

The models had their own organization, the Artists and Models Club, founded in 1933 by Doris Harman and located at 6879 Alta Loma Terrace in Hollywood. The club held an open house every Friday afternoon, which casting directors and others were encouraged to attend. The club also hosted an annual ball, "Mystery Bacchanale," often sponsored by one of the studios. The history of the Artists and Models Club is not well documented, but it was certainly extant as late as 1940, with Doris Harman still serving as president. Club secretary was Lynn Bailey, "recognized as the outstanding model on the Coast,"[13] when not working in the cutting department at Paramount.

For extras of the silent era, the coming of sound did not herald a new era like the exuberant one depicted in *Singin' in the Rain*. No instant stars were plucked from their ranks. Many extras from an earlier age decided to leave the industry and embark on new, possibly more lucrative careers.

One became a taxi driver, another a manicurist, and many became waitresses. Frances Johnstone, described as one of the most attractive extras ever to wear a pair of false eyelashes, became a secretary to agent Jessie Wadsworth. Vampish Ouida Willis could be found working as a saleslady in a shop on Hollywood Boulevard. Natalie Napp joined a real estate company, while Dorothy Irving went to work in the salon of interior designer Howard Greer.

The situation at the beginning of the sound era was not a healthy one for most extras. The *Washington Post* reported that in 1928, the last major year for silent films, there were twelve thousand registered extras collectively working approximately twenty-four thousand days a month—two days each. In 1929, the first major year of the talkies, there were 17,500 registered extras, but only 22,500 monthly jobs. The surge in major spectacular productions in 1930 improved the situation somewhat, with eight to ten thousand reportedly at work on *Cimarron*, two thousand on *Beau Ideal*, three thousand on *Dishonored*, two thousand on *The Big Trail*, and two thousand on *Fighting Caravans*.[14] But in all probability, these figures were highly inflated by studio publicists.

It was not only long-time extras who faced an uneasy future with the coming of sound. Studio casting directors were now obliged to discover which extras and which bit players had voices. Fred Datig supposedly carried the images of twenty-five thousand actors and actress in his head, but he could not identify them by voice. He might know what an actor or actress sounded like in conversation, but he did not know how they would sound on film. He could cast by type and by looks, but now a third dimension was added: the voice. One newspaper came up with the suggestion that Central Casting keep voice tests of extras on file:

> A girl could have a talking-film test of herself made in Chicago or Cleveland or Philadelphia, and airmail it to Central Casting in less time that it would take her to travel here by train. Her speaking image of the screen would tell more about her qualifications than she could tell in person, and if it showed her obviously unfitted for a picture career she at least would not have to buy a railroad ticket home.[15]

One positive aspect of the coming of sound was better pay for the extras in the chorus lines. Once these extras had been trained for a specific number, the studio needed to keep the chorus happy and could not risk losing even one member, as a new girl would have to learn the steps. Studios put

Extras at the Selznick Studios in the 1930s.

extras in the chorus lines under contract, paying them on average sixty or seventy-five dollars a week while working and thirty or forty dollars a week while rehearsing. "Not bad money for any miss in her 'teens. And not bad money for the highest paid chorus girls in New York."[16] In fact, the pay scale was infinitely superior to the monies paid by Broadway shows, where rehearsal time was not recompensed and where a production might last only a few weeks before closing. However, the life of a chorus girl was far from easy, with strenuous rehearsals often lasting from 8:00 a.m. through until 2:00 p.m. without a break. It is not necessarily accurate to assume that the male extra's life was any happier.

Chorus girls were not always willing to accept whatever a director might demand. Incensed at the amount of clothing they were being asked to remove, a group of sixty-five angry chorus girls from *Murder at the Vanities* (1934) surrounded their director, Mitchell Leisen, and removed his trousers. The somewhat effeminate Leisen responded by hitting some of the girls and then fainting. Two of the chorus girls, Jeannette Dixon and Katherine Hankin, were reported as having received considerable bruising. A contrite Mitchell Leisen sent flowers to all of his attackers.[17]

By the late 1930s, there were four classifications of extras: (1)"day" or "dress" extras who earned the highest pay, $16.50; (2) "day" extras with smart street clothes, who earned eleven dollars; (3) extras with very good street clothes, who earned $8.25; (4) extras for mob scenes, etc., who earned $5.50.

If an extra happened to be given a line to read in a scene, he or she would automatically earn twenty-five dollars a day.

However, a decent pay schedule was of little relevance without a regular work schedule. And the latter was not guaranteed. In 1933, reportedly only 187 female extras averaged one day a week or better, with 101 averaging between one and one-and-a-half days, forty-two averaging between one-and-a-half and two days, and only sixteen averaging between two-and-a-half and three days a week. The reality was that a stenographer could take home an average weekly salary of between twenty and thirty dollars, while even the highest-paid and most active of female extras could seldom look forward to such a substantial paycheck. Stenographers did not have to worry about their working clothes, while female dress extras would need to maintain a wardrobe of at least five evening gowns and spend regular sessions at the beauty parlor attending to hair and nails.

Of course, there were always those who would insist that extras were actually overpaid. For example, Winston Churchill's son, Randolph, visited the set of *Parnell*, which had a scene set in the British House of Commons, in June of 1937. Acknowledging the extras playing members of parliament, he commented that the $7.50 a day they were earning was in excess of the amount paid to his fellow parliamentarians.

As the 1930s progressed, extras received other perks aside from a guaranteed salary. Both female and male extras were given twenty-minute rest periods every hour during dance and marching sequences.[18] Dying on camera also proved lucrative to the extra. Dying in bed resulted only in the minimum pay of $2.50. However, dying as part of a stunt—such as falling down a flight of stairs—could bring in additional pay from between $2.50 and fifty dollars, depending upon the violence of the death. Unfortunately, dying on the battlefield—the most common of deaths for extras—brought in only five dollars. "Some extras can die very naturally, so they are in demand," reported the *Baltimore Sun*.[19]

Once the initial enthusiasm for Hollywood musicals declined, many chorus girls once in heavy demand were suddenly and permanently out of work. Life for the average female extra in the 1930s was far from glamorous. They would live five or six to a bungalow apartment, with two sleeping on the bed, one on the Chesterfield, one on the reclining chair, and one on the floor with a pillow. One extra would always have to stay in to answer the telephone. Whoever worked paid for the groceries. None had a car. "Without the thousands of 'boy friends' who dutifully haul extras back and forth, the movie industry in Hollywood wouldn't last ten minutes," noted one reporter.[20]

One typical extra from the late 1930s was Alberta Hamblem, who worked at most of the studios and whose credits include *Sitting Pretty* (1933) at Paramount, *San Francisco* (1936) and *The Great Waltz* (1938) at MGM, *Music for Madame* (1937) at RKO, and *Angels with Dirty Faces* (1938) at Warner Bros. In 1938, she reported that she earned $565. In the summer of 1939, during one month, she worked ten days, earning $8.50 per day. When not working, she would spend her days on the telephone. She needed to cultivate the assistant directors, both on and off the set.

Former child star Baby Peggy, along with her family, eked out a living in Hollywood in the 1930s. As she recalled:

> Actually there were two Hollywoods, the packaged export on which our very lives depended, and the real thing, on which most of us practically starved to death. . . .
>
> Some extra people managed to pay their rent with fair regularity, but among a dozen of our close friends not one family could stay on top of the electric, gas, water and telephone bills as well. One or other was always being shut off or "temporarily disconnected." This brought into existence an unspoken code of conduct that helped us cope with an abnormal situation which, for the time being at least, was our way of life.
>
> If we were the ones whose telephone was working (but whose water had been turned off), we let the next-door neighbor, who was without phone service, call Central at our house and she in turn gave us enough water to make supper. If our gas was off it was no disgrace to put the makings of dinner in a roaster and march upstairs to Mrs. Lundquist's kitchen. There we cooked the meal while Mrs. Lundquist was downstairs using our phone. The combinations and reciprocations were endless, and fortunately everyone possessed a sense of the ridiculous, which made it possible to laugh instead of cry over the way things were.[21]

Baby Peggy was not the only child star of the silent era working as an extra in the 1930s. Also in the ranks were Peaches Jackson and Mary Jane Irving, both of whom had been well-known child players a decade earlier.

No matter how desperate the situation, extras remained on the whole a politically conservative bunch, unwilling to support a socialist agenda. "We don't want any of that Russian stuff, is all I know," said one extra. Asked if he meant communism, the man replied, "Yea. We don't want that. We'll get along—somehow."[22]

The film industry itself was anything but recession- or depression-proof. In the 1930s, it became more cost conscious, perhaps cutting down from two days to one the employment of an extra or bit player. It has been suggested that on the set, a script might be modified to eliminate the need to use a bit player, or to have the player appear in, say, two scenes, when one would suffice. The studios failed to acknowledge what elsewhere would be defined as "industrial accidents." There producers showed no concern for Florence Oberle, bitten in the face by a dog while working at Pathé in 1930, or for Rose Plumer, who lost two teeth when struck in the face with a club while filming *The Bowery* in 1933.[23]

Aside from the musical, another genre inextricably linked with Hollywood in the 1930s—and in particular with Warner Bros.—is the gangster film. An obvious problem developed when the gangster types available in the silent era proved unsuitable with the coming of sound. As Central Casting's Dave Allen explained:

> In the silent picture days we had no end of tough types in our files—hard-boiled fellows who would scare a man half to death. The talkies have cut the list down tremendously, since about four out of five of these rough-looking gents have tenor voices and high tenors at that.
>
> They come up here, these gorillas, and pipe out, in a shrill treble, "Any work for me today?" It's hard to keep from laughing sometimes.[24]

A group of tough guy extras actually got together in the fall of 1931 and placed an advertisement in local newspapers, announcing: "For Hire—twenty-eight mugs, rough, tough and scarred, with cauliflower ears and barrel chests—ready for anything but gangster work preferred. Available for $7.50 and $10 each per day." Appropriately, members of the group had names like Kid Wagoner, Big Pat Rooney, Sailor Sharkey, and Hap Hogan.[25]

Dave Allen reported, "Most of our regular boys are very easy to work with . . . As a matter of fact, they're easier to handle than the 'dress' extra people. But then again maybe we are a little kinder to them, for they are pretty tough customers once they get mad."[26] If Central Casting could not fulfill its requirements from registered extras, it would turn to the athletic clubs on Los Angeles's Main Street. Here, it might find former boxing champions such as Frank Goddard, Jack Perry, Charlie Sullivan, "Sailor" Vincent, Phil Bloom, and wrestler Jack McKenzie. The ex-fighters knew how to take care

In the early 1930s, Fox casting director James Ryan (left) hands some of his records over to his successor, Jack Gardner. AMPAS.

of themselves on the set, avoiding physical injury, but, as was reported, "The assistant director usually gets the mugs together before the scene and says, 'Now, boys, there's $5 apiece extra coming to you today if this fight is a good one.' And believe me, the assistant gets a wow of a battle."[27] By the 1940s, ex-fighters and wrestlers could generally be found congregating at the corner of Hollywood Boulevard and Vine Street. Among their number—the "Mug Colony," as they were called—were LeRoy McGuirk, world's junior heavyweight boxing champion, John Swenski, former junior heavyweight champion, Yukon Jake, Bob Gregory, European heavyweight champion, Mike Nazarian, Red Lyons, Paul Orth, and Dude Chick.

The circus could also provide "tough guy" extras, such as Al Rosen, who began his movie career as an extra with Joe E. Brown in *The Circus*

Clown (1934). Rosen recalled working with the circus in the season and in Hollywood out-of-season as an extra.[28]

One of the busiest and ugliest of extras was English-born Harry Wilson, who happily billed himself as "Hollywood's ugliest man," and had appeared in more than four hundred gangster and prison films by the early 1950s. Wilson came to Hollywood in 1924 upon leaving the merchant navy. While visiting a friend who was an assistant director at Paramount, the ex-sailor was quickly signed up by the studio. One of his first major productions, *Old Ironsides*, in which he was typecast as a member of the crew of the *USS Constitution*, was released in December 1926. Later appearances include one as a caveman in *One Million B.C.* (1940), one as a bodyguard in *All the King's Men* (1949), one as a Kansas City hood in *The Enforcer* (1951), another as a prisoner in *My Six Convicts* (1952), and even as one a bear in *The Yearling* (1946). His massive hands have been featured in close-ups in many films, including *Gone with the Wind* (1939) and *Samson and Delilah* (1949). In 1952, he reminisced, "I've been in Alcatraz, Leavenworth and all the other federal prisons—in pictures—and Sing Sing, San Quentin and most of the state pens, and a lot of foreign jails besides. I've been hanged, electrocuted, shot by firing squads, flogged and forced to walk the plank. . . . I've never had what you'd call a really sympathetic role . . . I'll leave all that romantic stuff to the pretty boys."[29]

With their cauliflower ears and frightening features, these tough guy extras might give the impression of being criminals, but they were not. One genuine extra turned criminal was thirty-seven-year-old, average-looking Kenneth Scott. He had often appeared on screen as a card dealer and even taught some card tricks to Humphrey Bogart, Lauren Bacall, John Garfield, and Dennis Morgan. Unfortunately, as most extras could testify, there was little money to be had in his chosen profession, and so Scott adopted a new one—that of safecracking. Between January and August 1946, he robbed more than fifty Safeway supermarkets in Los Angeles, Ventura, and Santa Barbara of some sixty-five thousand dollars. Obviously, the Los Angeles Sheriff's Department viewed extras with suspicion, and in April 1940, the police suggested to Central Casting that as part of the registration process all extras be fingerprinted. The interest in fingerprinting extras came about as a result of the revelation that New York-based contract killer Irving "Big Gangi" Cohen had worked briefly in Los Angeles as an extra.

Sometimes, rather than use Central Casting, studios in the 1930s would directly hire individuals who seemed appropriate for the extra roles. For *The White Angel* (1936), in which Kay Francis was an unlikely Florence

Extras relax between takes while making *The Prisoner of Zenda* (1937). The photograph was taken by one of the film's stars, David Niven (who had himself begun in Hollywood as an extra). AMPAS.

Nightingale, Warner Bros. hired fifteen real hospital nurses, along with assorted crippled World War I veterans. The latter, it was reported, hobbled from Burbank to Hollywood rather than spend forty cents on carfare. For *Suns o' Guns* (1936), Warner Bros. hired two hundred members of the 160th Regiment of the California National Guard to play German soldiers.

A very unusual group of extras was created in 1936 by Captain Richard von Opel, who had come to the Olympic Games in Los Angeles in 1932 as a member of the Austrian fencing team. When he read about the number of injuries sustained by extras appearing as soldiers in *The Charge of the Light Brigade*, he came up with the notion of creating a brigade of men to be known as the Cinema Troop, consisting of one hundred individuals between twenty-two and twenty-seven years of age, and ranging in height from five feet, eleven inches to six feet, one inch.[30] The group studied the military methods of various nationalities, the types of weapons used, the commands, the customs, and the regulations. They practiced horsemanship and cavalry movements. Subsequently, the men of the Cinema Troop hired themselves out at a day rate of between ten and twenty-five dollars. They played colonial soldiers in *Maid of Salem*, Germans in *The Road Back*, Poles in *Madame Walewska*, Spaniards in *The Firefly*, Austrian officers in *The Great Waltz*, and Ruritanian troops in *The Prisoner of Zenda*. They were unlike other extras in that when the assistant director called lunch, they would not disband until ordered to do so by Captain von Opel, and they would not dismiss from the set until told to "stand at ease."

Captain Richard von Opels's Cinema Troop in costume for *The Prisoner of Zenda* (1937). AMPAS.

Very different from von Opel's "soldiers" was the neo-fascist California Light Horse Regiment, created by actor Victor McLaglen to uphold the values of "Americanism." This group also provided appropriate extras for Hollywood films of the period, including *Under Two Flags* (1936).

Richard von Opel's Cinema Troop prospered because of the number of spectacular films that Hollywood was making in the 1930s. Such films provided work for other specialized types of extras. *If I Were King* (1938) boasted more than its share of beggars, providing work for those registered with Central Casting as hunchbacks, cripples, and dwarfs. *Suez* (1938), chronicling the building of the canal, required among its extras some fifteen stuntwomen, along with four hundred horse wranglers to handle Arab steeds. A reported 750 extras were kept busy on location for *Gunga Din* (1939). Spectacles on screen translated into extra groceries, explained the *Los Angeles Times*.[31]

The variety of types of extras available indicates just how varied the casting call for any one production could be. For example, a South American café scene for a 1931 film required the following:

three well-dressed Spanish men, thirty-five to forty years of age, palm beach suits and pajamas

two well-dressed American engineers, aged thirty, Palm Beach suits

one young Chinese girl, native costume, age twenty

one Spanish character, ordinary tropical clothes

four Spanish women, twenty-five to thirty-five years, tropical clothes

three Spanish men, hard types, thirty-five to forty years, dirty tropical clothes, unshaved

two South American policemen, costumes furnished

four Mexican men, big and tough, old white clothes

six Filipinos, ordinary old clothes, small men not over five feet or five feet, one inches

one hard type women, cheap tropical clothes

two South Sea island women

two hag types[32]

The look, age, and clothing required all determined not only the type of extra but also the pay. These elements also created an obvious caste system among the extras. Those with full wardrobes looked down on those classified as "mob" players and paid five dollars a day. "The last-named actor is the nobody of pictures," reported the *Los Angeles Times*. "His main thoughts, to all appearances, are concerned with his daily pay check and a comfortable place to sit and listen for the closing whistle."[33]

Extra Paul Bradley recalled:

In the morning when you reported to work, they would see if you were well dressed or not. If you weren't well dressed, there was a man from the Screen Actors Guild and from the studio would look you over. And if you weren't dressed in clothes to do the job, they wouldn't give you a check.

In order to get better work, you had to be very well dressed and you must have a good wardrobe. So I had a few dollars [and] I went to a place called Mackintosh in Hollywood. There was an Italian man there called Henry, who used to take measures, and he made beautiful suits. I had four suits, a top coat, a tuxedo and tails, and a cutaway. I had over thirty suits in my wardrobe—all kinds of evening clothes. There was a lady named Mary

> Webb Davis, on La Cienega near Melrose, and she would hire me to model clothes. Sometimes I'd do such a good job that they'd say you can have the overcoat or you can have the suit, which was nice.[34]

Paul Bradley recalled that the life of an extra on the set was not always a pleasant experience. In the summer of 1939, he was working at the RKO ranch on *The Hunchback of Notre Dame*:

> William Dieterle was the director. It was a hot day, and he said, "You bum extras, why don't you do this, why don't you do that." I was so damn mad, I threw the spear down and walked up to him with a check in my hand. I said, "Mr. Dieterle, these people are not bums. These people are hard-working people. It's a hot day. And you don't have the courtesy to talk to these people civilly." I said, "You can have that check. Now go and apologize to those people." And every time I would work for him, he would come over, put his arm around me, and say, "Paul, my Italian friend."[35]

The specificity of type worked against many extras. Gossip columnist Jimmie Fidler visited the set of MGM's 1939 production of *Thunder Afloat*, where he was impressed by the extras and the care that had obviously been employed in their selection:

> One and all, blowsy, strident-voiced women and weather-beaten, salt-encrusted men, they fitted that seaport set like so many barnacles. They BELONGED on the water front—couldn't possibly belong anywhere else.
>
> And that, of course, is the tragedy of the "successful" extra's lot. He is a sacrifice on the altar of authenticity, for he is hopelessly typed and labeled as a flesh-and-blood property, suitable for this background, or that.
>
> If he looks like a desert rat, he is "background" when a desert picture is made; if he looks like a wharf rat he prospers only when the studios launch a cycle of sea pictures. Hollywood doesn't want extras who suit any background fairly well; it demands types who suit particular locales EXACTLY. And it doesn't want actors and actresses from the extra ranks; it only wants human pigment for the director's brush.[36]

In 1939, the Standing Committee of the Motion Picture Producers and the Screen Actors Guild published a survey, to which 2,860 extras responded. The survey revealed that almost one-third had no other earnings other than those gained as an extra. Seventeen percent earned up to five hundred dollars annually as extras. Six percent earned between five hundred and one thousand dollars annually as extras. Five-and-a-half percent earned in excess of one thousand dollars as extras.[37] It was depressing news and should have served as a warning to those considering employment as extras, but, as in the past, enthusiasm always won out over cold reality. Would-be extras were governed by the heart and not the mind.

Also in 1939, the *Hollywood Reporter* struck terror in the hearts of all extras with an announcement in its issue of December 4 that Hollywood producers were so disenchanted with extras and their behavior that they planned to close Central Casting. Even worse, producers were considering the need for stories that did not involve the use of extras at all. "Pictures can be made without extras," claimed an analyst hired by the studios. If films did require extras, they could be shot outside California, in states where labor laws were less stringent. The piece noted that initial production on Columbia's Western, *Arizona*, took place in Tucson, where all types of extras were readily available at three dollars a day.

According to the producers:

> The extra has come to believe himself to be an actor—which he was never designed to be. No skill or experience is needed for extra work.
>
> The fact that some former actors have been forced by age or other circumstances to do extra work doesn't affect the situation. The extra always has been an occasional worker—to be used when there was work for him the same as any migrant field worker.[38]

It was an insulting comment, and one both Central Casting and the Screen Actors Guild decried. The extras should ignore the *Hollywood Reporter*—and they did. With a reported typical average daily wage of $10.52 as of March 1939,[39] working extras had enough to worry about.

On a more positive note, a standing committee of the Screen Actors Guild came up with some new proposals for extras, none of which, unfortunately, was implemented:

> We recommend that in casting, those extras, who by past employment experience appear to be best suited for extra work be accorded priority or preference over other extras, the demands for whose services have resulted in only casual or infrequent employment.
>
> We recommend that if the requirements of the industry warrant it the Guild admit to probationary membership each year a number of young

> people who shall be admitted to full membership at the end of one or two years only if their employment record in the industry indicates that they have the minimum qualifications for extra work.
>
> We recommend that all casting be done through Central Casting Corporation.[40]

By the 1930s, the hiring of extras, and all that activity entailed, had become incredibly efficient. The assistant director would report the project's requirements to the unit production manager. The latter would make out a form, which would be mimeographed and distributed throughout the studio by messenger. The studio casting department would select bit or part players and turn over the provision of mobs and crowds to Central Casting. The studio café would be advised by the production manager as to how many extra hot dinners were needed for the night. The wardrobe department would confirm that costumes, if necessary, were available. The makeup department would prepare for an appropriate morning rush. If necessary, the studio transportation department would ensure that buses were available. A first aid man would be assigned, dressing room space would be made available, and the studio police were notified. It took a mere fifteen minutes to put all these details into operation.[41]

Chapter Seven

THE STAND-IN

Audience familiarity with the role and purpose of the stand-in is evidenced by the 1937 Walter Wanger production titled, appropriately enough, *Stand-In*. Based on a story of the same name by Clarence Budington Kelland (published in the *Saturday Evening Post* from February 13 through March 20, 1937) and directed by Tay Garnett, *Stand-In* features Leslie Howard as a Wall Street financier who comes to Hollywood to investigate what is wrong with a film company in which his firm is heavily invested. He meets Lester Plum, played by Joan Blondell, a former child actress who is the stand-in for star Thelma Cheri (played by Marla Shelton), learns all about the film industry from her, and eventually decides to propose to her. The film is unusual in that it is perhaps the first to suggest that the source of many of the problems in Hollywood—including the treatment of extras—is not studio executives but rather New York bankers interested only in profits and the bottom line. (For the record, both Leslie Howard and Joan Blondell have stand-ins for the film: Richard Foster for the actor and Connie Rae for the actress.)

A gentler image of the stand-in is provided by former silent star Charles Ray in his 1935 short story of the same title. Here, the stand-in enjoys her life, appreciating the free time it provides for her to wander around the studio, "like a chastised child she was seen and not heard." As Ray writes, "She was the stand-in, just a girl with a makeup on, never to be photographed. Her peculiar studio duty was to stand under the hot arc lights until the camera men obtained the proper light balance and focus; then she could retire, awaiting another call, privileged to watch the star on her photographic throne, as a maid might look at a queen."[1]

The concept of a stand-in, someone who would "stand in" for an actor or actress when a scene was not actually being filmed—for example when the lighting of the shot was being determined—originated with Pola Negri in the 1920s. The legendary and often temperamental Polish-born star had begun her American career at Paramount in 1923. It was definitely not to her

Humphrey Bogart and Marla Shelton in *Stand-In* (1937).

liking to hang around the set when not working, and so she suggested that a dummy or manikin be used to replace her. Thus was the stand-in created.

There are, however, earlier examples of a stand-in or stunt double—if not in an entire film, at the least in one sequence. For example, Jean DeKay doubled for star Norma Phillips in a scene in which the actress was supposedly thrown from a racing automobile in the 1916 series *Our Mutual Girl*. The earliest documented use of a double is by D. W. Griffith in his 1914 production of *The Escape*. While she was working on the film, Blanche Sweet contracted scarlet fever, and a minor actress named Claire Anderson was hired to double for her in some of the scenes. There were rumors that Sweet left the film before completion, and Anderson took over, although Sweet denied this interpretation of events.[2] Certainly, Sweet and Anderson are similar in appearance, and it is possible that Anderson appears in some of the still photographs from the film, which were deliberately shot so as to show the leading lady's face indistinctly.

According to director Robert Florey, who knew all of the principals involved, in D. W. Griffith's *Intolerance* (1916), the chariot supposedly driven by Constance Talmadge in the Babylonian sequence is actually under the control of Annette De Foe (1889–1960), who commenced her career with the Kalem Company in Jacksonville, Florida, and played bit parts for Griffith. In the same production, Willam Dark Cloud doubled for Miriam Cooper in the "Modern Story" after she has killed the Musketeer of the Slums and jumped to the ground from a second-story window.

Extra Lila Stevens, active in the late 1910s, bears an extraordinary resemblance to Lillian Gish. Stevens would have been a perfect double, as *Photoplay* reported.[3] However, as far as can be ascertained, Stevens never did work as a stand-in for Gish. In 1919, Dorothy Phillips was set to play two sisters in Universal's production of *The Right to Happiness*. The studio decided to advertise for a double for the actress to play alongside her in long shots, but after casting director Lillian Greenberger had interviewed more than one hundred potential doubles, not one was found to be satisfactory.[4]

In the silent era, it is believed that cowboy star Buck Jones stood in for William Farnum, although the slim cowboy star bears little bodily resemblance to the somewhat stolid Farnum. Don Alvarado may have worked at some point as a stand-in for Rudolph Valentino; certainly both men have a Latin look. Jack Montgomery, the father of silent child star Baby Peggy, doubled for Ronald Colman in the riding sequences in *The Winning of Barbara Worth* (1926). In the 1920s and 1930s, Carmen La Rue was Dolores Del Rio's stand-in. German-born Karl Holl had worked as an extra in crowd scenes on films as varied as the Lon Chaney vehicle *The Hunchback of Notre Dame* and *King Kong*. He was also a stand-in for Tom Mix in the 1920s, selected because he had a similar nose and could ride a horse. Holl claimed actually to have doubled for Mix in two unidentified films, one in a train ride sequence after the star failed to appear one morning, and the other a sequence featuring an escape from a burning building.

By the 1930s, stand-ins were commonplace on the studio set. Some stars actually had stand-ins who had been or were to be performers in their own right. In the early 1930s, Ann Harding's stand-in was Julie Haydon, who was to be a leading lady on screen and, more prominently, on the Broadway stage. At one point, Joan Crawford had as her stand-in Ann Dvorak, prior to the latter's rise to stardom at Warner Bros. Baby Marie Osborne's career as a child star of the 1910s was long over when she became the stand-in for Ginger Rogers. By 1939, Osborne had returned to playing roles, albeit small ones, and was superseded as Rogers' stand-in by Dorothy Panter.

C. Aubrey Smith's stand-in, Brigadier General R. D. Napier Raikes.

However, in the 1940s, Osborne went back to being a stand-in, this time for Deanna Durbin. Durbin's stand-in in the 1930s had been Dorothy Sherrill, her agent's daughter. "B" Western leading man Buddy Roosevelt was a stand-in for Ronald Colman, an actor not associated with the Western genre. When Ronald Colman became ill while shooting *Lost Horizon* (1937), for five weeks extra Paul Bradley stood in for him, earning three hundred dollars per week. Some leading ladies required two stand-ins. Sonja Henie had a number of non-skating stand-ins—Lillian Baer, Frances Sawyer and Joan Taylor—while Bert Clark handled requirements on the ice.

Katharine Hepburn used two sisters, Mimi and Patricia (Patsy) Doyle as her stand-ins. The latter, who also worked as a dancer, was a stand-in for

Barbara Stanwyck and continued on screen through 1942, when she married editor and director-to-be Robert Wise. Patricia Doyle's last appearances were as a sharecropper's daughter in *The Grapes of Wrath* (1940) (although she may have been cut from the film) and as a servant in *All That Money Can Buy* (1941).

At least one major character actor, C. Aubrey Smith, had a stand-in, Brigadier General R. D. Napier Raikes, whose name suggests that he was every bit as prominent a figure in the British military as Smith's performances might suggest he was. While Smith represented the British Empire on screen, it might be argued that Napier Raikes had served as its representative in person. However, there is no record of Napier Raikes holding any rank in the British army. Certainly, he regarded working in motion pictures as a comedown. But as Napier Raikes explained, "I am now about the lowest form of life within the studio but, nonetheless, I am actually participating in the making of a film production—and I came here to learn."[5]

Among the documented stand-ins for female stars in the late 1930s are Edna Eckert Noyer (Mae West), Mae Warren (May Robson), Fern Barry (Helen Hayes), Ruby Wilson (Marie Windsor), Jeanette Rudy (Martha Raye), Pluma Noison (Claudette Colbert), Helene Holmes (Alice Faye), Dayle Jensen (Patricia Ellis), Daisy De Witt (Margaret Lindsay), Jane Downey (Gloria Stuart and Jean Muir), Kasha Haroldi (Joan Crawford), Mary Jane Irving (Janet Gaynor in her later films), and Kathryn or Kay Stanley (Irene Dunne). Greta Garbo's stand-in is documented as Chris Marie Meeker, but it is unclear that the star ever acknowledged the latter's existence. In the late 1920s, Garbo also had a double named Geraldine De Vorak, who bore an incredible resemblance to the star—except that she lived not in a mansion but at the Hollywood Studio Club. When De Vorak appeared at a restaurant or store, she was often mistake for Garbo, and *Photoplay* suggested that she acted more like a star than the star herself did.[6] Unfortunately, De Vorak acted a little too much like Garbo, and she was downgraded from double to a typical studio extra.

Kasha Haroldi, who was also known as Hasha Harold, was Joan Crawford's stand-in for many years. Because Haroldi had been married to Crawford's brother, Hal Le Seuer, from 1931 to 1935, the star would always refer to her as "sister." Hal Le Seuer (1903–63) spent most of his life as an extra, apart from a short period when he worked as a make-up artist at MGM. His last screen appearance is believed to have been in 1957 in *Jeanne Eagels*. Joan Crawford was not a fan and was quoted as saying:

> Hal was a louse, an out-and-out bastard. He could charm the skin off a snake, but nothing, not his jobs, not the men and women in his life, lasted long. Liquor, then drugs, and always his distorted ego took over. I supported that son-of-a-bitch until the day he died . . . At least Norma Shearer's brother, Douglas, was brilliant and self-sufficient, and made his own career at Metro [as a sound engineer]. But I was stuck with a schmuck. That man—or did he ever become a man—was a monster. God, I hated him.[7]

Sally Sage was a stand-in for Bette Davis at Warner Bros., beginning with *The Big Shakedown* in 1934. At the studio, she had a stock contract guaranteeing her fifty dollars a week. Sage was the subject of a lengthy article in the pages of *Good Housekeeping* magazine, in which it was reported, "She isn't discontented, for she has no illusions about her work. She knows that so far no stand-in has ever risen to stardom, has ever gone higher than the rank of bit player."[8] But as one reads the piece, it becomes obvious that Sage is far from content with her lot. She tells the journalist to approach William Wyler, the director on *Jezebel*, and ask him what her name is. Wyler responds to the question with a blank look and "Who?," suggesting that he has never even noticed Sage.[9]

A 1933 graduate of Hollywood High School, Milwaukee-born Sally Sage got her job with Bette Davis when the star's former stand-in, Mary Windsor, decided to become a chorus girl for Busby Berkeley. Windsor introduced Sage to Bette Davis, and the actress was happy to welcome her to the set. It was not easy being a stand-in, as Sage was to learn. While she did not look like Bette Davis, she was the right height and weight and had the right coloring. But it took some time to learn that while the star could take an hour for lunch, the stand-in was limited to thirty minutes, that she had to read the script closely, that she had to copy the star's walk and body language, that she must never keep a cameraman waiting, that she must never be overfriendly with the star—and, above all, that she must mind her own business:

> She found that stand-ins must make themselves up in the morning. She discovered that the dresses they wear are not copies of the ones that stars wear in scenes—they are garments from wardrobe that match in color, but seldom in style, the costumes the star wears. She learned that a stand-in can shoulder part of a star's burden by knowing the action of a scene.[10]

Bette Davis and Sally Sage worked well together. The latter doubled for the star for a scene in *Satan Met a Lady* (1936) when the director was concerned that running through the rain on a cold night might give Davis a cold. During the shooting of *Jezebel* (1938), Bette Davis arrived on the set prior to Sage, and decided to stand-in for herself, unbeknownst to the director or cinematographer. When Bette Davis walked out on Warner Bros. in a contract dispute, she made certain that her stand-in had an unbreakable stock contract, and while the star was away, Sage worked as a bit player in *The Charge of the Light Brigade* (1936) and *San Quentin* (1937).

Sally Sage's relationship with Bette Davis appears to have ended in 1940, when Sage married her second husband, Clifford Hutchison. She has a bit part in *Meet John Doe*, released the following year, but after that date there are no recorded appearances on screen. Sally Sage died in Glendale, California, on January 1, 2000, at the age of eighty-five.

As of 1944, Mildred Crawford had been Rosalind Russell's stand-in for eight years. Betty Hall was a stand-in for Karen Morley and Shirley Ross before becoming Carole Lombard's permanent stand-in from *Nothing Sacred* (1937) onwards. Often there was little facial and physical similarity between the stand-in and the star; one major exception was Phyllis Yates, who bore an incredible resemblance to her star, Ann Harding.

Male stand-ins include: Victor Chatten (Lew Ayres), "Dutch" Petit (Richard Barthelmess and later Paul Muni), Tommy Noonan (Tyrone Power), Pat O'Shea (Joe E. Brown), Guy Gabriel (Cesar Romero), Nick Borgani (Adolphe Menjou), Walter Coffey (Richard Arlen), Frank McGrath (Warner Baxter), Art Berry, Jr. (Herbert Marshall), George Loller (Richard Dix), Delmar Costello (Peter Lorre), Ray Stewart (Lionel Barrymore), Bert Kennedy (Pat O'Brien), Ted Hall (George Raft), Henry Kraft (Ray Milland), Henry Wise (Fred MacMurray), Eddie Hall (Edward Everett Horton), Arnold Grey and Carl Andre (Joel McCrea), Jack Goodrich (Dick Powell), Malcolm Merrihugh (Cary Grant), Bill Meader (Fredric March), Jack Leeman (Fredric March), Carter Glass and Ben Splane (George Brent), Frankie Van (Hugh Herbert), and Bill Hoover (Charles Laughton and Edward Arnold).[11] Unfortunately, Hoover looked so much like Edward Arnold that it was virtually impossible for him to gain even extra work in his own right. Directors would complain that his presence could confuse audiences, and it certainly confused fans for whom Hoover would sign autographs in Arnold's name. Leo Lynn, a former plumber, was Bing Crosby's stand-in, and also worked as the crooner's chauffeur.

For most of his career, Will Rogers refused a stand-in, but by the mid 1930s, he was using Leonard Taylor, who was later to work in a similar capacity for Fred Stone. Wallace Beery used his brother-in-law, Mat Gilman, as

William Powell and his stand-in, Dr. W. W. Dearborn, fooling around during filming of *Double Wedding* (1937).

his stand-in. Hedy Lamarr's first stand-in was Melba Snowden, but she was replaced by Sylva Lamarr, who resembled the star, but surprisingly, was no relation. Sylvia Lamarr initially tried her luck at the studios early in 1937, but discovered that her facial similarity to Joan Crawford put her at a disadvantage—one Joan Crawford was enough.

Even supporting players and character actors had stand-ins: Richard Foster for Charles Butterworth; Joe Hinds for James Gleason; Boris Chamur for Akim Tamiroff; Pat Malone for Henry Stephenson. Not only did Gus Tallon serve as Barry Fitzgerald's stand-in, he also lived with the bachelor actor.

William Powell's stand-in was actually a chiropractor by the name of Dr. W. W. Dearborn. Dearborn became prominent promoting rights and appropriate salaries for extras, and when he died in May 1940 after an automobile accident, he was much mourned by his fellow extras and stand-ins. Gary Cooper's stand-in and stunt double was often Slim Talbot, whom the actor had first met in Helena, Montana. One day during the shooting of *Souls at Sea* (1937), Talbot did a scene for Cooper. After it was completed, director Henry Hathaway turned to the star and said, "Do it that way. It was perfect! Do it just like Slim did." The cast, crew and even the star greeted the comment with laughter.[12]

Some stand-ins, such as Cliff Lyons, worked for a number of stars and also served as a stunt double. Working as both a stand-in for Errol Flynn and a stunt double at Warner Bros. in the 1930s was Don Turner, who had a special stock company contract. Turner also worked occasionally as George Brent's stand-in. Don Turner was replaced as Flynn's stand-in by James Fleming, who had been what is described as a "house business manager." When Flynn claimed that Fleming was actually his butler, the stand-in responded, "Mr. Flynn has quite an imagination."[13]

Also closely associated with Errol Flynn is Howard Hill (1899–1975), who shot the arrows for the actor in *The Adventures of Robin Hood* (1938). Flynn would raise the bow for the long shots, and Hill would move in for the close-up. He doubled for Herbert Mundin, killing a deer with an arrow, and also shot a steel mace from the hand of Basil Rathbone when the latter played the Sheriff of Nottingham (and did not use a double for the shot). During eight weeks of location filming, Hill "killed" eleven stuntmen for the production—as well as a wild boar for the extras. Because he was also appearing on screen as a stuntman, Hill had to kill himself in one of the studios scenes. First there was a close-up of Flynn shooting the arrow. Then Hill took the star's place on the staircase and a stuntman took Hill's place, receiving an arrow fired by Hill himself.

Howard Hill also worked with Errol Flynn on at least three other films: *The Private Lives of Elizabeth and Essex* (1939), *They Died with Their Boots On* (1942), and *San Antonio* (1945). Generally, Hill is credited as a technical adviser rather than as a stunt double, although he does have a supporting role in a 1937 "B" Western, *The Singing Buckaroo*. Howard Hill's screen career, which includes many short subjects, began in 1935 with the documentary feature, *The Last Wilderness*, in which he plays himself filming (and killing) the last of America's big game.

Charles "Jumpy" DeBeaver was a parachute jumper until he was severely injured after his chute failed to open at Roosevelt Field, New York. He changed careers, becoming a stand-in for Edward G. Robinson. Frankie Van was a flyweight boxing champion in 1922, but he gave up fighting in 1928 and became comedian Hugh Herbert's stand-in.

In November 1935, it was announced that Donald Woods's stand-in at Warner Bros. would be Bryan Hargreaves, the nineteen-year-old grandson of William Jennings Bryan. The *Los Angeles Examiner* (November 25, 1935) published a photograph of Woods and Hargreaves, urging its readership to note the resemblance. Doing so must have taken a lot of imagination on the part of the readers.

Mary Jane Saunders (foreground), making her screen debut in *Sorrowful Jones* (1949), is seen with her stand-in, Della Downing.

Some stand-ins worked for multiple stars. Starting in the mid- 1930s, Leonard Mann could be found doubling for Eddie Bracken and Dick Powell, and then for Bing Crosby and Wendell Corey in the late 1940s. As a utility stand-in, Mann explained, "This sometimes means that I must wear shoe-lifts to elevate my height to correspond with that of my star. But utility work has its advantages. I'm in constant view of the director and quite often land a bit part. This means extra pay, of course, which comes in very handy between picture calls."[14] Another stand-in similarly engaged was Gale Mogul, who had understudied Eddie Cantor on Broadway in *Whoopee*. When the comedian came to Hollywood, Mogul came with him, standing-in not only for Cantor, but also, on a film by film basis, for Ronald Colman, Adolphe Menjou, Leslie Howard, Robert Donat, and Charles Boyer. Understudying the considerably taller Boyer in *Private Worlds* (1935), Mogul had to wear a pair of shoes with four-inch soles. Syndicated gossip columnist Dan Thomas explained, "He has dozens of pairs of shoes, with soles measuring from a quarter inch to six inches in thickness. With these he achieves the necessary height."[15]

Shirley Temple with her stand-in, Mary Lou Isleib.

Both child stars and supporting child actresses had their own stand-ins. In the mid-1930s, Marilyn Granas stood in for Shirley Temple. Granas was replaced, at least in 1938, by Mary Lou Isleib. Gloria Fisher stood in for Jane Withers, Carol Ann Saunders for Margaret O'Brien, and Barbara Campbell for Virginia Weidler.[16] Even Paramount's Baby LeRoy had his own stand-in, Ronald Smith, when the infant star became too raucous or difficult to direct.

When Paramount decided to film *Alice in Wonderland* in 1933, it undertook a highly publicized search for "Alice." Charlotte Henry was eventually selected. The runner up was Sue Kellogg, and she was hired to be Henry's stand-in. "Now she does everything but act Alice," reported *Literary Digest*.

Some stand-ins were used for hand close-ups, as was Lucille Brewster, here standing-in for Jean Arthur on *The More the Merrier* (1943).

"When Miss Henry works, she stands on the side-lines with a forlorn look, possibly imagining how well she could have played the part."[17]

Documented stand-ins from the 1940s and later include Jean Vernon (Ruth Hussey), Byron Fitzgerald (William Holden), Neil Collins (George Raft), Pearl Miller (Nancy Olson), Gordon Clark (Douglas Fairbanks, Jr.), "Fig" Newton (Charles Boyer)(replacing Richmond Lynch, who had worked with the star in the 1930s), Tommy Summers (Alan Ladd), Jack Robbins (Bob Hope, beginning with *The Princess and the Pirate*), Lyle Moraine (later Bob Hope vehicles), June Kilgore (Paulette Goddard), Ruth Peterson (Rita Hayworth), and June Smaney (June Duprez). Jimmy Cornell had worked as an extra since the early 1920s, and from *Shane* in 1953 through *The Carpetbaggers* in 1964, he was Alan Ladd's stand-in, while also finding time to work on a regular basis as a stand-in for Lloyd Nolan and J. Carroll Naish.

On *Casablanca* (1942), Betty Brooks stood in for Ingrid Bergman, and Russ Llewellyn performed the same role for Humphrey Bogart. *Gone with the Wind* (1939) boasted a complete cast of stand-ins, headed by [Millicent] Mozelle Miller, who stood in for Vivien Leigh. Miller had played bit parts in earlier films and was later to stand in for Vivien Leigh in *That Hamilton Woman*, before becoming a stand-in for Merle Oberon, the wife of that film's producer. Leslie Howard's stand-in on *Gone with the Wind* was Arthur Tovey, who had also served in the same capacity on *Intermezzo* (1939).

A not very believable publicity shot showing Lucille Ball indulging in "one of her favorite pastimes," fixing the hair of her stand-in, Wanda Cantlon. AMPAS.

Tovey made his screen debut as an extra in the 1924 Marion Davies vehicle, *Yolanda*. As with all aspects of the production, David O. Selznick gave careful thought to the use of extras in *Gone with the Wind*. He contemplated the proportion of male to female extras for the Atlanta sequences, noting, "care should be taken that we clearly have more women than men and a decreasing number of men as the picture progresses and as we get deeper into the war."[18] Selznick was also surprisingly careful with money when extras were involved. Rather than hire live men to play dead soldiers on the Civil War battlefield, he resorted to the use of dummies, thereby "depriving extras of badly-needed work," as gossip columnist Jimmie Fiddler noted.[19]

The role of the stand-in was instrumental in providing an extra with access not only to the star with whom the extra was associated, but also to others—particularly producers and directors—who might be able to advance the extra's career. Jules Garrison lied his way onto a studio lot by pretending to be Henry Fonda's double.[20] A stand-in could also aid the star. Tony Orlando, stand-in for Jack LaRue, pretended to be the leading man when a New York court summons was issued for LaRue. Aside from a somewhat sleazy look adopted by both men, their actual facial similarity was slight.

Typically, a stand-in might move from one star to another, moving up a ladder comparable to the one aiding a star's progression. For example, Ann Robinson began as Ann Dvorak's stand-in at Warner Bros., hired by Max

Olivia De Havilland and her stand-in, Ann Robinson, dry off after a scene in *The Charge of the Light Brigade* (1936).

Arnow at five dollars a day. She worked as a stand-in for Kay Francis and Margaret Lindsay before becoming Olivia De Havilland's permanent stand-in, beginning with *A Midsummer Night's Dream* in 1935, at a guaranteed weekly salary of twenty-five dollars. The pay was initially somewhat low, as most regular stand-ins at this time would make six dollars a day or thirty-three dollars a week. But in additional to her weekly paycheck, Robinson would routinely receive gifts from the star, including, for example, an antelope bag and a crate of soup from a company for which De Havilland recorded radio commercials.

De Havilland was not the only star noted for her generosity towards extras. Other names cited for treating extras to bottles of cola and dishes of ice cream are James Cagney, Claudette Colbert, Joan Crawford, Bob Hope, and Ginger Rogers.[21] When Bette Davis's stand-in, Sally Sage, married small-time actor Ed Price in the summer of 1937, the star gave the couple a complete silver dinner service for six as a wedding present. Myrna Loy became a close friend of her MGM stand-in, Shirley Hughes, and when the star married producer Arthur Hornblow, Jr. in Mexico in 1937, Hughes attended as maid of honor.

Stars did not, however, always understand what might constitute an appropriate gift for the extras. While Polynesian extra Satini Puailoa was appearing in *Waikiki Wedding* in 1937, its star Bing Crosby gave Puailoa a set of golf clubs. Puailoa did not play golf, but he did need money to survive, and so he sold the gold clubs for one dollar and fifty cents, enough for a few days' carfare.

Cary Grant's stand-in, Malcolm Merrihugh, had the opportunity to tell his story to the fan magazine *Silver Screen*. He had worked in *Holiday* and *Gunga Din*. He drove the car that Cary Grant sends crashing in *Topper*, and he drove another car for Cary Grant in *When You're in Love*. He was still Grant's stand-in as late as *Night and Day* in 1946. Merrihugh became so close to his star that in conversation he would always refer to the two of them as "we," as in, "We made three pictures last year," or "We did this," or "We did that."[22]

Merrihugh explained:

> A good stand-in takes care of his principal's make-up box, his principal's make-up, his clothes, sees that they are pressed and hung properly, checks the assistant director to find out when the star is working, sees that he's at work, keeps the dressing room orderly, makes and breaks dates on the telephone, does secretarial work, acts as a companion, runs errands, sees that certain people come on and off the set, and does everything in general.
>
> The star gets his stand-in better than the wage minimum and, when the stand-in works for the star, puts a little more in the pay envelope. Grant's a swell fellow when it comes to that extra help.
>
> The star has more responsibility than the stand-in, but the stand-in works harder.[23]

Sometimes, Merrihugh would also work, with the star's permission, as an extra on the same film in which he was standing-in for Grant, and that extra work could raise his daily salary to $16.50.

In his own right, Malcolm Merrihugh played small roles in a number of films, including *Sons of Steel* (1934) and *Ladies Day* (1943). While he was working on a Chesterfield production, he met Grant's first wife, Virginia Cherrill, and she suggested that he stand-in for her husband. She noted that Merrihugh was slightly lighter than Grant and also an inch-and-a-half shorter, but that difference was nothing that Cuban heels could not take care of.

As Ed Sullivan pointed out in a 1939 fan magazine article, there was nothing romantic about being a stand-in. The pay was better than that received by the lowest-paid extras after the Screen Actors Guild had won a basic pay contract for them of $6.50 a day. But stand-ins were only paid when the stars they doubled for were working, and no Hollywood stars worked fifty-two weeks a year or anything approaching that number. "A stand-in for Charlie Chaplin, who makes one picture every four years, would starve to death."[24] While stand-ins would get to know directors and assistant directors, and perhaps, as a result, get recommended for other jobs, stand-ins generally did not care to work as extras and would probably learn no more about the industry than extras. However, as Sullivan wrote, "the stand-ins do not feel at all morbid about the situation. To them, it is all in a day's work and, most important, it is a day's work. They have no illusions of grandeur, these kids."[25]

Stand-ins did attempt to form an organization, which might have grown to have some standing as a bargaining agent. In December 1939, a small group of stand-ins filed for incorporation as Hollywood Standin [*sic*] Players, Inc., which later changed its name to the Hollywood Stand-Ins Guild. The 1940s saw the organization of the Associated Stand-Ins of Hollywood. It sponsored the annual Elmer Awards, presented for outstanding achievement for standing-in, a category an outsider might consider difficult to define. In March 1944, in honor of work performed the previous year, Sally Wood won for her stand-in work for Susanna Foster in *This Is the Life*, and Jack Parker received the award for his stand-in work for Randolph Scott in *Gung Ho*.

The only documented example in the 1930s of a stand-in becoming a star is Anita Weber, who worked for Rosemary Lane in *Hollywood Hotel*. The photograph of the star and her stand-in was published in a Berlin magazine, and when it was learned that Weber was a Swiss citizen, she was hired by an Austrian film company to star in a film set in the Swiss Alps. One American stand-in who might have become a star, but did not, is Mary Dees. When Jean Harlow died on Jun 7, 1937, she left unfinished her last film, *Saratoga*, a horse-breeding and racing drama co-starring Clark Gable and directed by

Malcolm Merrihugh and Patricia Doyle stand-in for stars Cary Grant and Katharine Hepburn on the set of *Bringing Up Baby* (1938).

Jack Conway.[26] MGM initially decided to shelve the production, but when fans clamored for its release, the studio decided to complete the film, using a double for Harlow. Mary Dees, a dancer, was hired for the part because she had a similar build and hairstyle to that of Jean Harlow. She was photographed only from the back, and the Harlow voice was provided by radio actress Paula Winslowe. The concept did not work in that it was obvious that the actress in the later scenes was not Harlow. The film, released on July 23, 1937, also failed to generate interest in Mary Dees, and she disappeared from the scene.

A very different film with a very different reason for using a stand-in is *Salt of the Earth* (1954), a story of striking mine workers in New Mexico made by a group of blacklisted Hollywood filmmakers, including director

Mary Dees doubled for Jean Harlow after the star died prior to completion of *Saratoga* (1937). It is unclear whether this "art" pose was shot prior to Dees's appearance in the film, or if the photo was circulated with the intent to fool viewers into believing it shows a topless Jean Harlow. AMPAS.

Herbert Biberman and screenwriter Michael Wilson. The Mexican leading lady, Rosaura Revueltas, came to the attention of US authorities, who were incensed by the film's pro-communist storyline, and she was voluntarily deported to Mexico during the production. An unidentified double was found, and she appears in a number of scenes, shot in half-profile or over-the-shoulder, with Revueltas speaking her lines. As Biberman notes, the double was "the only player who used make-up in the entire production."[27]

There are other examples of stand-ins attempting to break through into the big-time, but generally such players' ambitions meet with little success. In the fall of 1937, Richmond Lynch, who had been a stand-in for Charles Boyer and also worked in a similar capacity for Spencer Tracy, signed with

Fanchon and Marco to put together a touring program titled "Richmond Lynch and His Stand-Ins of Hollywood." The act played the few surviving vaudeville houses, as well as theatres presenting joint film and stage presentations. When Lynch approached the various studios about contacting potential players, according to the *Hollywood Citizen-News* (October 5, 1937) he was told, "Stand-ins . . . don't have talent." It is a statement, of course, with some merit, in that stand-ins do not act and need show no indication of any artistic creativity at all.

For thirty years, Maurice Elliott worked as a dresser, secretary, and stand-in for rotund character comedy star Victor Moore. Elliott graduated to minor speaking but uncredited roles in the mid 1930s. The 1951 Frank Capra production of *Here Comes the Groom* boasted seven stand-ins with credited roles. In addition to their regular assignments as stand-ins for Bing Crosby and Jane Wyman, stars of the film, Alan Calm and Pat Marlowe were given parts in the production, as were stand-ins Lyle Moraine, Tommy Summers, Neil Collins, Byron Fitzgerald, and Pearl Miller.

While there are obvious similarities between the work of a double and the work of a stand-in, the two occupations are not generally interchangeable. The stand-in need possess nothing more than a passing resemblance to the star, whereas the double generally should be of the same build and height and have a strong facial resemblance to the star (although the last is not always true in terms of the stunt doubles, discussed below). Outside of scenes involving stunts, doubles are not terribly important to most productions.

Just as *Stand-In* glorified that particular occupation, another 1937 production—this time from Columbia Pictures—paid tribute to the work of screen doubles. *It Happened in Hollywood* tells the story of a silent Western film star, played by Richard Dix, who is unable to make the transition to sound. As a result, he cannot keep a promise to a young, disabled boy that he will introduce him to various Hollywood celebrities. This problem is solved by the decision to host a party to which doubles for the stars are invited. If nothing else, the film introduces the film going public to a number of actual Hollywood doubles, although it is not totally clear that all were actually active in that capacity. Featured at the party are: Phil Waldron (Clark Gable), Doc Dearborn (William Powell), Robert O'Keefe (James Cagney), Howard Bruce (Edward Arnold), Joan Beauchamp (Myrna Loy), Margaret Wormser (Loretta Young), John Bohn (John Barrymore), Arthur McLaglen (Victor McLaglen), James May (W. C. Fields), Eugene DeVerdi (Charlie Chaplin), Charles Clark (Joe E. Brown), Frank Brown (Harold Lloyd),

Stunt double Richard Talmadge.

Virginia Rendell (Mae West), Carol Dietrich (Marlene Dietrich), Frank E. Farr (Eddie Cantor), Earl Haddon (Bing Crosby), Berna Mack (Claudette Colbert), Zeffie Tilbury (May Robson), Mary Miner (Irene Dunne), Al Constance (George Raft), Don Eddy (Fred Astaire), Lillian Tours (Ginger Rogers dancing), Beatrice Coleman (Ginger Rogers non-dancing), and Betty Dietrich (Greta Garbo).

Some of the "doubles" had never actually worked in that capacity, despite their physical similarity to the stars they substituted for. Earl Haddon looked and sounded like Bing Crosby, while Charles Clark had only ever impersonated Joe E. Brown in high school. Like Loretta Young, Margaret Wormser was born in Salt Lake City, but she had never worked in Hollywood. Phil Waldron worked at MGM, but as a prop man, while James May (who at seventy was considerably older than W. C. Fields) worked at everything from set electrician to dialectician. Others had impersonated the star not on screen but on the variety stage or, in the case of Frank E. Farr, at the Chicago World's Fair.

Al Constance had doubled George Raft in long shots, and Jean Seale had undertaken similar duties for Jean Harlow, while also serving as a member of MGM's stock company. Mary Miner bore such a striking resemblance to Irene Dunne that RKO kept her under contract while the star was also under contract to the studio. Robert O'Keefe had doubled for James Cagney in *A Midsummer Night's Dream*. As might be expected, Arthur McLaglen was the brother of Victor. Carol Dietrich was no relation to Marlene Dietrich, but had impersonated her and other stars on the vaudeville stage. Her sister, Betty Dietrich, worked as a dress extra.

Stunt doubles are the most commonly recognized of such players. While the earliest of screen stars (even before the term was known) generally performed their own stunts without argument and with little concern for personal safety, the notion of the stunt person as a stand-in or double for the leading player can be dated back to the 1910s. Many stunt persons from the silent era remain anonymous. One female stunt performer who did generate some interest from the fan magazines is Arizona-born Winna Brown, who was noted for her riding skills. She played Indian women at Universal in the 1910s, and by the 1920s, she was stunt doubling for Norma and Constance Talmadge and even Pola Negri, who persuaded Brown to dress off-screen in more feminine attire. When Joseph Schildkraut was signed to play opposite Norma Talmadge in *The Song of Love* (1923), it was discovered that he was afraid of horses, and so Talmadge arranged for Winna Brown to double for him. Stunt doubling in the 1920s paid little more than what an extra might earn. Brown seldom earned more than ten dollars a day, and sometimes was paid five dollars for each fall from a horse.[28] There was talk in 1922 that Winna Brown (or Winnie Brown as she was described at the time) was going to become a star in her own right, discovered and about to be directed by scenarist Frances Marion, but nothing came of the notion. "Winna can talk to a cowboy in his own language, matching slang for slang and profanity for profanity, and strength for strength," reported *Picture-Play*. "Of course, some of the cowboys working in pictures are a lot of hams and don't know anything about taking care of animals. Or as Winna will tell you, 'They're short on horses and long on bull.'"[29]

A former circus and vaudeville performer, Richard Talmadge came into films in the 1910s, performing stunts in both serials and features, and doubling on a fairly regular basis. Among the best-known stars for whom he performed stunt doubling are Douglas Fairbanks, Sr. (*Robin Hood*, *The Black Pirate*, and *The Gaucho*), Slim Summerville, and Laurel and Hardy. Talmadge's dedication was such that while doubling for cowboy star Al Hoxie in the 1920s, Talmadge managed to break his neck. Little wonder that one fan magazine wrote that, "He has risen from an obscure 'double' to one of the best stunt stars in the world."[30]

One pioneering Hollywood stuntwoman from the 1930s is Lila Finn (1909-96), who appeared in more than one hundred films. She was twenty-six years old, and as she recalled there were ten other stuntwomen active in the industry, when she was hired to double for Dorothy Lamour in *The Hurricane* (1937), swimming and diving on location on the island of Pago Pago in Samoa and later off the California Coast for pick-up shots. Working conditions in Samoa were primitive, as she recalled: "As a dressing room, they had a little tent with one of the big heaters in the centre. And [leading man] Jon Hall's double and myself, when we got cold, we'd have to go into the tent and turn our backs on each each—just change our clothes in there with each other."[31]

She doubled for Paulette Goddard, riding the rapids, in Cecil B. DeMille's *Reap the Wild Wind* (1942) and *Unconquered* (1947), and for Donna Reed, when the star dances with James Stewart and falls into the swimming pool underneath the gym floor in *It's a Wonderful Life* (1946). Other actress for whom Finn doubled include Ida Lupino, Frances Dee, Veronica Lake, Joan Fontaine, and, in later years, for Jessica Tandy in *Batteries Not Included.* (1986). In Alfred Hitchcock's *To Catch a Thief* (1955), she doubles for thief Brigitte Auber, jumping from one roof to another and eventually rolling off the roof and catching herself as she falls. Finn's colleague on *The Hurricane* was Paul Stader, who doubled for leading man Jon Hall. Stader later worked as a stunt coordinator with Finn on the 1981 television movie, *Goliath Awaits*, in which Finn played a grandmother.

Proficient as a horsewoman while still a teenager in Hollywood, Martha Crawford gained both Screen Actors Guild and Screen Extras Guild membership cards in 1947. Among the stars for whom she doubled, on horseback, are Debra Paget in *Love Me Tender* (1956) and both Jean Simmons and Carroll Baker in *The Big Country* (1958).

While some doubles worked steadily in that capacity because of their stunting abilities, others came to doubles work in almost a casual, even accidental fashion. For example, on the evening that star Ava Gardner was to film a sequence in which she would swim out to James Mason's yacht in *Pandora and the Flying Dutchman* (1951), she had a date planned with fiancé Frank Sinatra. The actress agreed only to film the close-ups, while script girl Angela Allen doubled for her in the long and medium shots in the water. Allen recalls that on *The Third Man* (1949), it is director Carol Reed's fingers audiences see through the grating, doubling for those of Orson Welles. Because of the latter's late arrival on location in Vienna, assistant director Guy Hamilton stood in for the actor in several shots, and when Welles refused to go down into the sewers for the climactic scenes, it was again Hamilton who did the honors.[32]

Pauline Wagner became friendly with one of the employees at Central Casting, who learned of her riding ability. Wagner recalls:

> Bette Davis made this costume picture where she rode horses all the time, side-saddle, English-style. Well, she wouldn't get on a horse if it was lying down. So he called me and asked, "Would you like to do this horse stuff?" I said, "What's in it for me?" He said, "Whatever the studio wants to pay you. Name your own price." They couldn't find anyone that could ride side-saddle. So I did all this side-saddle stuff for her.[33]

RKO put Wagner under contract, but because she looked so similar to Ginger Rogers, the star's mother would not permit Wagner to appear on screen. "They couldn't fire me. They put me on all her pictures, and I never worked a day. I sat there for almost three years." One day Wagner was on her way to the Ginger Rogers set, when she was stopped and asked to talk to one of the directors of *King Kong* (1933). She was told to show her legs, which proved satisfactory, and to put on the clothes worn by star Fay Wray, who had left the production to start on a new movie being filmed out of the country. With the help of a wig, Pauline Wagner doubled for Fay Wray on the Empire State Building (which was, of course, a miniature): "All that stuff on the Empire State Building that was me. No close-ups. Fay Wray was in England and they couldn't get her and they had to do retakes. So I worked there about three or four hours."[34]

In more recent years, a number of stuntmen/stand-ins have gained a modicum of fame, something their earlier counterparts seldom achieved. Martin Grace, who died in 2010 at the age of sixty-seven, had studied fencing, body building, and acting before making his screen debut as one of the Thals in *Dr. Who and the Daleks* (1955). He performed stunts in the first James Bond film, *You Only Live Twice* (1967), and went on to be Roger Moore's stunt double in *The Man with the Golden Gun* (1974), *The Spy Who Loved Me* (1977), *Moonraker* (1979), *For Your Eyes Only* (1981), *Octopussy* (1983), and *A View to a Kill* (1985). Accepting his Academy Award for best actor for his work in *Crazy Heart* in 2010, Jeff Bridges paused to praise his stand-in and stunt double, Lloyd Catlett, who had worked with Bridges since 1971 and *The Last Picture Show*.[35]

Jack Russell terrier "Uggie," the acclaimed canine star of The Artist was present at the 2012 Academy Awards presentation, at which his film was honored as Best Picture. Absent and unacknowledged was Uggie's younger brother "Dash," who stood in for him in the climactic race through the streets of Los Angeles to rescue the leading man from a fiery death, along with a second, unrelated stand-in named "Dude."

Chapter Eight

CELEBRITY EXTRAS

It is true that a handful of stand-ins gained celebrity status—very much passing fame—as a result of articles in the fan magazines, although the emphasis was as much on the star for whom they worked as on the stand-in. Fan magazines also displayed an interest in extras with unusual backgrounds, unusual wardrobes, or unusual stories.

An extra who literally steals the entire show is J. Jiquel Lanoe, who appeared in more than one hundred American Biograph films between 1910 and 1913. He was never the subject of any news story, and made no impact, except in *Judith of Bethulia*, D. W. Griffith's first feature-length production, released in 1913. As the eunuch in the court of Holofernes, he gives an incredibly "camp" performance, guaranteed to have audiences riveted and sniggering from 1913 to the present.

J. Jiquel Lanoe's performance has certainly stayed in the memory of all those who saw it originally. In 1971, I was having lunch with the great Irish actor Micheál Mac Liammóir, and I mentioned that I knew the star of *Judith of Bethulia*, Blanche Sweet. Immediately, he leapt up from the table and asked, as only he could, "But do you remember the eunuch?" And preceded to give an impersonation of Lanoe.

One of the first extras to be the subject of a profile in his own right in the pages of *Photoplay*, Colonel T. Waln-Morgan Draper is described as "the Mt. Everest of the supernumeraries."[1] He was a striking figure, with a large, bushy yet carefully trained beard whose very appearance suggested strength of character, a strong family background, and the military career that he had once led. "As a jurist, as soldier, as financier, surgeon or savant, he preserves the eternal fitness of things. He always registers. He is to the manor born."[2] Waln-Morgan Draper had begun his career on October 25, 1914, with an appearance in the serial *The Perils of Pauline* at the Pathé studios. Within a couple of years, he had worked for virtually every film company active on the East Coast.

Judith of Bethulia (1914): J. Jiquel Lanoe as the eunuch, with Henry B. Walthall and Blanche Sweet in the foreground.

Waln-Morgan Draper was approaching sixty years of age when he made his screen debut. If anything, in the 1910s age was far from an issue when it came to extra work. Another extra featured in *Photoplay*[3] was "Dad" Taylor, a favorite of director Edwin Carewe, who was born in Brownsville, Texas, on July 9, 1828. At the age of 101, with his long, flowing beard and long, flowing hair, Taylor was undoubtedly the oldest of working screen extras. If Taylor had not been hired for his age, he would undoubtedly have been hired for his facial hair, a physical commodity in heavy demand, particularly in films featuring juries or the aging members of gentlemen's clubs. Billed as "Pop" Taylor, he receives screen credit—the only one in his life—for Metro's *As the Sun Went Down* (1919). Taylor died in 1932 at the age of 104. But Hollywood had already found an extra to take his place in the person of John Mouster, a mere one hundred years of age.

An infrequent extra from the 1920s onwards was a Hollywood eccentric by the name of Peter the Hermit, who lived somewhere in the Hollywood Hills. Sometimes laughingly described as a vagrant to the stars, Peter the Hermit was a gentleman by the name of Peter Howard. His life story is largely unknown, but he was apparently born in Knocklong, Ireland, on June 26, 1879, and had been a wealthy San Francisco businessman until deciding to renounce worldly wealth. He died in Los Angeles on March 14, 1969. "Thoughts of the world and the flesh concern Peter but little," wrote

Peter the Hermit, at the age of eighty, entertains Count Ilya Tolstoy, son of the Russian novelist. The two were kindred souls in that neither ate meat and thrived on raw vegetables.

one fan magazine writer in the 1920s, "though occasionally when pressed for funds he works in mob scenes, preaching his beliefs in a loud voice as he does so, and quite frankly elated that his audience can not arise and leave him, as one man."[4]

The 1928 Paramount film *The Last Command* features Emil Jannings as the former Grand Duke Sergius Alexander, now reduced to being a Hollywood extra. He is driven to madness after being cast as a Russian general by the film's director, played by William Powell, who had been a revolutionary leader. Jannings was most enthusiastic about the American extras with whom he worked. He thought them the most colorful personalities in the world, telling the *New York Times*:

> The American extra is totally different from the European. Abroad, the professional extra is virtually a tramp. Picture production has not become systematized to a great extent, and furthermore it is not concentrated to the extent it is in America. In London, Paris and Berlin when extras are wanted they are picked up from the highways, probably taken from some other job from which they can gain temporary freedom.
>
> Hollywood . . . has become a haven for artists of the world. They drift into pictures because it suits their artistic temperament in more ways than one. They don't mind doing extra work. To them it's preferable to the drudgery of routine employment. There never was an artist who didn't prefer leisure to money, and a little of both seems just about the right mixture for these temperamental souls.[5]

There were obviously others just like the Jannings character in *The Last Command*, White Russians who ended their days eking out a living in the film industry. According to the *New York Times*, such persons numbered close to 1,500 in 1932.[6] Among them were: Alexander Novinsky, commander of the ports of Theodosia and Archangel; General Alexander Ikonikoff of the Finnish infantry guard; and Theodore Lodijensky of the cavalry.

In another, "lost" Emil Jannings starring vehicle from 1929, *The Patriot*, Nicholas Kobliansky, who had served as a member of the Art Committee of the Imperial Theatres of St. Petersburg, was employed both as an extra and as the production's technical director. Also appearing in the film were Viacheslav Savitsky, a general with the Kuban Cossacks, and now "just a private of the extra army in Hollywood,"[7] and General Alexander Skonnikov, an extra remembering his days with the Kolchak White Army, fighting from Omsk to Vladivostok, and now fighting for a seat on the tramcar to the Paramount studios.

The 1932 production of *The World and the Flesh* provided openings for a large number of Russian émigrés, including Major Nicholai Kolovaloss, Lieutenant George Blagol, George Polonsky, Lieutenant Nicholas Veher, and Lieutenant Alexander Woloshin. Lieutenant Colonel Alexis Davidoff served as a technical advisor. Among the Russian-born female extras in the film were Carrie Ysave Daumery, Nina Miatleva, and Nadja Efron. Warner Oland's stand-in, Alex Chirva, had held a commission in the Russian Imperial Army.

In 1928, no less a celebrity than Elinor Glyn wrote in praise of Russian Princess Natalie Golitzin, who had fled the Revolution with her parents. Glyn was so enamored of the young lady's beauty that the actress offered to

The Last Command (1928): William Powell is on the right, (as director Leo Andreiev) and Emil Jannings (as General Dolgorucki/ Grand Duke Sergius Alexander) on the left. AMPAS.

provide the princess with a wardrobe. The princess declined but did agree to borrow the necessary funds from Glyn's maid. While the latter helped financially, Glyn persuaded Cecil B. DeMille to cast the princess as a lady-in-waiting to Pontius Pilate in *King of Kings* (1927).[8] The 1930 Wheeler and Woolsey comedy, *Half Shot at Sunrise*, featured among its extras former Russian major general Alexander Ikonnikoff, as well as Englishman Owen Martin, who had commanded the British Somaliland campaign in East Africa, and former Canadian war ace Stanley Campbell.

Other North American war heroes at work in Hollywood in 1932 include Lieutenant Cedric B. Davis and a Major Farrell, who it was claimed was the oldest flying officer in World War One and who had served with the French forces for more than four years. From the French Foreign Legion came Lieutenant Louis Van den Ecker, a genuine French war hero whose English reportedly was limited.

Aristocratic extras were not limited to those from Russia. In 1927, it was reported that Archduke Leopold of Austria was working as "a full-fledged motion picture extra."[9] The major difference between the archduke and the typical Hollywood extra was that he came to work accompanied by a male secretary, who would mop his brow after each shot.

While hungry, impoverished extras might be in the majority, they were definitely in the minority when it came to press coverage. The fan magazines were far more interested in individuals like Sylvanus Stokes, Jr., who enjoyed life on board his own yacht until he decided to sell it to Paramount. Still in his twenties, Stokes, Jr. became enamored of Hollywood life and, in the late 1920s, began appearing on screen as an extra—an extra who didn't need the money and who lived in a Beverly Hills mansion—and was featured in a 1927 fan magazine in a piece headed "Poor Little Rich Boy!" He promised to stick it out for a year, adding, "If, at the end of a year of extra work, no director in the whole business has seen fit to give me even a bit, I'll give it up as hopeless."[10] Stokes, Jr. was not the first or last of his type, best described as the dilettante extra. In the 1950s, Max-Anne Viault, the daughter of the president of the Los Angeles Grain Exchange, consented to appear as an extra simply because she didn't want to just sit around and go to the occasional luncheon and tea.

Many ex-sporting figures appeared as extras in the early 1930s, including Frank Goddard, the former heavyweight British boxing champion, who could be seen in *Dr. Jekyll and Mr. Hyde* (1932). Also working as an extra in the same film was a nephew and namesake of the author of the original novel, Robert Louis Stephenson. (This sounds suspiciously like a publicity stunt, and perhaps a reporter should have demanded both a birth certificate and a family tree.) There were other boxers in Hollywood, including lightweight Meyer Grace, and sportsmen such as: Florida All-American Dale Van Syckle; Notre Dame All-Americans Marty Brill and Jack Elder; Olympic swimming champion Josephine McKim; and Olympic track athlete Ida Schnell.

For filmed football matches, extras were recruited from the ranks of the USC and UCLA teams. In the off-season, they were regularly active in movies, but, unfortunately for their game, lost weight appearing on the field during the hot California summers. In addition, some coaches objected that team members, some of whom had gained a considerable sports reputation, were required to play in comic football games the comedic heroes won with a final touchdown.

Bob Steele (no connection to the leading man of the same name) was a popular radio announcer and sportscaster on WTC-Hartford for many years. Prior to joining WTC, he had come to Hollywood in the early 1930s, often appearing on screen as a motorcycle cop, and also teaching Spencer Tracy how to ride a motorcycle in *Disorderly Conduct* (1932).

An extra might gain fleeting fame, as with the anonymous extra on *Tortilla Flat* (1942) who was singled out by director Victor Fleming to throw out his arms and kiss star Hedy Lamarr as she came out of a doorway. The extra refused, insisting that kissing the star entitled him to a higher daily rate. He got it. Robert M. Parrington Jackson was a British naval officer who worked briefly as a Hollywood extra in *The Adventures of Robin Hood* (1938) and other films of that period. On May 29, 1946, he was murdered while managing the Odeon Cinema in Bristol, England, which was showing *The Light That Failed.* His death remained an unsolved mystery until 1993, when the son of the murderer walked into a police station and identified his late father as the killer. In the summer of 1935, Rose Rockne enjoyed her fifteen minutes of fame not for her work as an extra but for her novelty wooden handbags, sold to the likes of Ginger Rogers and Sally Eilers.

Some extras have gained fame after their careers, and often their lives, were over—in large part thanks to enthusiastic and highly observant film buffs. Thanks to this group, Italian-born Gino Corrado (1893–1982) is credited with appearances in some 355 films between 1916 and 1954. He is the only actor to have appeared in three of the most important films of all time: *Gone with the Wind* (1939), *Citizen Kane* (1941) and *Casablanca* (1942). While Corrado's appearance in the first cannot be verified, he is easily identifiable as the waiter asking Kane's second wife if she wants another double in *Citizen Kane*, and as the waiter taking Conrad Veidt's order for champagne and caviar in Rick's Café in *Casablanca.* Corrado was often cast as a waiter, although his heavy build might suggest he play gangster types. Billed as Eugene Corey during the silent era, he actually had three credited roles in obscure films of the early 1920s.

Extra or character comedian? How exactly does one categorize Vince Barnett, who made a living out of "ribbing" people both on screen and off, just as his father, Luke, had done? Among the celebrities whom Barnett—often in the guise of a waiter—ribbed and insulted were Winston Churchill, Henry Ford, Clark Gable, Franklin D. Roosevelt, and George Bernard Shaw. In 1936, Barnett approached the last, identifying himself as reporter Timothy Glutzspiegel, in search of an interview. When the writer pointed out that he had already spoken with the press, Barnett retorted, "But that was old stuff you gave them—you only repeat yourself." Vince Barnett came to Hollywood from vaudeville and the Broadway stage, first appearing as an extra in the 1931 Samuel Goldwyn production of *One Heavenly Night.* He generally dated his film career from an appearance as Angelo the following year in *Scarface*, in which at director Howard Hawks's request, he repeated a gag he had played on golfer Bobby Jones. Typical roles for the comedian were as bartenders, for example in *A Star Is Born* (1937), in which his appearance was uncredited, or as petty criminals, such as Muggsy in *Brute*

Vince Barnett.

Force (1947). On average, from the 1930s onward, Barnett could be spotted in more than sixty feature films a decade. He died in Encino, California, on August 10, 1977, at the age of seventy-five.

As has already been pointed out, extras and bit players came in all manner of guises, but certainly the most original, and the one with the highest credentials, was Father Neil Dodd (1878–1966), who was billed as the chaplain to the stars. Not only did he officiate at celebrity weddings, such as those of William S. Hart and Winnifred Westover in 1921, and Jack Pickford and Marilyn Miller a year later, he also appeared on screen overseeing some three hundred motion picture weddings. He was the only minister to be a

The Reverend Neal Dodd.

member of the Screen Actors Guild, and as director Nick Grinde once told me, "You could always rely on Father Dodd never to forget his lines, and he didn't cost as much as an actor because he supplied his own Bible."

The Reverend Neal Dodd had arrived in Los Angeles in 1917, and he probably made his first film appearance that same year in the Roscoe "Fatty" Arbucke comedy, *His Wedding Night*. Dodd's favorite screen roles were that of the clergyman in *It Happened One Night* (1934), and the Senate Chaplain in *Mr. Smith Goes to Washington* (1939). Other films include *Tillie's Punctured Romance* (1927), *Anna Christie* (1930), *Blue Skies* (1946), and *The Secret Life of Walter Mitty* (1947). Perhaps wisely, the clergyman never attacked the industry, noting, "I am not called upon to criticize. I am called upon to give my services in as kindly and as sincere a manner as is possible." Dodd took his film work seriously, and he refused to marry a divorced character on screen. "Marriage is a solemn service, not a circus," he told the *New York Times* (September 3, 1950). As well as appearing on screen, in the early 1930s, the Reverend Neal Dodd also had a choir, billed (perhaps somewhat unfortunately, in view of today's jaundiced view of the clergy) as "Father Dodd's Boys." The choristers could sing, dance, and act, according to casting directories of the period, and may be seen in at least three 1930 productions: *Holiday*, *King of Jazz*, and *Romance*.

At least one earlier clergyman appeared as a bit player, the Reverend A. W. McClure, who ministers at the potential hanging of the Robert Harron character in D. W. Griffith's *Intolerance* (1916). The gentleman overacts rather badly, and it has been claimed that he was not, in reality, an ordained minister. If he was actually an actor rather than a priest, there is no excuse for his performance.

One of the most prominent of leading men from the sound era began his film career as an extra—and has written about his experience with affection—is British-born David Niven. He came to Los Angeles in 1934 and visited Central Casting. He was granted an interview, but then rejected for registration because he had no work permit. As a result, Niven traveled to Mexico, obtained the appropriate visa, returned to the United States at the beginning of 1935, and was registered by Central Casting as "Anglo Saxon Type No. 2008." Despite the typecasting, Niven often worked in Westerns, thanks to his ability to ride a horse well, and commenced his career as an extra under the direction of Aubrey Scotto. In his autobiography, *The Moon's a Balloon*, Niven writes:

> My fellow extras, I discovered during the next few weeks, fell into two distinct categories. There were the professional "crowd artists" and the actors who were "would-be stars."
>
> The professionals were content to remain extras. They had no acting ambitions. They worked all the angles and were not above slipping a percentage of their daily salaries to unscrupulous assistant directors to guarantee being called the next day. Among these "professionals" could be counted the specialists such as mounted extras who worked almost exclusively in Westerns and the dress extras. The latter group were much more highly paid, getting as much as twenty dollars a day because they provided their own modern wardrobe for every occasion. . . .

> The acknowledged leaders of the professional dress extras were two elderly English people, Mrs. Wicks and a white-mustached ex-Indian Army man known as Major.
>
> This couple were in great demand, lending dignity and refinement to the drabbest pictures. They had their own little coterie of friends, and sitting in full evening dress, they all played bridge together from morning to night.
>
> There were a few younger professional dress extras also totally devoid of acting ambition and perfectly content to put on their smart clothes and work two or three days a week. Stuart Hall was one of these. Born in Cyprus, he had been brought to California as a child and had drifted into the movies. Stuart was a striking-looking man of my age. He was constantly being offered small speaking parts; he always refused them.
>
> I did not have the finances to set myself up as a dress extra, but Stuart became a good friend and if we were called to the same studio, he always gave me a lift.[11]

Generally, it was the dress extras who were singled out for special attention by reporters, thus becoming celebrities in their own small way. One of the first to be so acknowledged was Jane Arden, whose real name was Jane Slease and who selected her screen name because of the Arden Apartments in Hollywood. She was identified in 1930 by *American Magazine* as the most successful of Hollywood extras. Despite this claim, her name does not appear among the credits of any Hollywood film of the 1920s, 1930s or 1940s, except one. She has a bit role in a 1926 Universal Western melodrama, *The Escape*, starring Pete Morrison, on which she worked for one week at a salary of one hundred dollars. No other credited roles were ever offered to her. "I have no ambition to play parts," she claimed. "Not any more than a stenographer in an office has an ambition to become general sales manager. They say to get along as an extra girl is to keep in the background. That's what you're for."[12] Described by Central Casting's Marian L. Mel as "O.K. Dress and good figure," Jane Arden was five feet, three inches in height, with dark blue eyes and long hair, and weighed 116 pounds. She could drive a car, swim, dive, and dance.

On the male side was Myron C. "Babe" Green, a thirty-three-year-old standing five feet, eleven inches, with blue eyes and grey-brown hair, and weighing 170 pounds. Green had been working as an extra for eight years, and could ride, swim, dance, golf, drive, and play tennis, but he was unable to dive.

Up against Arden and Green in the stakes for highest paid extras were: William Boardway (who worked 427 days in two years); Fred Lee (391 days); James Kilgannon (305 days); Ellinor Vanderveer (397 days); Paula Drendell (378 days); and Margaret Gray (346 days). Their average weekly wage was $43.94 cents. Each of the women possessed a wardrobe valued at two thousand dollars. The men had smaller wardrobes valued at half that amount.

In 1934, it was dress extra Oliver Cross's turn to receive publicity as the highest paid extra, earning $2,846.25 that year. Cross had been working in the industry since 1921, but his only screen credits were in three silent films from the early 1920s.

Gwen Zetter was identified by *New Movie Magazine* and by Central Casting as the most successful extra in Hollywood in 1935. Statuesque, and with the appearance of someone who might be identified as an Edwardian beauty, Swedish-born Zetter was, of course, a dress extra, one who had at that point been in Hollywood for three years. She had previously been a model and claimed, "I came to Hollywood already equipped with a much better than average wardrobe."[13] Noting that she designed her own clothes, Zetter dismissed the notion that dress extras needed at least two thousand dollars for an acceptable wardrobe. The cost of maintaining her wardrobe was between twenty-five and thirty dollars a month. Unlike most of her contemporaries, Zetter worked on average three days a week, and was occasionally assigned a line or two of a dialogue. The only known credits for her are *She Wanted a Millionaire* (1932) and *Vagabond Lady* (1935).

In 1938, the *Los Angeles Times* and *American Magazine* identified Herschel Graham and Betty Kimbrough as Hollywood's leading dress extras and Central Casting's top earners. Graham had worked as an extra for twelve years, after coming to Hollywood from Stillwater, Oklahoma, and boasted a wardrobe valued at two thousand dollars. Twenty-nine-year-old Kimbrough, a former photographer's model and chorus girl with the *Ziegfeld Follies* and *Earl Carroll's Vanities* in New York, was divorced and a single mother. A brunette, five feet, five inches tall, with green eyes, she also worked as a lingerie model and owned a wardrobe valued at five thousand dollars.

Among child extras, the highest wage earner was eight-year-old Moyer "Sonny" Bupp, with an annual income of $1,500. His thirteen-year-old brother, Tommy, also worked as an extra. Both "Sonny" and Tommy Bupp were busy extras and bit players in the 1930s. Probably as a result of military service, Tommy's career ended in 1941—appropriately enough with a film titled *Naval Academy*—and Sonny's ended the following year.

Herschel Graham claimed that it was not luck that brought work, but being known: "If you were selling drugs and called on the trade year after year, they'd buy from you rather than from some newcomer . . . It's the same in the picture business. Everybody knows me."[14] Kimbrough earned an estimated $2,500 in 1937, and Graham brought in $5,000. Despite their fame in the pages of the *Los Angeles Times*, one searches in vain for the names Herschel and Kimbrough in film credits of the 1920s and 1930s. Kimbrough has no credits in the 1940s, but beginning in 1943 and continuing into the 1950s, Graham does have a few, including *It's a Wonderful Life* (1947) and *Joan of Arc* (1950).

In a 1934 gossip item, the *Los Angeles Times* described Bess Flowers as a "one time prominent silent screen actress." Well, she was not exactly that, although she certainly was featured in silent films. The reality was that Bess Flowers was to become far better known, far better remembered, and generally recognized as—if not Hollywood's most famous extra—at the least the industry's most prominent dress extra. She had so many costumes in her wardrobe that after her retirement and her move into the Motion Picture Country House, special storage facilities were needed for her clothes. No way did they fit into the one-room cottages at the facility. It was not, however, for her costumes that Bess Flowers first came to prominence in 1923 in Chaplin's *A Woman of Paris*. In a sensational sequence, she is pictured as a model, naked except for a band of cloth that is slowly unrolled from her body as she stands on a pedestal.

Born in Sherman, Texas, on November 23, 1898, the statuesque Bess Flowers came to Hollywood after an argument with her parents. Upon her arrival in 1922, she went for an interview and was immediately hired for an unidentified production. Never a star, Bess Flowers would be a leading lady to minor actors such as Lefty Flynn, John Bowers, and Fred Thomson. As she explained it, "They liked tall women, because they didn't have to bend down to kiss them and ruin their profile." Director Frank Lloyd told her, "You'll be selected to work with principals because you're tall, but when you get old, you'll be a good character woman."[15] In fact, long before she got old, Flowers was working both as a leading lady and as an extra. For example, in 1926, she has a prominent role in the Colleen Moore vehicle, *Irene*, and a walk-on in the Paramount epic *Old Ironsides*. With the coming of sound, she still had dialogue scenes, but more and more, she became a recognizable, elegantly attired extra (as in 1950's *All about Eve*, in which she is one of the guests congratulating Anne Baxter at the awards ceremony at the film's close).

Bess Flowers with Herbert Marshall in *Forgotten Faces* (1936).

Did Bess Flowers's marriages help her career? Perhaps. Her first was to Cecil B. DeMille's assistant director, Cullen Tate, and the next, in August 1929, was to Christie Film Company vice-president William S. Holman. Whether it was luck, marriage, or— as I suspect—talent and reliability, Bess Flowers can be seen in more than 350 films, including such classics as *Blonde Venus* in 1932, *Now Voyager* in 1942, and *Singin' in the Rain* in 1952. As she told me before her death in Los Angeles, on July 28, 1984, "I never amounted to a row of pins in the picture industry, but I made a good living. I'm lazy, from the South, so I never took anything that was hard. I was always good to Bess."[16]

Another prominent dress extra, heavily involved with the Screen Extras Guild, is Dulcie Day, who also worked as a singer, and died at the Motion Picture Country House in December 1954 at the age of forty-three. Both Dulcie Day and Bess Flowers were founding members of the Screen Extras Guild, and both served as the guild's original second vice-presidents. Flowers was a strong union advocate. She was actively involved in the Screen Actors Guild's September 1939 strike plan, and the new collective bargaining agreement of May 1950 covering extras at major studios. And on May 6, 1959, she was elected recording secretary of the Screen Extras Guild.

There are celebrity extras whose appearances were limited to one film each, and whose casting was perhaps influenced by publicity potential. Both Benito Mussolini and Britain's Prince of Wales were extras in *Chasing thru*

Europe (1929), in which a newsreel photographer and a wealthy American travel through Europe photographing various landmarks, including presumably living ones in England and Italy. In 1939, a British headmaster (at Rose Hill Preparatory School in Gloucestershire) appeared as an extra in MGM's *Goodbye, Mr. Chips*.

One extra who gained celebrity long after his time in Hollywood was Werner Plack, who combined his film career with diplomatic duties as an assistant to the German consul in Los Angeles, George Gyssling, during the Nazi era. It is more than likely that Plack kept a watchful eye on refugees from Nazi Germany working in Hollywood, who might be harming the regime through appearances in anti-German productions. Plack's only known appearance on screen was as a conductor in Universal's *Madame Spy* (1934), set in Warsaw during World War I. He was better known in the film community for partying with Gert von Gontard, scion of the Anheuser-Busch family. Plack left the United States, via San Francisco and Japan, in August 1940, and subsequently worked in the radio division of the German foreign office in Berlin, where he boasted of his subversive activities in Hollywood. It may well be that Plack met British novelist P. G. Wodehouse in Hollywood in 1936-37, while the latter was working as a screenwriter. Certainly Plack is responsible for persuading Wodehouse to broadcast propaganda for the Nazis during the war. Plack's return to America was less than prestigious when, in 1948, he testified at the Boston treason trial of Robert H. Bert.

Incorrectly identified as the most "famous" of extras to appear on screen is Russian revolutionary Leon Trotsky, who supposedly can be glimpsed in Vitagraph's 1914 production of *My Official Wife*, starring Clara Kimball Young. There is certainly an extra in this Russian-themed film who looks like Leon Trotsky, presumably deliberately so. But while he may have been known to Americans both by name and appearance, Trotsky was not in the United States until early 1917, long after *My Official Wife* had been released. The story of the Russian's appearance in the film dates from 1918, and appears to have gained credibility through the years.

Chapter Nine

THE SILENT STAR AS EXTRA

Ironically, just as many stars of the silent screen began their Hollywood careers as extras, they ended their careers in the same capacity a decade or so later out of necessity rather than choice. In June 1927, *Variety* published a front-page, headline story headed "'Has Beens' Can't Come Back." The unfriendly heading was followed by a listing of former "stars" who were no longer active in major screen roles, with the trade paper noting that that an extra had a better chance at screen popularity than a faded "name" player. None of the listed players was reduced at this point to taking on the role of an extra—some in fact had married well or retired—but with the coming of sound, and the continuing Depression, such demotion was to be more and more the norm.

Commenting on the unhealthy state of the film business in 1931, *Variety* reported, "The extra list is the refuge of has-beens and layoffs," noting, "In a mob of 250 at one studio the other day an executive counted two former directors, a dance director, six featured players and a score or more bit actors."[1] Former silent stars and leading players were at their busiest as extras or bit players in the 1930s and 1940s. If they were still alive in the 1960s or 1970s, job offers had either slowed to a trickle, or the players had found these offers neither financially nor physically worth pursuing.

The Screen Extras Guild boasted as its third president Franklyn Farnum,[2] a major dramatic actor of the early silent era. In 1957, what was claimed as his 1,110th film, *Top Secret Affair*, was released. Farnum succeeded Edd X. Russell, who had been the guild's president since its inception and retired in January 1959. The previous year, on June 8, 1958, Farnum had presided over an annual membership meeting, at which thirty-five extras were honored with gold life memberships.[3] Among them was Lily Teitelbaum, who had worked as an extra since 1922, with her silent credits including two screen classics, *What Price Glory?* (1926) and *7th Heaven* (1927). Teitelbaum died in

May 1972 at the age of seventy-five. Presenting the award to Teitelbaum was former silent comedian Snub Pollard, by then an extra and a member of the board of the Screen Extras Guild.

It is fair to say that it is the coming of sound that can be blamed for the transition from star to extra. However, there were certainly a handful of leading players who fell from stardom prior to *The Jazz Singer*. One such individual is Barbara Tennant, who had been acclaimed as a star with the Éclair Company as early as 1912. She was spotted by a fan magazine writer on the set of the 1925 Alice Joyce vehicle, *Daddy's Gone a-Hunting*. When asked if she was Barbara Tennant, the actress replied that she was, "But I fell by the wayside . . . I was ill for two years and that is fatal. It is funny—a few years ago Alice Joyce and I were neck and neck in popularity. To-day she is still successful, while I am—an extra. . . . I love it all so . . . I can't leave it. Since I can't get anything else I shall do this work rather than completely lose touch."[4] Tennant does not appear to have acted on screen after 1931. There is no record of her death to be found; perhaps she returned to her native England.

One of the screen's first stars was Florence Turner, "The Vitagraph Girl," named after the studio she joined in 1907. At the height of her fame in 1913, she moved to the United Kingdom to star in films for her own production company. World War I forced her return to the United States, but in 1922, she again went to England. Unfortunately, she arrived at a time when the British film industry was on the brink of collapse, and, of course, her star was in rapid decline. Penniless, she was stranded in London until Marion Davies paid for her return fare to the United States, where Davies gave Turner a small part in *Janice Meredith*. That small role was a portent of what lay ahead. In July 1928, the fan magazine *Motion Picture Classic* painted a pathetic picture of the actress: "She waits for the studio telephone call that will give her a few days' work. Young-looking and slim, a capable actress, a brilliant pantomimist . . . What does she ask? Stardom? No. Meaty little parts. Character roles. A chance to come back." As Turner explained:

> Certainly I cling to pictures. And why not? I was big once. I can be big again as a character actress. Experience has taught me that there's only one way to the top. That is to hang around, ready to grasp, or fight for, the slightest opportunity. I don't feel humble or ashamed because circumstances have temporarily whipped me. True success, I believe, is founded upon determination inspired by failures. I know that eventually I shall be a "star" again.[5]

Maurice Costello in 1936. AMPAS

It was, of course, never to be. There were extra roles in *The Animal Kingdom* (1932) and *The Sign of the Cross* (1933), among others, in the early 1930s—but that was all. A decade later, Florence Turner was again penniless and living in the Motion Picture Country House, where she died on August 28, 1946, at the age of sixty-one.

Turner's leading man at Vitagraph had been Maurice Costello (1877–1950), and he, too, ended his days as an extra. In an emotional 1928 interview with *Motion Picture Classic*, Costello raises the issue of ageism, noting as actors ever have, that directors are too young to know who they are: "And the insulting part of it is, they try to direct *me*! I've made eight hundred pictures—and some little squirt of a director who was promoted from the wardrobe room tells me how to act!" The interviewer continued, "Not long ago, he relates, he was playing the heavy in a picture featuring a famous woman star. He came to the fight scene. For a moment the pain at playing a small part was swept away by the old joy of acting, but the director as he watched him was nervous. "'That's very nice, Cos,' he told him when the scene was finished, 'but once more. And this time don't give quite so much.'"

> Maurice Costello understood him perfectly. The director was afraid that the attention of the audience might be taken for a moment from the blonde and beautiful star whose acting specialty was wearing low-cut evening gowns. He said nothing but he played that scene for all that it was worth! Five times, the director made him go through it, and then Costello addressed him. "I'll do the scene once more," he told the director quietly, but dangerously, "and only once. Remember! This is the last time."
>
> "I gave it everything I had," Costello says grimly. "He couldn't stop me. Nobody could have stopped me! *It was my scene and I was going to have it.* And they left every foot of it in the finished picture, too."[6]

In 1938, Maurice Costello claimed his first "featured" role in a talkie was MGM's *Stand Up and Fight*. He worked three days at twenty-five dollars a day. In fact, Costello had appeared briefly a couple of years earlier in *Hollywood Boulevard*. He does not appear in the cast list for *Stand Up and Fight* and in all probability was cut from the film, but later that same year, he does play a headwaiter in Columbia's *There's That Woman Again*. Maurice Costello was an occasional extra through the mid-1940s, with his last two (uncredited) roles in *The Doughgirls* (1944) and *Delightfully Dangerous* (1945).

Using an approach that Bette Davis was to try some decades later, Claire DuBrey (1882–1993) decided to advertise her availability. DuBrey had been an extra with Thomas H. Ince in the mid-1910s, and she and Alice Terry, who starred opposite Rudolph Valentino in *The Four Horsemen of the Apocalypse*, had both appeared, uncredited, in the producer's 1916 spectacle, *Civilization*. DuBrey went on to become a leading lady at Universal in the 1910s, but by the 1930s, her career was in decline—although she was to continue to work in films, generally as an extra, into the 1960s, as she did in television. In the June 1930 issue of the *Standard Casting Directory*, DuBrey took a full-page advertisement, complete with four photographs of her, one at each corner, in very disparate roles. The copy read:

> Is This a Sporting Proposition?
>
> I was a featured screen player for years and have appeared on the stage in many fine productions including three with Pauline Frederick, two with Rob't Ames, "The Great Necker," "One Man's Woman," "The Youngest," etc.
>
> I will do extra work, bits, dead bodies off stage or what have you? With the sincerity which dictates this drastic step, plus the above experience, I ought to be a rare bargain as an extra woman.
>
> Obviously, I am gambling on the chance of establishing myself in talking pictures.
>
> If you don't believe I mean this, try me.

As a result of the advertisement, Du Brey received more work that she could handle. "Motion Picture people are attracted by the unusual," explained *Photoplay*.[7]

Also in 1930, *Photoplay* asked, "Where are the stars of yesterday?" After noting some of those who had retired well, it continued: "You don't hear of the others—the girls who didn't marry millionaires and the men who did not succeed after their brief heyday. Hollywood doesn't like to talk of its failures. Success is all that really matters in Hollywood."[8] Among those now documented as extras were two serial stars, Carol Holloway and Helen Holmes; Ethel Clayton, Del Henderson, Rose Tapley, Neil Hart, Franklyn Farnum, Edward Hearn, Rosemary Theby, and Ben Wilson, who had just died on August 25, 1930, at the age of fifty-four, "unknown and moneyless, as a seven-dollar-a-day extra."[9]

Two years later, the *New York Times* explained why silent stars had become extras this way: "The fascination of screen work is such that those who have once been famous directors and stage and screen stars never want to do anything else."[10] Among that group, it listed Ed Coxen, Ella Hall, Vola Vale, Frank Beal, and Edward Le Saint (the two former directors appearing together in the 1932 production of *The Miracle Man*). Wilfred Lucas, who had once been a leading man with D. W. Griffith, worked uncredited in the 1931 Marx Brothers vehicle, *Monkey Business*. Many vaudevillians had seen their careers disappear along with vaudeville, and were appearing as little more than extras on screen. For example, Ted Doner, who had once been a vaudeville headliner, was now an uncredited dancer in films such as *Music in the Air* (1934). Two prominent vaudevillians, singer-comedienne Trixie Friganza and comedian Billy Dooley, appear as extras in *A Star Is Born* (1937). And then there was Fay Lamphier, for two years Miss America, who had once been an extra and was now a stenographer at Paramount.

Claire Dubrey, a Universal star of the 1910s and an extra in the 1930s.

It is apparent reading the names in the *New York Times* of those now working as extras, and the roster of former silent players working as extras in the 1930s and later, that the majority had careers dating back to the early 1910s and the early years of the motion picture. There are very few extras who were stars or even leading players in the 1920s. For whatever reason, those who were seem to have survived better.

It might well be said that Cecil B. DeMille never met anyone that he did not want to use in one of his films. The number of silent stars appearing as extras in DeMille productions of the 1930s and 1940s is staggering. For example, in *Cleopatra* (1933), one can find William Farnum, Julanne Johnston, Wilfred Lucas, Mary MacLaren, Jack Mulhall, Phillips Smalley, George Walsh, and Bryant Washburn. *Reap the Wild Wind* (1942) used Monte Blue, Max Davidson, Mildred Harris, Claire McDowell, and Dorothy Sebastian, as well as two former directors, Christy Cabanne and George Melford.

The one silent star who had money and a unique and starring career in the sound era was Charlie Chaplin. He used a handful of individuals from the silent era in his films: Wilfred Lucas in *Modern Times* (1936); Chester Conklin in *The Great Dictator* (1940); former juvenile Barry Norton, Franklyn Farnum, Frank Reicher, and Phillips Smalley in *Monsieur Verdoux*

Billie Bevan, smiling, to the left of leading man John Derek in *Rogues of Sherwood Forest* (1950).

(1947); and Snub Pollard in *Limelight* (1952). Chaplin's most famous leading lady from the silent era, Edna Purviance, did not work for him after her starring role in 1923 in *A Woman of Paris*. According to director Robert Florey, she would have liked to have appeared as an extra or bit player in Chaplin's sound films, but he would not allow her to enter his studio. He did, however, keep her on his payroll—as his ex-mistress.

Before Chaplin, there was John Bunny, the first of what may be considered the legendary screen comedians—although, of course, there is no similarity between the two in terms of style and appearance, or, if truth be told, comedic talent. John Bunny died in 1915, at the age of fifty-one. As fat and probably just as talented as John was his brother George Bunny (1867–1958), whose silent career was based on exploitation of the family name. When that was forgotten, with the coming of sound, George soldiered on as a bit player and extra.

Some silent comedians survived well into sound era thanks to their country of origin. Both Billy Bevan (1887–1957) and Clyde Cook (1891–1984) had worked as prominent comedy leads with Mack Sennett in the silent era: Cook, with his wiry acrobatics, in the 1910s, and Bevan, with his trademark walrus moustache (toned down for the talkies), in the 1920s. Both had also been born in Australia, and, as far as Hollywood was concerned, there was little to differentiate between an Australian accent and an English one. Thus,

Bevan and Cook were in demand for character and smaller roles in sound films with English backgrounds. Bevan is memorable as the batman Trotter in the screen adaptation of R. C. Sheriff's *Journey's End* (1930), and in the prominent role of Joseph Sedley in the 1932 modern-dress adaptation of *Vanity Fair*. He can also be seen in such "English" films as *Cavalcade* (1933), *Lloyds of London* (1937), *Mrs. Miniver* (1942), *Jane Eyre* (1944), *The Picture of Dorian Gray* (1945), and *That Forsyte Woman* (1949). Clyde Cook was as busy as Bevan, but his parts were generally smaller and sometimes uncredited, including such English-themed productions as *Oliver Twist* (1933), *A Tale of Two Cities* (1935), *The Little Princess* (1939), *The Sea Hawk* (1940), and *Forever and a Day* (1943).

Harry "Snub" Pollard (1889–1962) was also born in Australia, but he was more closely associated as a comedian with Hal Roach. Curiously, he wasn't utilized in "English" films, but was at his busiest in Westerns. In later years, he was frequently used by Jerry Lewis and often could be seen in the television series *Gunsmoke*. His last appearance was in *Pocketful of Miracles* (1961). Pollard's most enduring, and endearing, appearance as an extra is in *Singin' in the Rain* (1952), in which he is the old man to whom Gene Kelly hands his umbrella at the close of the title song. *Singin' in the Rain* does not boast any other prominent players of the silent era, but one can spot there, among the extras: former 1930s leading lady Mae Clarke, as a hairdresser; Fred Datig, the son of the casting director, as a ticket taker; and Norma Zimmer, Lawrence Welk's "Champagne Lady," in the "Beautiful Girl" number.

Some silent comedians associated with Mack Sennett did better than others with the coming of sound. Al St. John became a reliable Western sidekick, with roles too important for him to be included here. Bobby Vernon switched from acting in silent comedies to working on the production side with sound comedies. Hank Mann tried to mix work as a bit player in the early 1930s with running Bot [*sic*] and Hanks Café on Sunset Boulevard, which specialized in charcoal broiled steaks and chops. Eventually, in 1943, he made the step down to extra, continuing to work in that capacity into the 1950s. But he also found time to open a malt shop in the community of Sierra Madre.

Like Billy Bevan, Chester Conklin (1886–1971) was famed for his walrus moustache and was one of the original Keystone Kops. Conklin retired in 1929, but he returned to the screen ten years later in bit parts. "Conklin doesn't work too often nowadays," reported an April 2, 1948, Paramount press release.

> Once he earned a four-figure weekly paycheck, but those days are long since past. Today he gets the occasional bit, sometimes a few lines, sometimes just atmosphere. But he's not unhappy. Mrs. Conklin died ten years ago and Chester never re-married. He lives by himself in a Hollywood apartment, cooks his own meals and spends evenings chinning with old cronies like Mack Sennett and his fellow Keystone coppers, [Jimmy] Finlayson and [Hank] Mann.

Conklin permanently retired to the Motion Picture Country House in 1961.

Victor Potel (1889–1947) was a skinny comedian of lesser order, but he was still a leading player in the 1910s. By 1930, he was advertising himself in the *Standard Casting Directory* as an actor able to speak French, Italian, Hebrew, and German dialects. Yet what came his way was never anything more than a bit part—more than eighty in the 1930s and more than forty in the 1940s, with the last in the year of his death. Potel liked to paint in his spare time, and so did Jean "Babe" London (1901–80), an extremely plump character comedienne in silent films, closely associated with producer Al Christie, who spent the sound era playing largely uncredited roles in films, appearing as late as 1970 in *Dirty Dingus Magee*.

In April 1935, Earl Theisen, veteran Hollywood commentator and the man responsible for the first "Hollywood Museum" at what was then the Los Angeles County Museum, wrote:

> Even though the old-timer is no longer at the top of the motion picture pile, there is still needed a lot of persons to keep the pile together, and the old-timer would be satisfied and happy too with a small part in the pile. He would be satisfied with an extra part, or a furniture mover job. He was both in the old days. . . .[11]
>
> Some day a producer or a director with an eye for business will quietly round up all these men and women and sign them up on a long term contract as extras. No, he won't be a philanthropist. He will be a smart business man who will realize that the talent scattered among the old timers will save him money and help him make better pictures through their ripened experience of years before the camera.
>
> The background will be worthy of the best he can put in the foreground.[12]

Who knows if he actually read what Theisen had to say, but exactly a year later, in April 1936, Louis B. Mayer made the surprise move of announcing

the placement of some dozen former silent stars and leading players on the payroll at MGM as extras. It was explained, "Realizing the pioneer work performed by the earlier-stars in the film industry, instructions were recently passed on to directors, producers and casting officials by Louis B. Mayer of Metro-Goldwyn-Mayer that the screen pioneers were to be given preference in casting roles in MGM productions."[13] The financially needy group included: former director King Baggot; Helene Chadwick; Naomi Childers; John Bunny's leading lady, Flora Finch; Mahlon Hamilton; Del Henderson; Rudolph Valentino's first wife, Jean Acker; and Florence Lawrence, who had the distinction of being the first star of the American film industry. All had worked as extras, with Florence Lawrence's last pre-MGM extra work probably appearing in *One Rainy Afternoon* (1936), produced by two giants of the silent screen, Jesse L. Lasky and Mary Pickford.

The Florence Lawrence story has a particularly tragic ending. She was living in a West Hollywood home that she shared with another MGM employee and his wife, when on December 28, 1938, she committed suicide, poisoning herself with a mixture of cough syrup and ant paste. That same morning, she had called the studio to cancel a scheduled appointment for work at 1:00 p.m.

The reason for Louis B. Mayer's apparent generosity is unknown. There was assuredly no attempt to humiliate the former stars by promoting their new employment (although certainly photographs of the group were released for publicity purposes). One historian has suggested that the studio

Former silent stars under contract to MGM in the 1930s, here costumed for *San Francisco* (1936). Left to right are: Rhea Mitchell, Naomi Childers, Rosemary Theby, Eddie Hearn, Fritiz Brunette, Frank Mayo, Helene Chadwick, Flora Finch, Harry Myers, Lillian Rich, and King Baggot.

head might have been aware of his own advancing age, or perhaps that such a move would present MGM in a highly positive light.

At the beginning of April, *Variety* had suggested that "old- time film personalities" were still fresh in the memory of many moviegoers, and that perhaps their appearance on screen might generate box office. The trade paper mentioned a group of films with casts that included such silent era performers as Gertrude Astor, Reginald Denny, Hoot Gibson, Conway Tearle, Rosemary Theby, and Henry B. Walthall.[14] But, of course, these players were billed, whereas the MGM extras would be precisely that—extras—and receive no billing. In all probability, they would not be recognizable in the crowd to moviegoers, no matter how enthusiastic the latter might be for stars of the past.

By all accounts, the former silent players found nothing demeaning about working as extras. Indeed, such work provided them with a steady, and most welcome source of income. Some had lost their money as a result of the Wall Street crash, which tragically hit exactly as their careers as silent stars came to a close. Others were simply unemployable. Typical of the latter category was King Baggot (1879–1948), whose career as a director ended in 1928 with *The Romance of a Rogue* because of his alcoholism. Towards the end of his life, Baggot appeared as an extra in seventeen films, concluding with *Holiday in Mexico* in 1946.[15] As Fred Datig recalled, "He'd come to work three sheets to the wind. He could hardly talk. He'd sort of stand in a stupor the whole day long. Pathetic really. I didn't see any brilliance out of him, but people would talk about him behind his back—how great he had been."[16]

Another extra at MGM was Mahlon (pronounced May-lon) Hamilton. "Mahlon was quite a character," remembers Datig. "He had gone through all of his money. One time he told me, 'Freddie, I've been everywhere in the world I've ever wanted to go. I've owned everything I ever wanted to own. I've had every woman I've ever wanted to have. And I really don't have any regrets. It's been a great ride.'"[17]

An extra who had saved her money was May McAvoy. She didn't need to work—particularly as an extra at MGM—but she enjoyed the camaraderie, and she liked coming in to work every day and sitting around with her former peers. She recalled, "Most of the time my scenes were shot over my shoulder—and I was eternally some middle-aged secretary with her back to the camera. You could blink your eyes and miss me altogether in some of those parts. Or I was an off-scene voice."[18]

One former silent star to whom Louis B. Mayer did not offer a contract as an extra was Gertrude Astor. In the 1920s, he had chased her around the desk in his office, but she refused to be caught. When he passed her on the lot a couple of decades later, he commented to one of his accompanying "yes" men, "There she goes; she was such a foolish girl."[19]

Some former silent stars had contracts as extras or bit players with other studios, particularly Warner Bros., which appears to have sponsored a scheme similar to that instigated at Metro-Goldwyn-Mayer. Myrtle Stedman (1885–1938) was under contract to Warner Bros. in the 1930s, making her last (uncredited) appearance in *Hollywood Hotel* (1938). Until her death in 1971 at the age of eighty-eight, Leah Baird had been under contract to Warner Bros. for seventeen years. Similarly, former silent leading man Monte Blue (1887–1963) was under long-term contract to Warner Bros. starting in the mid-1930s.[20]

Paul Panzer (1871–1958) had appeared as the villain in the 1914 *The Perils of Pauline*. That film had been shot on the East Coast, and Panzer remained there, in later years under contract to William Fox, until 1925. After coming to Hollywood, he was placed under contract to Warner Bros. as an extra in 1934. He told the *Los Angeles Times* (June 18, 1944) that Jack Warner had said to him, "You can stay here as long as you want." And through the 1950s, he was still at the studio. The Warner Bros. Archives contains a sad letter, dated January 29, 1937, from Panzer to studio head Jack L. Warner, asking for a pay raise. In it, the actor writes, rather badly:

> Am now starting on my third year with you and I want to thank you as well as my family from the bottom of our hearts for the happiness you have brot [*sic*] us.
>
> Being such a big Company now and knowing of the many important and big problems always on your mind, I hesitate in writing to ask if it is at all possible for you to grant me a slight increase. Am receiving $35.00 and during the past 3 years have never requested a raise. However, my children are getting older, going to high school now and need many things now that they heretofore did not require.
>
> In any event you know Mr. Warner I shall always put forth an untiring effort for you and our wonderful company.

At the bottom of the letter is scribbled: "increase to $40.00 wkly starting Feb. 1, 1937," initialed by J. L. W.[21]

Just as at least two studios did their part in keeping former silent stars active as extras or bit players, so did at least one Hollywood director, French-born Robert Florey, who a few years earlier had been responsible for the

Hollywood Boulevard (1936): director Robert Florey at rear, with, from left to right, Charles Ray, Esther Ralston, Francis X. Bushman, and gossip columnist Sidney Skolski.

short, *Life and Death of 9413—A Hollywood Extra.* French-born Florey had a great love for Hollywood and its history, and, indeed, published a number of volumes on the subject. In late 1935, he began production on *The Preview Murder Mystery,* which has a storyline that obviously owes much to *The Phantom of the Opera.* Florey used several former silent leading players in speaking roles—Rod La Rocque, Conway Tearle, Jack Mulhall, and Bryant Washburn—and even a large number as extras: Hank Mann, Chester Conklin, Phillips Smalley, Wilfred Lucas, and others.

A few months later, at the same studio, Paramount, Florey began dictating a new storyline to script girl Marguerite Roberts, whom he later insisted should take sole screenplay credit. The subject was that of a former

Hollywood Boulevard (1936): a group of former silent leading men surround star John Halliday. Among those present are Albert Conti, Creighton Hale, Jack Mulhall, and Bryant Washburn.

unemployed and penniless star, played by John Halliday, who is persuaded to write his memoirs. The little-known film is a remarkable treatise on Hollywood hypocrisy and compromise. The basic theme is summed up by a waiter at the Hollywood Brown Derby: "When they put the skids under you in this man's town, you're out." Happily *Hollywood Boulevard* provided employment for an incredible number of silent players. In relatively important roles include: Mae Marsh as the mother of the film's female lead, Marsha Hunt; Esther Ralston as a movie star; Francis X. Bushman as her director; Oscar Apfel as a doctor; Herbert Rawlinson as the manager of Grauman's Chinese Theatre; and Charles Ray as an assistant director. Florey's intention was to begin each sequence by opening on the exterior of a well-known Hollywood landmark, inside which might be spotted a large number of recognizable silent players, such as: Creighton Hale (who actually shares equal screen time with Gary Cooper as a couple at the bar of the Trocadero), Maurice Costello, Betty Compson, Jane Novak, Roy D'Arcy, Ruth Clifford, Frank Mayo, Harry Myers, William Desmond, and Edward Burns. Unfortunately, after production ended, the editing was taken over by a former gagman and director from the silent era, Eddie Cline, and he cut down the scenes featuring many of the silent players and completely eliminated others, including Evelyn Brent, Louise Brooks, Alice Lake, Florence Lawrence, Rosemary Theby, and even Harold Lloyd (in a prominent cameo role at the bar).

One bit player and extra in Hollywood who had been a silent star in his native England was Jameson Thomas, whose decline in status had nothing to do with the talkies or the Wall Street crash. London-born Thomas had commenced his screen career as leading man to American star Betty Blythe in the 1923 production of *Chu Chin Chow*. As a former stage and musical comedy star, he made an easy transition to sound and might have continued in British and European films had his wife not contracted tuberculosis. In 1931, Thomas decided that his only option was to move to the warm climate of Los Angeles. Here, he made his uncredited American film debut in the World War I aviation drama, *Body and Soul*. Many other films followed. His best role was *It Happened One Night*, in which he plays a fortune-hunting playboy. Sadly, not only did Thomas's wife die, but he himself contracted TB. During the last years of his life, he augmented a small allowance from the Motion Picture Relief Fund with occasional, equally small screen roles. He died on January 11, 1939, at the age of forty-five, at a tubercular rest home in Sierra Madre, just outside of Los Angeles. Jameson Thomas had been working, uncredited, in *Marie Antoinette*, and his funeral was paid for by the Motion Picture Relief Fund.

It was the Motion Picture Relief Fund (today known as the Motion Picture and Television Fund) that took care of so many of Hollywood's aged extras who had once been "names." While there was no legal obligation for anyone in the industry to contribute to the fund, the general consensus was that all those earning more than one hundred dollars a week should give one half of one percent to the charity. Of course, no extras fell into that wage category.

Another Hollywood extra and bit player who had gained fame in the United Kingdom was André Charlot. Paris-born Charlot had not been an actor, but rather a leading theatrical producer, noted for the *Charlot Revues*, first seen on the London stage in 1924. He was a frequent visitor to the United States, and in 1937, for reasons that remain unclear, he became an American citizen. It is equally unclear why he chose to appear on screen in more than forty, generally uncredited roles from 1942 onwards. He was as autocratic as one might imagine a theatrical producer to be, and while working at Paramount as an assistant to George Cukor in 1938, he insisted on bringing his dog onto the lot in defiance of studio rules. André Charlot died at the Motion Picture Country Hospital on May 20, 1956, at the age of seventy-three.

Like André Charlot, there were other non-actors who had gained a modicum of fame behind the camera who ended their careers and their lives

Lloyd Ingraham, a director in the 1910s, working in the 1930s as an extra.

in the 1930s among the ranks of the extras. Thomas Ricketts had been directing with the Essanay Film Manufacturing Company in Chicago as early as 1909. On stage since 1882 and in films since 1906, Ricketts claimed to have made one of the earliest films to be shot in Hollywood. And he died in Hollywood on January 20, 1939, at the age of eighty-six, having spent the last twenty years of his life in slow decline from minor character actor to extra. He had contracted pneumonia after insisting upon showing up for work, despite having a cold, at Universal the week prior to his death. He left no funds, and the Motion Picture Relief Fund paid for his funeral.

Oscar Apfel might have gained a prominent place in film history as the first credited co-director of what is erroneously described as the first

Oscar Apfel, a director in the 1910s, working in the 1930s as an extra.

Hollywood feature film, *The Squaw Man*, released in 1914. Unfortunately, he shared credit with Cecil B. DeMille, whose grasp of the potential of publicity and place in cinema history is firmly secured. Apfel continued to direct obscure films into the late 1920s, but with the coming of sound, he was reduced to working as a bit player and extra. Somewhat plump, distinguished, and balding—but looking good in a business suit and sporting a monocle—Apfel appeared in more than one hundred films in the 1930s before he died March 21, 1938, at the age of fifty-nine.

Phillips Smalley was an equally distinguished-looking bit player and extra of the 1920s and 1930s, playing good, solid, and often slightly suspect

George Melford, who directed Valentino in *The Sheik* and *Moran of the Lady Letty*, works as an extra in the 1951 production of *Valentino*, starring Anthony Dexter in the title role.

businessmen or politicians. Like other directors-turned-extras, his career started on stage, but Smalley gained fame thanks to his co-director and wife, Lois Weber, the first and most prominent of American-born female filmmakers. Smalley died in Los Angeles on May 2, 1939, at the age of seventy-three.

Emile Chautard had enjoyed a successful career as a director both in his native France and in the United States, but by the mid 1920s, he had become a character actor, generally cast as a Frenchman—even though the films were silent. With the coming of sound, his accent did help him secure small parts in films with French themes or characters. Even if he didn't have a line of dialogue, he still gave the appearance of being French. He is, for example, the French officer in the Marlene Dietrich/Josef von Sternberg production, *Shanghai Express* (1932). Chautard died in Los Angeles at the age of sixty-nine, on April 24, 1934.

German-born Frank Reicher (1875–1965) had been a prominent stage director before turning to film direction in 1915 with the Famous Players-Lasky Company. He continued to direct through the silent era, but with the coming of sound, he soon became a busy, but unknown extra. Likewise, legendary producer Thomas H. Ince's brothers, John (1878–1947) and Ralph

Clara Kimball Young, a glamorous star of the 1910s and an extra in the 1930s and later. AMPAS.

(1887–1937), were both directors during the silent era, and both became extras in later life.

Jerome Storm (1890–1958) had been a major director in the 1910s, responsible for more than a dozen feature films starring Charles Ray in 1919–20. Storm became a bit player and extra with the coming of sound, often billed (when he was credited) as Jerry Storm. In the 1930 issue of the *Standard Casting Directory* he advertised himself for "Characters, Comedy, Heavies." Typical of his work in the 1930s is the courtroom spectator he played in *An American Tragedy* (1931), a title that might well apply directly to him. After Storm's star, Charles Ray (1891–1943), faded from popularity in the mid 1920s, the actor appeared in his first sound film, *Ladies Should Listen*, in 1934. He ended his career with bit parts, often unbilled, which he played through 1942. Once a perennial juvenile, in later years his looks remained the same—influenced only by the ravages of time.

Francis Ford (1882–1953) had been a director and actor in the silent era, more important in the early years than his younger brother, John, was as a director. Francis was a familiar figure in sound films, with roles varying in importance (some did not even have dialogue), but always adding to the story and to the audience's viewing pleasure. In 1935, very sensibly, 20th Century-Fox put him under long-term contract as a character-comedian. Francis Ford was at his best under the direction of his brother in more than twenty films from 1931 through 1953.[22] In fact, Francis Ford's penultimate appearance on screen was in his brother's *The Sun Shines Bright* in 1953. He ended his career—378 films as actor, director, or both—with *The Marshall's Daughter*, also released in 1953.[23]

Francis Ford was married (in 1913) to actress and occasional director and screenwriter Grace Cunard (1893–1967), and the two usually appeared opposite one another in Universal productions until their divorce in the late 1910s. With the coming of sound, Grace Cunard generally worked as an extra, sometimes, as with *Show Boat* (1936), at Universal, the studio where she had once been a star. Her second husband, Jack Shannon (1892-1968), whom she had married around 1925, was a stuntman.

The number of "names" from the silent era active as extras or bit players is too numerous to list. There was Adda Gleason (1888–1971), who in 1940 was one of the Rock People in *One Million B.C.* and a maid in *Abe Lincoln in Illinois*. Silent ingénue Barbara Bedford (1903–81) was in more than fifty films in the 1930s and over twenty-five in the 1940s, making her last recorded appearance in 1944. Niles Welch (1888–1976) had been a leading man of the 1910s. In the 1930s, he worked as an extra, but thanks to his earlier stage experience, he was able to end his film career not as an extra but as the narrator of two 1942 wartime documentaries, *Invasion* and *"Kukan": The Battle Cry of China*. Similarly, Bryant Washburn (1884–1963), who had been a leading man in almost two hundred silent films, appeared in over fifty films in the 1930s and thirty-five in the 1940s, playing his last role in 1946. Rudolph Valentino's first wife, Jean Acker (1892–1978) made sporadic screen appearances from 1935 through 1955, with her last probably being in *Friendly Persuasion*, released in 1956. "My story," she was quoted by the *Los Angeles Times* (August 19, 1978) as saying, "is short, simple and not so sad as you may believe. In 1926 I left motion pictures and toured New York and the nation on the stage and in vaudeville. In 1929 I had amassed a fortune of $300,000, and the same year the market crash swept it all away."

Serial star Eddie Polo (1875–1961) retired from the screen in 1930 with the coming of sound, but he returned thirteen years later to work as an extra. Claire McDowell (1877–1966) and her husband, Charles Hill Mailes (1870–1937), were prominent character players in the silent era, with both becoming extras in the 1930s—although McDowell always seemed to obtain better parts than her husband (whose last credited appearance was in 1935).

Mailes, who is distinguished in appearance, advertised himself to casting directors in the 1930s as having played "Irish, Scotch [*sic*] & German characters." In 1912, Clara Horton (1904–76) was billed as the "Éclair Kid," after the studio for which she worked; in the 1930s and through 1943, she appeared unbilled as an extra. Clara Kimball Young (1890–1960) had been a beautiful star, with expressive eyes and face, at Vitagraph in the 1910s. In 1932, she saw the auctioneering off of her estate, and that same year, she returned to films as a bit player or extra, considerably plumper than in her starring days. Her older, matronly figure appeared onscreen in some twenty films through the mid-1940s.

Nigel De Brulier (1877–1948) was positively cadaverous in appearance, and most of that extremely skinny body was on display in Nazimova's 1922 production of *Salome*, with De Brulier as a loin-clothed Jokaanan (John the Baptist). So ascetic was his appearance, De Brulier was often cast as clergymen, playing Cardinal Richelieu in the 1921 version of *The Three Musketeers*, the 1929 version of *The Iron Mask*, and in the 1935 sound version of *The Three Musketeers*. He was even considered for the 1939 screen version of *The Three Musketeers*. Despite the prominence of the Richelieu role in the sound film, De Brulier was, in reality, little more than an extra in the 1930s and into the early 1940s. For example, he is uncredited in MGM's *Rasputin and the Empress* (1933).

Silent leading man Kenneth Harlan (1895–1967) was active in the sound era as an extra and bit player through 1943, with his last appearance in Monogram's *Death Valley Rangers*. From extra work, Harlan moved to operating a restaurant and then had an agency booking strippers before he retired to Sacramento in the late 1950s. Herbert Rawlinson (1885–1963) enjoyed a successful career as a silent leading man starting in the early 1910s. He had many unbilled roles in the 1930s and 1940s, and, with a fine, English accent, he was equally busy as a regular on the *Lux Radio Theatre*. His last appearance on screen was in *The Stranger Wore a Gun* (1953). Rudolph Valentino's brother, Alberto, worked as an extra in the 1930s, including his appearance in *Fatal Lady* (1936).

A silent star-turned extra might be lucky like Mary MacLaren (1896–1985), who was very busy in the 1930s and 1940s. In *Cavalcade* (1932), she was nothing more than "atmosphere" as the woman who sees her husband on the list of war dead and faints. Even so, she stands out, commanding audience attention and sympathy. Betty Blythe (1893–1972) had starred as the Queen of Sheba in 1921. With the coming of sound, her roles varied considerably in stature; she could be an extra in *Man-Proof* (1938) and the leading

Herbert Rawlinson, once like Robert Montgomery a leading man, later worked as an extra.

lady playing opposite Harry Langdon in *Misbehaving Husbands* (1940) (in which Mary MacLaren appears as an extra, as does Gertrude Astor [1899–1977]). Blythe obviously took whatever was available; the importance of the role grew along with the unimportance of the studio involved.

Motion Picture Classic (January 1928) wrote of Astor when she was a silent star: "[She] [e]nters a room like an African tigress in quest of food. Sinuous, graceful, alert. Has the hauteur of a queen, and lends the impression of one till someone calls: 'Hi, Gert!' and she replies: 'Lo kid!'" That just about sums up Gertie (as she was fondly called) Astor, who never worried about the reality of life and her fall from predatory silent star to Hollywood extra. She had no interest in clinging to the limelight once her time as a leading lady was up, and to a large extent, the joy had gone out of her work. In silent films she was slightly taller than most leading ladies, and, luckily, in later years, she had the presence and the statuesque appearance to play socialite extras in films like *The George Raft Story* and *All in a Night's Work*, both released in 1961. Along with Minta Durfee, who was once married to Roscoe "Fatty" Arbuckle and comedian Ernie Kovacks's mother, she can be seen, laughing and applauding on cue, in a night scene from *Kiss Me, Stupid* (1964). She is in *Around the World in Eighty Days* (1956), *The Music Man* (1962), *Gypsy* (1962), and *My Fair Lady* (1964). She had been John Ford's

Gertrude Astor, still glamorous in her later years.

leading lady in 1917, and he insisted she appear in virtually all of his films through *The Man Who Shot Liberty Valance* in 1962.

The director of *My Fair Lady*, George Cukor, was also a fan, casting Astor in *Camille* (1937) and *A Star Is Born* (1954). He also paid homage to her at a tribute organized at Universal by *Los Angeles Times* film critic Kevin Thomas on September 30, 1975. At that time, she said, "I used to be ashamed of myself—thought I didn't do a lot of big things—but now I'm not. I am very proud. I thought life was over and I should just crawl in a corner and die. I have no family. I haven't a soul in the world to enjoy this, but I'm going to do plenty of that."

From left to right: extras Gertrude Astor, Eva Prentice, Gypsy Gould, and Blanche Rose. The film is probably *Montana* (1950).

Kevin Thomas remembers Gertie Astor with great affection as "the most unpretentious, unassuming actress I ever knew. She was full of fun, sensitive, intelligent and free spirited, although she did not have wonderful luck with men."[24] Thomas recalls that the actress was at one time involved with director Robert Florey. After their breakup, she was the only silent leading lady with whom he would have nothing to do and whom he never cast in any of his films.

Gertrude Astor retired in 1967 following a back injury. Her last appearance was in the ABC television series *Judd for the Defense*, starring Carl Betz—who, in reality, is probably less known today than the extra on his show.

Minta Durfee (1889–1975) was always grateful for any work she could find. She had no money. She could not drive a car, and so her brother, Paul, would dutifully bring her to whatever studio was employing her. Minta had a number of memorable scenes as an extra, for example in the opening of *Some Like It Hot* (1959) and as a hairdressing assistant in *The Legend of Lylah Clare* (1968). While costumed for *Hello, Dolly!* (1969), she wore a magnificent cameo brooch given to her by Roscoe "Fatty" Arbuckle. When star Barbra Streisand spotted it, she sent word that Minta should send the

At the September 30, 1975, Universal luncheon to honor Getrude Astor, she is surrounded by three of her directors: George Cukor, Henry Hathaway, and Allan Dwan.

jewelry to her for inspection. Minta was affronted by Streisand's attitude and responded, "If she wants to see it, she can come to me."[25]

Aristocratic Aileen Pringle (1895–1989) was busy in the 1930s after the demise of her career as a star of the 1920s. However, despite the pretense that her roles—generally those of elegant socialites—were important, in reality, they were little more than walk-ons and sometimes did not even survive the final cut. She was last seen in 1943.

In the summer of 1938, a group of former silent players was appearing as extras in *The Young in Heart*. On the set, they talked about the old days, noting, "We drew the highest salaries, got the choicest roles, heard the loudest cheers." They conceived of a plan, which on June 18, 1939, they submitted to California Governor Frank P. Merriam:

> We ask that "Career Insurance," or the "Mandatory Film Savings Law" provide that the studios be required to deduct from each star's salary check ten per cent of the total, this sum, in turn, to be handed over to the state treasurer for safe-keeping, against the time when a star's career is ended. Only those who have worked in Hollywood can appreciate the amount of heartache and disappointment this would save in the future years. We know.
>
> We ask nothing for ourselves, but speak only for the good of the film industry.[26]

The petition was signed by Jean Acker, Harry Myers, Rosemary Theby, Alice Lake, Ann Luther, Henry Otto, Mahlon Hamilton, Gertrude Astor, and Elinor Fair. As might be expected, nothing came of the proposal.

Records of appearances by extras, no matter their name value today, are often difficult to find. I can recall back in the mid-1970s being asked by the Motion Picture and Television Fund if I could help document screen appearances by Yola D'Avril, who hoped to move into a cottage on the fund's campus. Sadly, I found the task impossible, and D'Avril was denied the support to which she was undoubtedly entitled. Despite once enjoying major careers on screen, without later credits, many leading men and women of the silent era were ineligible for the largesse of the Motion Picture Relief Fund (as it was originally known). Yola D'Avril always played French characters on screen (although she was born in Belgium on April 8, 1906) and is best known for her small part as the French girl, Suzanne, who tempts the young German soldiers in *All Quiet on the Western Front.* (1930). She had quit films after a marriage in the 1930s, but she returned in 1941 after her divorce, playing smaller and smaller parts. D'Avril died in Port Hueneme, California, on March 2, 1984.

The studio where Yola D'Avril began her later career as a bit player and extra was Paramount. Other silent players working there as extras in 1941 include Dorothy Sebastian, Anna Q. Nilsson, Monte Blue, Ethel Clayton, Julia Faye, James Kirkwood, Raymond Hatton, Mildred Harris (a former Mrs. Charlie Chaplin), Claire McDowell, and Chester Conklin.

Being a former silent star or leading player did not guarantee work as an extra. In 1940, many older extras complained to Central Casting that they were being discriminated against "under a policy favoring 'new faces.'"[27] The reality, as Central Casting pointed out, was than in the first five months of 1940, there had been only thirteen calls for men over fifty. In that same period, the agency had received 248 calls for 1,580 players of miscellaneous ages. As the Screen Actors Guild rightly pointed out that same year:

> Because of the character of the work, seniority alone is an unsatisfactory criterion upon which to base assurance of continued employment. However, we believe it advisable to assure certain prior rights with respect to available employment to those extras who by their employment experience appear to be most useful and best qualified for such work.[28]

To emphasize its basic premise, as expressed by Gloria Swanson's Norma Desmond that "We didn't need dialogue. We had faces," *Sunset Blvd.* (1950)

Yola D'Avril.

features a scene with a group of "waxworks," as William Holden's character, Joe Gillis, describes them. They are all representatives of Norma Desmond's era: Buster Keaton, H. B. Warner, and Anna Q. Nilsson. Warner has one word of dialogue, Keaton has two, and Anna Q. Nilsson has three. Of the group, Nilsson (1888–1974) is perhaps least known to modern audiences, and she is the only who came closest to being an extra—despite having insisted to the *Los Angeles Times* (April 13, 1947) that she would never work as such. From the mid-1930s onward, she took small roles as Swedish housekeepers, cooks, frontier women, and the like, playing Loretta Young's mother in *The Farmer's Daughter* (1947). The parts became smaller, not larger, after *Sunset Blvd.* She was a seamstress in *Show Boat* (1951) and a pioneer woman in her last film, *Seven Brides for Seven Brothers* (1954).

In 1951, Universal-International released *Hollywood Story*, directed by William Castle and starring Richard Conte as a Hollywood producer wanting to make a movie about the unsolved murder of a Hollywood director in 1929. Universal-International denied the film had anything to do with the 1922 unsolved murder of director William Desmond Taylor. Critic Ezra Goodman noted in the Los Angeles *Daily News* (December 12, 1950) that, "If Conte looks just a smidgeon better than most movie producers you are likely to encounter on or off the Universal-International lot, that can undoubtedly be attributed to dramatic license." As part of the storyline, William Castle decided to cast a number of former silent stars in bit parts,

but playing under their real names. Initially announced to appear were Marie Osborne, William Farnum, Betty Blythe, Francis X. Bushman, Helen Gibson, Cleo Ridgely, Elmo Lincoln, Dorothy Vernon, Spec O'Donnell, Arline Pretty, Stuart Holmes, and Marjorie "Babe" Kane. Eventually, only Bushman, Farnum, Blythe, and Gibson appeared in scenes shot on the then-abandoned Charlie Chaplin lot in Hollywood.

Hollywood Story (1951). Left to right: Richard Neill, Marie Osborne, William Farnum, Betty Blythe, stars Richard Conte and Julia Adams, Francis X. Bushman, Helen Gibson, Cleo Ridgely, Elmo Lincoln, Dorothy Vernon, "Spec" O'Donnell, Arline Pretty, Stuart Holmes, and Marjorie "Babe" Kane.

Several of the stars-turned extras (including Pauline Garon, Julia Faye, Elmo Lincoln, Hank Mann, Eddie Polo, and Herbert Rawlinson), along with legendary comedy producer Mack Sennett, did show up for the film's premiere at the Academy Theatre in West Hollywood on May 8, 1951. Ronald Reagan, as president of the Screen Actors Guild, was on hand, Jack Benny was the master of ceremonies, and to escort the former stars there was a "Young Players Committee," a group that included Tony Curtis (with Helen Gibson) and Rock Hudson (with Pauline Garon). Each star was presented with a citation from the Hollywood Chamber of Commerce: "For your outstanding contribution to the art and science of Motion Pictures . . . For the pleasure you have brought to millions the world over . . . For

Creighton Hale bending forward in *Million Dollar Mermaid* (1952).

your help in making Hollywood the film capital of the world . . . in grateful acknowledgement."

Responding to an ovation, Heine Conklin commented, "If only we could get a similar enthusiastic reception at the casting offices." Conklin's comment was ironic in that, of course, Hollywood was happy to exploit former silent celebrities to promote a new film, but not—by the 1950s—to offer them substantial work on screen in any capacity. Equally incensed, Elmo Lincoln pointed out that the previous week he had been working as a bartender at Universal. "Honor. Huh," he snorted, "I'd rather have the groceries . . . I'm writing the proper authorities to suggest they put us old-timers in a stock company . . . The major studios could pay us steady salaries, and we wouldn't expect big ones. They could use us in small character parts whenever they wanted to. We'd earn our keep."[29] Lincoln was the screen's first Tarzan, appearing in *Tarzan of the Apes* (1918), *The Romance of Tarzan* (1918), and *The Adventures of Tarzan* (1921). He had worked steadily as an extra in the 1930s and 1940s, including as a roustabout in *Tarzan's New Adventure* (1942), with Johnny Weissmuller, and playing an uncredited part in *Tarzan's Magic Fountain* (1949), with Lex Barker. Using the original star—now a bit player or extra—in a remake was good publicity. For example, William Farnum had been the star of the 1914 version of *The Spoilers*, worked steadily as a bit player and extra in the sound years, and was cast as a lawyer in the 1942 version of *The Spoilers*.

One of the featured silent players in *Hollywood Story* was Helen Gibson (1892–1977), who had made her name as the second actress to play the lead in the serial *The Hazards of Helen* in 1915. Her career had basically ended in 1921, and she worked in vaudeville and Wild West shows through the 1920s, before returning to the screen in 1927 as a double for Louise Fazenda, Marie Dressler, Edna Mae Oliver, Esther Dale, Marjorie Main, and Ethel Barrymore, and as a bit player and extra. She continued to work through into the late 1950s. *Hollywood Story* is a reminder that silent stars may not have had any substantial film roles, but they were willing to work as extras into the 1950s. Among the silent stars active as extras in the new decade were:

Monte Blue in *The Story of Will Rogers* (1952)

Clyde Cook in *Rogue's March* (1952) and *Loose in London* (1953)

Helen Gibson in *Ma and Pa Kettle at the Fair* (1952), *The Treasure of Lost Canyon* (1952), and *City That Never Sleeps* (1953)

Creighton Hale in *The Girl in White* (1952), *Scarlet Angel* (1952), *Million Dollar Mermaid* (1953), and *Take the High Ground* (1953)

Stuart Holmes in *The Band Wagon* (1953) and *Tribute to a Bad Man* (1956)

James Kirkwood in *Winning of the West* (1953)

Mary MacLaren in *Androcles and the Lion* (1952)

Hank Mann in *Son of Paleface* (1952)

Mae Marsh in *The Model and the Marriage Broker* (1951), *Night without Sleep* (1952), *The Quiet Man* (1952), and *Powder River* (1953)

Former director George Melford in *The Bandits of Corsica*, *Blueprint for a Murder* and *The President's Lady*, all released in 1953

Matt Moore in *Plymouth Adventure* (1952) and *Vicki* (1953)

Anna Q. Nilsson in *The Great Diamond Robbery* (1953)

Barry Norton in *The Strange Door* (1951) and *What Price Glory?* (1953)

House Peters in *O. Henry's Full House* (1952) and *Treasure of the Golden Condor* (1953)

Herbert Rawlinson in *The Stranger Wore a Gun* (1953)

And then there was Mae Clarke, who had been the fiancé of Dr. Frankenstein in the legendary 1931 film, and was now glimpsed as an extra in *Pat and Mike* and *Skirts Ahoy!*, both released in 1952. Carli Elinor, who had conducted his own score for the first Los Angeles screening of *The Birth of a Nation* in 1915, was an extra in *The World in His Arms* (1950). Gertrude Astor was busiest of all, on screen in *Elopement* (1951), *Crazy over Horses* (1951), *Angel Face* (1952), *Fort Osage* (1952), *Loose in London* (1953), and *Money from Home* (1953). The 1954 version of *A Star Is Born* included among its extras Mae Marsh as a Malibu party guest, Josef von Sternberg's first wife, Riza Royce, as a secretary, and, of course, Gertrude Astor as a spectator at the racetrack.

If any film is symbolic of the aspiration of every Hollywood extra in the 1930s, it is William Wellman's 1937 production of *A Star Is Born*, the story of Esther Blodgett from Colorado, who comes to Hollywood in pursuit of the dream of becoming a movie star. She knows that she must begin as an extra, but reality quickly sinks in when she visits the offices of Central Casting, where a clerk, played by Peggy Wood, tells her that no extras have been signed in the last two years. Esther Blodgett has a "1,000,000 to 1" chance of becoming a star, but her luck changes thanks to a screen test arranged by prominent movie star Norman Maine, a change of name to Vicki Lester, and a subsequent marriage to Maine. Maine becomes a drunkard and takes his own life, but he lives on when his wife introduces herself at Grauman's Chinese Theatre as "Mrs. Norman Maine." Fittingly, former silent director Marshall Neilan appears among the extras in a Santa Anita racetrack scene.

Chapter Ten

ETHNIC EXTRAS

In 1917, one fan magazine reported that Los Angeles was a city with a population of over five hundred thousand cinematic souls, "to say nothing of a number of Mexicans." The magazine article goes on to say that the film industry employed seven thousand as actors—"and every Mexican."[1] There can be little dispute that if all those Mexicans really were working in the movies, they did so in only one capacity—as extras.

Rob Wagner, writing in 1918, identified one extra as "half Indian, half Mex., and half Chink." Because he possessed long, black hair, the extra would often double for "women who have to be handled rough."[2] Ill treatment of Mexican extras was commonplace in the early years, and often a group would be hired to play a scene if it held potential for injury during shooting— even if the parts were not written for actors of any particular ethnicity.

A good description of the manner in which Mexican extras were hired in the 1910s is provided by Rob Wagner:

> The Mexicans are the queerest bunch that work extra. They are employed by a *patrón*, and consequently take orders from him alone. A director can shout his fool head off, even in bad and violent Spanish, but they won't do a thing until their *patrón* tells 'em to. They work best in the battle stuff, for they are naturally better actors and more dramatic than Americans. The lowest-browed dub in the bunch has some artistic sense and will take a fearful drubbing for art's sake.
>
> Strangely enough, they fight with much more enthusiasm just before lunch. The studio lunches are banquets to fellas who've grown up strong on chili beans. I once heard a director tell a *patrón* to tell his men that he was goin' to pay 'em five dollars for their day's work; but he expected 'em to earn it. Say, you ought to 've seen those black devils fight! They'd liked to have killed one another.[3]

Arapaho Indians, who had appeared in *The Covered Wagon*, take part in a prologue to the film titled "Pioneer Days" at Grauman's Egyptian Theatre in Hollywood, beginning April 10, 1923. In the center of the photograph, from left to right, are: Sid Grauman, producer Jesse L. Lasky, director James Cruze, and Colonel Tim McCoy.

Producer Thomas H. Ince noted in 1915, "Los Angeles is a rendezvous for Mexicans of all classes alike, and particularly hundreds of peons who have fought in various revolutions. These chaps have smelled powder, have been acclimated to scenes bordering on the melodramatic, and consequently make excellent material for the purpose for which they are used before the screen."[4]

According to Angela Gomez (who worked as an extra along with her husband in the 1920s and 1930s), Mexican and other Hispanic types were provided to the studios by Pedro Carmona and Chris-Pin Martin, who lived and worked in the Chavez Ravine area of Los Angeles (where Dodger Stadium now stands). The studios would send runners to the pair, and Carmona and Martin would hire extras congregating around "El Arbol," a large tree outside a house owned by the Gamboa family on Temple and Diamond Street.[5]

There was always the more convenient possibility of finding all the Mexicans one might need if a film were actually shot in Mexico itself. Supposedly, the entire Mexican army appeared in the scenes where Villa makes his first entrance into Mexico City in *Viva Villa* (1934). The army was mobilized after Mexican officials complained that the original shoot did not contain sufficient soldiers. There were obvious reasons why American producers would prefer hiring extras on location in Mexico rather than in the United States: In 1938, it was reported that Mexicans in their own country were willing to work for five pesos or one dollar a day.

Generally, Mexican extras were badly treated in Hollywood. When one such extra, working for $7.50 a day on *Dancing Pirates* in 1935, was told to speak a line in Spanish, thus qualifying him for an adjustment in pay, this adjustment was denied. The assistant director excused the injustice by explaining, "because he [the extra] was a Mexican . . . [and] he [the director] did not pay Mexicans for speaking lines."[6]

Native Americans were probably first used on screen by producer Thomas H. Ince in 1910 or 1911 after the Miller Bros. 101 Ranch Real Wild West Show come to winter in Southern California. The company had utilized "real" cowboys and Indians in its live shows, with the latter coming from the Ponca tribes of Oklahoma. The Miller Bros. 101 Ranch joined forces with Ince to provide actors for his Western productions, filmed under the Bison-101 label. One of the earliest known Native American extras was Silver Haar, who appeared as an Indian rider in 1911, and received a gold life membership card from the Screen Extras Guild in 1958.

At least two Native Americans appear in D. W. Griffith's *Intolerance*. In the Babylonian sequence, in small, insignificant roles—and cast obviously because of their appearance—Charles Eagle Eye appears as a Barbarian chieftain and William Dark Cloud as an Egyptian chieftain. Director James Cruze filmed his 1923 epic Western, *The Covered Wagon*, on location in the Snake River Valley on the border of Utah and Nevada. Here, Colonel Tim McCoy (later a Hollywood celebrity in his own right) hired and supervised some 750 Indians, who were each paid five dollars a day, with an additional dollar for those providing their own horse and tepee.[7] The Arapaho and Shoshone Indians appearing in *The Covered Wagon* also appeared in other productions of the same period, most notably *Spoilers of the West* (1927).

In November 1926, the members of various Indian tribes met in Hollywood under the leadership of White Bird, a Cherokee, in order to establish a casting organization to which all twenty-five tribes participating in Hollywood productions might belong. Called the War Paint Club, its members would seek to provide producers with genuine Native Americas, thus precluding the hiring of substitute Mexicans and other dark-skinned Los Angeles residents. "We have just squirmed sometimes in seeing a picture supposedly with Indians in it and we knew they weren't," said White Bird.[8]

Traditionally, Indians were portrayed in leading roles by "white" actors, most notably Richard Dix in *The Vanishing American* (1925) and *Redskin* (1929). However, Native Americans living in California were frequently utilized as extras. Scenes for *Ramona* (1936) were shot in part at the Mesa Grande Indian Reservation in San Diego County, with local "Indians" participating as extras. Publicity had it that these "Indians" were descendants of those about whom Helen Hunt Jackson had written in her original 1884 novel.

Native Americans would generally be hired to play themselves, but they could also easily be used to portray other ethnic groups. Yuma Indians supplemented Hollywood extras portraying Arabs in location scenes shot in the California-Arizona desert—itself substituting for the Sahara—in *Under Two Flags* (1936). When *Lives of a Bengal Lancer* (1935), set in India, was shooting on location at Independence, California, one hundred Piute Indians were hired from nearby reservations. Additionally, Paramount found real Indians among the Hindu fruit pickers of the Napa Valley.[9]

Perhaps the most prominent but least known Native American in Hollywood was Charles Stevens (1893–1964), whose father was Welsh and whose mother was the daughter of Geronimo. Stevens worked with Douglas Fairbanks, Sr. on his first film, *The Lamb*, in 1915, and was, in all probability, in every one of Fairbanks's American productions. The star certainly kept Stevens on his payroll throughout his career, and it would appear that Stevens doubled for Fairbanks on many, if not all, of his films. Charles Stevens's career predates that of Fairbanks, beginning at American Biograph in Los Angeles and continuing with both Indian and non-Indian roles after Fairbanks's retirement. Two of Stevens's important non-Fairbanks appearances from the early sound era are as Pedro in *The Virginian* (1929) and as Injun Joe in *Tom Sawyer* (1930). Stevens's appearance, as an Indian, in *Escape from Fort Bravo* in 1953 was hailed as his 200th on screen.

For the Westerns he made in Monument Valley, including, most famously, *Stagecoach* (1939), John Ford would utilize local Navajo tribes. They would not play Navajo, but, rather Apache, Sioux, Comanche, and Cheyenne. To the audience, the tribal link was an irrelevancy. When asked to speak in their native tongue, the Navajo would often say what they wanted rather than what was required. For example, in Raoul Walsh's *A Distant Trumpet* (1964), what the Indian chief says to the cavalry officer is not what the subtitle claims, but rather, "You can't do anything to me, you're just a snake crawling in your own shit."[10]

In the 1940s, when a large number of Native Americans—more than Central Casting could provide—was needed for a specific production, an Indian chief by the name of "Many Treaties" negotiated with local reservations. (Similarly, a lady named Bessie Loo would help Central Casting out providing Chinese extras.) There was some aversion to Hollywood Indians, in that they could appear on screen to be over-fed and in need of physical exercise. As a result, for its production of *They Died with Their Boots On*, starring Errol Flynn and released in 1942, Warner Bros. imported sixteen Sioux Indians from Fort Yates, North Dakota. They were paid five dollars a day when idle and eleven dollars a day when working, and housed in individual rooms in a local hotel. As a major production, *They Died with Their Boots On* had more than its share of well-known extras, including Aileen Pringle, Anna Q. Nilsson, Vera Lewis (whose career dates back to D. W. Griffith), Frank Mayo, Francis Ford, and De Wolf Hopper (the only husband of Hedda Hopper).

When he was filming *The Green Goddess* in 1923 and in need of a mob of religious fanatics, director Sidney Olcott rounded up every available native East Indian. "And some of them were so carried away in the film frenzy that in their mad rush they punctured some of the mad ruggedness of our Himalaya sets." "It is difficult," continued Olcott, "to have absolute obedience in a mob. Some of them are cheeky, others are stubborn or believe they know better than the director."[11]

Filming the Gilda Gray vehicle *The Devil Dancer* in 1927, producer Samuel Goldwyn claimed to have major problems hiring ethnic extras. With two thirds of the film set in Tibet and one third in India, he wanted the audience to be able to differentiate between the two ethnic types. Authenticity was important, claimed the producer. Apparently, the Indian extras presented no problem, but what to do about the Tibetans? "Our job was to represent these strange, unknown people in the stark and rugged magnificence of their country," explained Goldwyn to the *New York Times*, ignoring the reality that their country was actually represented by a Hollywood backlot. "That's why we had to have extras who looked like authentic natives. More than that everyone of them had to be, in a sense, an actor." Orientalists were consulted, the name of the Dalai Lama thrown into the mix for good measure. Goldwyn reported "the most exacting care in the selection of extras."[12] There is no record of where in Hollywood the producer found Tibetan extras, but one suspects that ultimately they were not quite as realistic as was maintained.

One Hindu working on a regular basis as an extra in Hollywood was Profulla Kumar Ghosal, who could also portray not only Indians, but also Chinese, Japanese, Mexican, and Italian types.

MGM director Frank Lloyd traveled to Papeete, Tahiti, to shoot scenes for his 1935 production of *Mutiny on the Bounty*. The location easily provided him with 2,500 South Seas native extras. Shooting additional scenes on San Miguel Island, off the California Coast near Santa Barbara, the director had to make do with forty athletes from Santa Barbara State College, whose physiques suggest South Seas ethnicity.

While filming *The Hurricane* in 1937, director John Ford actually visited Samoa. Extras were recruited from the native population, but as they were under the guardianship of the Department of the Navy, the studio was not permitted to pay them in cash (which I am sure must have pleased producer Samuel Goldwyn immensely). Instead, the miserly two dollars a day that the native extras were supposed to be paid was turned over to the local authorities and converted into packages of chewing gum and cans of salmon, which were doled out over a long period of time.

There were certainly many Polynesian extras in Hollywood, but the most prominent was Satini Puailoa, who is credited as the first of his nationality to become a member of the Screen Actors Guild—back in 1937. Born in Samoa in 1905, Puailoa left there in 1919, eventually arriving on the United States mainland, via Honolulu, in 1924. He developed a nightclub and vaudeville act dancing and throwing flaming knives and supplemented his income working as a Hollywood extra, appearing in the 1926 release of *Ben-Hur*, among others. Puailoa was a fixture in films with Hawaiian settings, among them *The Hurricane* (1937), *Hawaiian Nights* (1939), *South of Pago Pago* (1940), *Pardon My Sarong* (1942), *Song of the Islands* (1942), *Lure of the Islands* (1942), *Tahiti Nights* (1944), *Call of the South Seas* (1944), and *Road to Bali* (1952). In *Waikiki Wedding* (1937), in which he can be seen performing his knife dance, his daughter plays "Sweet Leilani," to whom Bing Crosby sings the song of that name. Puailoa could also play other nationalities, as he did in *The Real Glory* (1939), in which he appears as a Filipino.

Unlike African Americans, Puailoa claims to have never experienced discrimination on or off the set. He knew his limitations. He knew what he could or could not do, and he knew that one of the best things that he could do was to teach stars such as Clark Gable and Betty Grable how to perform Hawaiian dances. As he recalled, "A lot of the extras, when the scene was over, they would go back and play cards to while [*sic*] away the time. I didn't do that. I would stay on the set. So when they suddenly wanted somebody for a stunt or something, I would say, 'Here I am!'"[13] Satini Puailoa retired in 1973 after appearing in more than eighty films. His more recent appearances included *Elephant Walk* (1954) and *Around the World in 80 Days* (1956). Aside from acting, he also worked as a technical advisor on films with Polynesian locations, such as *Rain* (1932).

Just as Puailoa might play a Filipino, so were Los Angeles Filipinos cast as Polynesians, with many appearing in the 1929 Ramon Novarro vehicle, *The Pagan*. Filipinos were also cast as natives of an unidentified civilization in the 1935 production of *She*, and actually as themselves in the 1939 production of *The Real Glory*. For reasons that remain unclear, Filipino extras were paid less than others. Only in July 1936 was it announced that their pay would rise from $3.20 a day to the standard, minimum rate of five dollars.

According to producer Thomas H. Ince, in the mid 1910s, Japanese male extras were readily available in Los Angeles, quickly understanding that they could make more money on screen than they could in any other occupation available to them. There was a problem with female Japanese extras in that "[t]hey are timid and modest and scarce, and it is necessary to pay them double the amount received by the men before they will step before a camera."[14] Chinese extras were less amenable, in large part because many were in the country illegally and feared arrest if they accepted work in the industry. As Ince wrote somewhat tongue-in-cheek:

> A modern Motion Picture camp certainly comprises a babel of tongues and a contrast of customs. Self-preservation demands that each distinct race be segregated from the other. The Indian [Native American] scorns every race but the white race, for which he has a filial respect. The Hindu keeps by himself, where the shadow of others than his own caste can't cross his food. The Jap eats his bean curd and drinks his green tea peacefully, contemplating his next door neighbor, the Chinaman, of whose territory he would like to annex. The Chinaman holds aloof from and casts furtive glances at the pepper-heated Mexican, whom he distrusts.[15]

One of the earliest known Chinese extras was James Wang, who began his career in New York and Chicago before moving in the 1910s to Los Angeles, where he became known as the "Mayor of Chinatown." He worked as a technical adviser on a number of films with Chinese themes, including two prominent 1919 releases, the Nazimova vehicle *The Red Lantern* (translating the director's commands to five hundred Chinese participating in a recreation of the Boxer Rebellion), and D. W. Griffith's *Broken Blossoms*, in which he also appears as a Buddhist high priest. "But most of all," he explained to a 1922 fan magazine reporter, "I am a villain. I have played in many serials; the last one with Tony [Antonio] Moreno, *The Unforeseen Hand* [actually, *The Invisible Hand*, 1920]. I was also with William Duncan, and I played with Louise Glaum in *The Lone Wolf's Daughter* (1919)."[16]

There was a sudden and inexplicable explosion of films with Chinese themes in 1920, with the production of the Ethel Clayton vehicle *Crooked Streets*, the Anita Stewart vehicle *The Yellow Typhoon*, and the Antonio Moreno serial *The Invisible Hand*. Suddenly, Chinese extras were in demand. Japanese extras refused to don Chinese attire and pretend to be Chinese, and so there was no choice but to recruit the real thing. Unfortunately for Hollywood, the real thing demanded 50 percent per day more than Caucasian performers. As one fan magazine writer reported, "Where five dollars a day will compensate the Caucasian extra for a day's work without evening clothes, the citizen of the Flowery Kingdom will listen to nothing less than the clink of seven and a half. They simply can't understand English when you quote lower terms."[17]

In 1921, Leatrice Joy had appeared as the Chinese heroine of *A Tale Two Worlds*, set in San Francisco's Chinatown, which used a fair number of Chinese extras. A few years later, in 1926, Leatrice Joy was starring as a boyish American in *Eve's Leaves*, set on the Chinese mainland. The Chinese villain was portrayed by Caucasian actor Walter Long, and his Chinese henchman by Japanese-born actor Sojin (whose roles were always too important for him to be classified as an extra). The film does, however, make extensive use of a large number of one hundred or more male and female Chinese extras. Chinese players are not generally identified by name, but we know the name of one Chinese extra, Kalo, who also worked as an assistant cameraman at the Lasky studios in the 1920s.[18]

Providing extras from Chinatown was handled in the 1920s by Caucasian Tom Gubbins, a thirty-something "highly educated" and "courteous" individual, who had spent eight years in China "and who [spoke] that peculiar language."[19] He claimed to have approximately 160 resident Chinese extras at his call, and to have been responsible for introducing Anna May Wong to Hollywood producers. Among the extras handled by Gubbins was: Chan Lee, the only "cross-eyed Chinaman" and one who could double for Ben Turpin; former Baptist minister Jimmie Wang (not believed to be related to the above-mentioned James Wang); Elena Juarado, a half-caste Chinese and Filipino who appears as a maid in *The Ten Commandments*; and Willie Fung, described as a second Roscoe "Fatty" Arbuckle. Gubbins explained in 1926: "My Chinese are trying hard—very hard to win the respect of Americans . . . They do not like to appear in roles which in any way seem degrading. . . . They would take part in no scenes which showed Chinese kidnapping white girls. . . . the Chinese believe in honor and honesty."[20]

By the mid 1930s, a handful of Chinese players was available. Among the women, there was one Chinese-American star, Anna May Wong, and four others: Ai-Li-Ling, Oie Chan, Yuen Tsung Sze, and Olive Young. Among the men, there was one well-known name, Keye Luke, thanks to the Charlie Chan series, in which he played the title character's number one son. There was also a substantial number of "atmosphere" players: George Chan, Jim Chan, Luke Chan, Spencer Chan, King Hou Chang, Frank Chew, Wong Chung, Jue Fong, William Fong, Willie Fung, Chester Gan, Eddie Lee, James B. Leong, Maurice Liu, Richard Loo, Loo Loy, Moy Ming, Kam Tang, Sam Tang, James Wong, Victor Wong, and Suan Yee.

The number of Japanese players available during this same period was very small. There were six women: Mia Ickioka, Lois Izumioa, Lotus Long, Tochia Mori, Iris Yamaoka, and Josephine Yamaoka. And there were only four men: Daro Haro, Tetsu Komai, Mike Morita, and Otto Yamaoka.

Chinese-American extras found work in great numbers with the filming of Pearl Buck's *The Good Earth* in 1937. They were again in heavy demand in 1944 for two films, *Dragon Seed* and *The Keys of the Kingdom*. Because of their involvement in war work, an insufficient number was available for the former film, which supposedly needed three thousand extras. As a result, Mexicans and Filipinos were hired, along with other racial groups that could easily be made up to appear oriental.

Four-year-old Eunice Soo Hoo and her six siblings appeared in *The Keys of the Kingdom*. The children worked regularly on screen, with five earning one hundred dollars a week and the sixth $150. Betty Soo Hoo was nine years old when she appeared in *The Keys of the Kingdom*. As an infant in *The Good Earth*, she had come to be known as "the one-take Chinese baby," according to the *New York Times* (April 2, 1944). That same report also identified two thousand Chinese extras who were available in the Los Angeles area, with 1,500 employed in *The Keys of the Kingdom*. This number is probably highly inflated, in that *Daily Variety* (August 25, 1944) identified only three hundred as "capable of working close to the cameras in the mob of several thousand extras required for Celestial scenes. Remainder were often other nationals in the guise of Chinese."

D. W. Griffith's *The Birth of a Nation* (1915) might have gained notoriety for its use of white actors in blackface, but the production did boast one prominent African American extra, Madame Sul-Te-Wan (1873–1959), born Nellie Conley, who was to appear on screen on a fairly regular basis into the 1950s. Her *Los Angeles Times* (February 5, 1959) obituary claimed she had been "in several hundred pictures since 1915." She could usually be found in films with Southern locations or themes, such as *Kentucky* (1938), *Maryland* (1940), and *The Story of Seabiscuit* (1949), along with other extras such as former silent players Gertrude Astor and Creighton Hale. Madame Sul-Te-Wan's characterization as a slave was not limited to *The Birth of a Nation*; she played the same role in *The Maid of Salem* (1937).

Madame-Sul-Te-Wan was a colorful character, given to wearing a turban and gold earrings, with hair in long, straight black braids down almost to her knees. She had been given a letter of introduction to Griffith by "Dad" Reddy, with whom she had worked in the circus and with whom, for reasons now unclear, the director was familiar. Not only did Griffith employ Madame for *The Birth of a Nation*, he also used her and her three sons (Otto, Onest, and James) by her first husband, Robert Reed Conley, whenever he could. Lucille Brown supposedly told the actress, "Mr. Griffith says you're the best of the race." Certainly, he was in no hurry to have Madame leave his company, and as Douglas Fairbanks told her, "When he gets rid of you—ain't no-one going to be here." And when there was no extra work available, Madame Sul-Te-Wan would serve as a maid—strictly on a voluntary basis, it would appear—to the Gish sisters or other actresses in the company. The devotion and respect between Griffith and Madame Sul-Te-Wan was absolute. When Griffith divorced his second wife, Madame took his three cats. While the director was dying in Temple Hospital in Los Angeles, Madame kept vigil. She was the only individual present, and when he died, she complained that he "should have gone with people around him and the sun blazing in the heavens."[21]

The earliest documented male African American extra is "Pop Purdy," an elderly gentleman who specialized in appearing as a coachman, footman, or manservant. "The enthusiasm he has for his parts, no matter how small, is almost pathetic," wrote Rob Wagner in 1917.[22]

African American extras were apparently noted for their versatility. An assistant to Lon Chaney was quoted in the 1920s as claiming, "Negroes are natural actors. You can pull one out of the mob and they can act. It is only a matter of makeup and costume to create anything from a Chinaman to an Eskimo."[23] A similar comment was made by a 1916 fan magazine: "Negroes are frequently used as 'extras.' They can be attired so as to represent a variety of strange peoples."[24]

Noble Johnson (1881–1978) may have played Uncle Tom in the 1927 production of *Topsy and Eva*, but he was no Uncle Tom among African American performers. He was just as likely to be cast as a Native American

King Vidor with African American extras on location for *Hallelujah* (1929). AMPAS.

as a black man. Similarly, he might appear as little more than an unbilled extra or as a major supporting character with screen credit. Johnson's film appearances were many and his roles varied. Prominent as he was as a black actor, Johnson is equally important as the co-founder in 1916 of the Lincoln Motion Picture Company, a Los Angeles-based all-black production company. Johnson starred in Lincoln's first films while also working as a featured actor at Universal.

Not surprisingly, African Americans constituted the largest group of ethnic extras, with a reported eleven thousand registered with Central Casting in 1924, of which fewer than half were ever fully employed.[25] By 1927, Central Casting had established an African American division, with Charles Butler as its "Coloured" manager. "Mr. Butler is responsible for the collecting, classifying and distributing of the Negro 'extras,'" reported the Urban League's *Opportunity*.[26] Butler had earlier been associated with the Cinema Auxiliary, which advertised itself as "filmland's coloured casting bureau," and which was headed by Jimmie Smith. In 1938, Central Casting considered dropping Charles Butler from its staff, but there was massive opposition from African American extras.

As Fred W. Beetson explained the situation in 1928, "All the casting of small town types [at Central Casting], colored people, Russians, Jewish, Mexicans, etc., is done by having people we call runners go into the particular neighborhood and gather them up." By way of explanation, he added, "Most of these people do not have telephones."[27] Sometimes the hiring of this casual labor could create a problem, as it did with *Uncle Tom's Cabin* (1927), which utilized a large number of African American extras. Liking the studio life, they were disinclined to return to their previous impoverished existence and could not be persuaded that there was simply no further work available at the studio (in this case Universal).

In the summer of 1938, Central Casting established a special department for all racial groups, to be headed by an unnamed individual

> who has a working knowledge of the picture business, who understands the problems of the racial groups, and who has no connection with runners. [Telephone] call girls who speak several languages will be assigned to the department. This department will have its own telephone numbers, and will conduct its interviews independent of those arranged for other members.[28]

Among African American extras known to have been registered with Central Casting in the mid-1940s are Martin Turner, Chester Jones, and Irene Allen.

It is not clear exactly what Charles Butler's title at Central Casting was. Presumably, he was not a casting director. In June 1962, a British Guiana-born playwright, director, and newspaper editor named Samuel A. Boyea made an appeal to the California (South) Fair Employment Practice Commission against Charles Boren, president of Central Casting, claiming racial discrimination when he applied for a job as the "first Negro casting director in the entire history of the motion picture industry."[29]

Obviously, productions with African locations provided African American actors with the best opportunities. MGM's *The Road to Mandalay* (1926) used a reported two hundred African American extras. Occasionally, there were also mainstream Hollywood films with prominent African American casts, most notably King Vidor's *Hallelujah* and Fox's *Hearts in Dixie*, both released in 1929. For Warner Bros. 1946 bio-film about Cole Porter, *Night and Day*, the studio hired twenty-four African American extras to play Senegalese soldiers moving to the accompaniment of beating drums, as the composer worked out the rhythm of the title song. In everything from Erich von Stroheim's *The Wedding March* (1928) to Cecil B. DeMille's *Cleopatra* (1934), there was demand for Nubian slaves. One African American newspaper reported in 1929:

> With the unusual demand for coloured extras during the year, mostly for talking pictures, 10,916 placements were made in Hollywood with 5,854 jobs at US $7.50 a day. Of the number placed, 1424 got tickets ranging from US $20 to $35 a day and made a total of US $11,700. Total amount of money paid coloured extras was US $9,702.89, with the daily placement a year being 30 and the average daily earnings US $8.22.[30]

The number of African American extras remained pretty much unchanged in 1930, but dropped severely in 1931 to a little over three thousand who were employed. The largest number of African American extras working in one film was reportedly five hundred, an unprecedented number for Central Casting to provide, to appear in the funeral sequence for the Louise Beavers character in *Imitation of Life* (1934). It was not, however, unusual for as many as three hundred African Americans to work on one production, as in *Kentucky* (1938).

Cecil B. DeMille's *Cleopatra* (1934) provided employment for African American extras, shown portraying Nubian slaves. AMPAS.

Those African American extras Central Casting could not provide were found around Central Avenue in Los Angeles by lowly black studio employees, such as bootblacks Oscar (Cutie Pie) Smith at Paramount and Harold (Slickem) Garrison at MGM. The latter also worked as assistant director on the 1929 all-black feature *Hallelujah,* rounding up as many as 340 extras for the film. Oscar Smith had been actor Wallace Reid's valet, and when he died in 1923, Reid requested that Smith be given a shoeshine stand at his studio, Paramount. By the end of the 1920s, Smith had supposedly appeared as an extra in some two hundred films, including at least two Paramount productions, *Beau Sabreur* (1928) and *Thunderbolt* (1929). He also worked with extra Zack Williams in the search for African American extras for independent Hollywood productions.

In the 1930s, a young actor named Ben Carter (1912–46) opened up an agency on Central Avenue for black extras and other African American actors and actresses. He claimed to have cast every black performer, except for the leads, in *Gone with the Wind.* Carter himself frequently appeared on screen. He played with a more famous African American entertainer, Mantan Moreland, in a double act in vaudeville and on screen in such productions as the Charlie Chan movies *The Scarlet Clue* (1944) and *Dark Alibi* (1946). Their act was known as the unfinished sentence routine. As described by the *New York Times* (September 30, 1973), "One would begin a sentence, the other would interrupt, and the exchanges would lead into mental brick walls. Nothing made sense to the viewer, but it did to them." Ben Carter died suddenly the day before an NBC television appearance, in which he and Mantan Moreland would have performed their unfinished sentence routine.

Only a handful of African American players advertised in the pages of the *Standard Casting Directory* in the 1930s. Generally, these were "name" performers, but occasionally there might be an extra, such as Mme. Elizabeth Ford, who proclaimed herself a graduate of the Ethel Cotton School of Expression and Dramatic Art, and advertised "My specialty Negro Dialect." Ford's name does not appear in association with any feature film of the 1930s.

The type of role that Ford was seeking was stereotypical and basically condemned in the early 1940s by the NAACP's executive secretary, Walter White. He wanted an end to the "old-time mammies, slothful servants, impish toadies, and grinning hoofers,"[31] roles African Americans had survived by in Hollywood. By diminishing such characterizations—and by extension, those who played them—Walter White was effectively limiting not only roles in which African American supporting players might find work, but also what was available to African American extras. Not surprisingly, many African American actors, from extras to character players, insisted that "so long as the roles were not burlesque nor reflecting on the race, they were willing to portray the characters assigned to them."[32]

Sadly, African Americans would sometimes exploit their brothers. In 1935, legendary tap dancer Bill Robinson accused Willie Covan, owner of the Covan School of Dancing, of charging an outrageous 20 percent commission for a large number of black dancers needed for Paramount's *Big Broadcast of 1935*. Supposedly, Covan threatened to blacklist any dancer who refused to pay his commission, a commission that was not only high but one he, as an unlicensed agent, had no right to require.

Directors might adopt novel if somewhat racist means of finding sufficient African American extras. While shooting *So Red the Rose* in the summer of 1935, King Vidor had problems recruiting five hundred Negro extras until he remembered that Thursday was the maid's day off throughout the city, and shot the scene that day.[33]

Deportment by African American extras was often the subject of commentary. In 1932, the African American newspaper, the *Pittsburgh Courier*, commented, "Hollywood needs high class, intelligent, self-respecting men and women, who possess fine qualities of character, deportment and integrity. People who are welcomed upon the lots because of their serenity and affable competence."[34]

Unlike their white counterparts, black extras could and did demonstrate against working conditions and pay at the studios. There was a general strike by African Americans, who demanded higher salaries, at various studios in September 1936. That same year, black extras on the set of MGM's *Tarzan Escapes* objected to the excessive makeup they were required to wear—as well as to the amount of skin they were required to bare. In August 1938, three hundred African American extras struck the MGM production of *Too Hot to Handle*, starring Clark Gable.[35]

With the formation of the Screen Extras Guild in 1946, there was some formal recognition of African American and other ethnic extras. The guild established admissions committees for "the Negro," headed by Anna Mabry; as well as for "the Indian," headed by Chief Many Treaties; for the Chinese, headed by Spencer Chan; and for Spanish and Mexican extras, headed by Trini Varela. The Screen Extras Guild was conscious of discrimination against African American extras. As was noted during its May 20, 1951, annual meeting, "We have a lot of racial boys that work at night with Johnny

Weissmuller that get $1.56 with a G-string. We have a lot of Indians do the same thing at night." Basically, African American extras were treated as if they belonged in the same class with migratory workers.[36]

In 1955, the Negro Actors Associated[37] organization was founded, with Mae Henderson as its business manager. The association had sixty black players registered and helped find and cast additional African Americans. It appears primarily to have been involved in local theatrical productions in Los Angeles, with its members performing under the leadership of Bob deCoy at the Dance and Drama Playhouse, located on West Washington Boulevard.

Through at least the early 1960s, only a handful of African Americans were members of the Screen Extras Guild, but that decade saw a general improvement in hiring and recognition of black performers. In October 1962, it was announced that Chester Jones had been elected to the board to become only the fifth Negro actor in the guild's history. He succeeded African American board member Anna Mabry, who had served nine years. Before Mabry, the board's sole African American members had been Edward "Ned" Boyd and his successor, Martin Turner.

In 1963, the *Los Angeles Times* reported, "In the last two months there has been a phenomenal increase in the employment of Negro extra players and actors, in marked contrast to the equivalent period one year ago and five years ago."[38] The wages earned by African American extras registered with Central Casting had increased over a five-year period by 1,500 percent. According to Douglas Dakin, general manager at Central Casting, the figures "clearly show that producers have recognized the fact that Negroes must be portrayed realistically and in proportion to their actual numbers."[39]

If life was improving for black extras in Hollywood, the situation elsewhere was not. The 1989 release, *A Dry White Season*, was shot on location in Zimbabwe, standing in for South Africa. The black extras in this anti-apartheid, MGM/UA release were outraged to discover that their salary of fifteen dollars a day was half that paid to a dog working on the production.

While it might be accurate to describe African Americans as marginalized in American films of the 1920s and later, in reality this ethnic group was almost invariably included in the pool of extras. Thus, African Americans were no more marginalized in the extra roles that they portrayed than were white Americans. Where the marginalization exists, of course, is in the general failure of Hollywood to offer leading or supporting roles to African Americans, a problem which continued until fairly recent times.

Theresa Harris was unbilled in *Professional Sweetheart* (1933). Adolphe Menjou, shown with hands on hips, and Franklin Pangborn, far right, were more fortunate.

African American extras did, however, suffer the indignity of being identified as "Zombres," which appears to be a corruption of "Zombies," meaning persons of the lowest order of intelligence, the walking dead. From the late 1920s onwards, an African American extra might also be identified as a "dinge," which derives from the word "dingy," meaning dark. When an African American did get a decent supporting role in a Hollywood film of the 1920s, 1930s, or 1940s, the actor may find his or her billing inappropriate to the size of the role—and sometimes simply the billing was non-existent. A typical example is the 1933 RKO production, *Professional Sweethearts*, starring Ginger Rogers, in which her African American maid substitutes as a radio singer for the star. She is crucial to the plot development, and yet Theresa Harris, the very obviously talented actress playing the maid, received no screen credit. In 1933, Theresa Harris also played a maid, Chico, working for star Barbara Stanwyck in *Baby Face*, and again her role and her performance stands out for modern audiences.

Theresa Harris is the quintessential, forgotten and unheralded African American performer from Hollywood's golden age. Born in Houston, Texas, in 1917, Harris and her family came to Los Angeles when she was just eleven years old. She studied at both the UCLA Conservatory of Music and Zoellner's Conservatory of Music, found work with the Negro musical comedy troupe, the Lafayette Players, and then entered the film industry, with her earliest known appearance in the 1930 production of *Morocco*, starring Marlene Dietrich. Despite her talents as a singer, Harris was looked on by the film industry as little better than an on-screen maid. In 1940, when Paramount needed a partner for Eddie "Rochester" Anderson, playing Jack Benny's servant in *Buck Benny Rides Again*, Theresa Harris was cast as a maid for Benny's co-star, Mary Martin. Theresa Harris died in Inglewood, California, on October 8, 1985. She was one of countless and talented African American players who were unrecognized in their lifetimes, and who might as well have been extras for all the attention and credit they received.

Chapter Eleven

THE 1940S, UNIONIZATION, AND BEYOND

Even before America's entry into World War II, Hollywood had a problem finding youthful, able-bodied young men among the ranks of the extras. Many had already joined the military. Many lacked the physical characteristics and capabilities necessary for the roles they were to assume. As early as May 1938, the Screen Actors Guild (SAG) had rounded up five hundred extras, the majority of them male, to determine their swimming ability for a production requiring three hundred extras to jump into the ocean from a burning movie barge fourteen miles off shore. The extras were ordered to participate in a 600-yard swim around the Hermosa Beach pier. Thirty lifeguards were luckily on hand to rescue the forty-nine male extras who couldn't complete the task.[1]

Filming *Meet John Doe* in the late summer of 1940, Frank Capra required a "mob" of the cheapest, $5.50-a-day extras to serve as a human background. The problem was that the Screen Actors Guild did not have a sufficient number of $5.50-a-day extras. When Capra asked for a waiver to use non-Guild extras, both the Screen Actors Guild and Central Casting set about trying to persuade the higher paid extras—those earning $8.50, $10.00 and $16.00 a day—to take the work at $5.50. The extras refused, suggesting that the director pay more and ignoring the reality of what was required. "The caste system among extras is incredibly strict," reported Morton Thompson in the *Hollywood Citizen News* (September 9, 1940). "I suppose everybody in Hollywood, figuratively speaking, pleaded with, or tried to plead with the extras to take those jobs. Some of the extras who refused were literally—not figuratively—starving." It was to no avail. Capra got his waivers, used them, and the extras impotently howled.

Among those advocating that extras accept the $5.50 a day pay was the Screen Actors Guild's Antrim Short, who had been a leading man in silent films. In order to block the use of waivers for large sets, heavy with "atmosphere" players, the Screen Actors Guild assured its members that Central

Crowds of non-union extras at the massive outdoor convention scene in *Meet John Doe* (1941).

Casting would not take away their regular wage classification, a pledge that the guild had first made as early as December 1933.

When Warner Bros. in 1941 needed young men of military age for two of its productions, *Dive Bomber* and *Sergeant York*, it had to turn to the University of Southern California to obtain 170 extras. The following year, the Screen Actors Guild granted a waiver to producer Samuel Goldwyn, allowing him to employ non-union extras to appear in the grandstands of his baseball film, *The Pride of the Yankees*. Plenty of female extras were available, but they were not what Goldwyn wanted.

Protesting the hiring of non-union extras, one extra who did make it to the set, Paul Cook, delivered a stump speech attacking the producer. Eventually, the *New York Times* (March 1, 1942) reported, "Cook was evicted from the set, and news of the fracas stimulated the chronic unrest of the extras all over town until some of their casual gatherings outside casting offices were described as protest meetings." As the *New York Times* reporter put it, the extras "cling desperately to their chance to starve to death," while

Screen Actors Guild activist James Cagney with extra/"bit" player Pauline Wagner in a scene filmed in the Cocoanut Grove for *Lady Killer* (1933).

dispirited officers of the Screen Actors Guild discussed the advantages of abandoning jurisdiction over $5.50-a-day extras hired for "atmosphere."

With a basic principle of advancing the economic interests of actors and actresses in the film industry, the Screen Actors Guild officially came into being on June 30, 1933, when articles of incorporation as a non-profit corporation were filed in Sacramento, California. Guild secretary Ken Thompson claimed, "For the first time in motion picture history, there are no class distinctions and no castes among the players. The star and the extra will work together to solve their mutual problems."[2] It was a noble claim, but one far from reality. In fact, at its first meeting, on September 8, 1933, the guild announced that it did not intend to accept extras into membership. It took four years for the guild to gain recognition and a contract with the producers, and its work was largely helped by the number of prominent stars involved in the organization's inception, most notably James Cagney.

There has been some suggestion that working conditions for extras were in some way instrumental in the guild's creation, but this is far from an accurate assessment. As actor Lyle Talbot remembered, "I don't think we knew too much about whether they had problems or not." Historian David F. Prindle wrote: "They didn't know if the extras had problems because they didn't know any extras."[3] It may be true that "actors" and extras did not mix, but almost from its inception, the guild's prominent members were aware of issues facing extras. The latter were not relevant to the guild's creation, but the guild was basically forced to acknowledge the financial and employment issues extras faced. First president Eddie Cantor was quoted in the *Screen Actors News* (December 13, 1933) as saying, "Despite the fact that we have most of the important stars in the Screen Actors Guild, the largest percentage of our membership must come from the extras and bit players. Our greatest work must be to protect the latter groups."

When several thousand actors met at the Hollywood Legion Stadium on May 9, 1937, to consider strike action—averted thanks to the producers' acceptance hours earlier of a union shop contract—bit players and extras were in attendance, along with stars and supporting players. The extras were allowed to join the guild not as full members, but rather as "B" class members, paying an initiation fee of ten dollars, reduced within months to two dollars, and quarterly dues of $1.25. "Predictions are that one-half and perhaps more will refuse to lay out $11.25 when there is no guarantee of even making the original investment back."[4] Throughout the early years of its existence, the guild experienced an ongoing problem as to the differentiation between an "actor" and an extra. The guild's attitude was that only "actors" could speak lines, not extras. The organization to which the extras belonged was dubbed the Junior Screen Actors Guild and formalized at a meeting in Hollywood on January 17, 1934. As junior members, extras were not permitted to vote in guild elections. Because they outnumbered all other groups of performers within the union, the extras could easily have staged a takeover had they been granted the right to vote. Surprisingly, all members of SAG—including extras—were permitted to vote, for the 10th Academy Awards, presented in 1938. According to the *Screen Guild Magazine*, this was the first year that all guild members, junior and senior, were allowed to vote: "Members of the Senior Screen Actors Guild voted on the nominations for acting awards, and finals were voted on by Senior and Junior members, making a total of more than 15,000 people voting."[5]

The Junior Screen Actors Guild was to all intents and purposes a continuation of a fledgling organization, the Motion Picture Extras and Supporting

Players Association, which came into being in 1933, with a charter membership meeting at the Hollywood High School auditorium on November 18 of that year. Character actor Allan Garcia (on screen since at least 1921)[6] lead a group of extras consisting of Larry Sleers, Lee Phelps, J. B. Russell, Una M. Hopkins, and Fred D. Burns, that formed the organization. It worked with the Academy of Motion Picture Arts and Sciences in an attempt to develop a motion picture code under the National Recovery Administration. Owing to problems with "favoritism shown to a very small group which keeps the majority of extras in privation and poverty,"[7] Garcia argued for a rotating schedule for extras. He also called for a top daily rate of pay of $25. The group was so short of money that in the summer of 1933, it actually appealed to Mary Pickford for funds to help send a representative to New York for meetings.

Sadly, Allan Garcia died in September 1938, never to see the eventual unionization of the extras for whom he had so nobly fought. As to favoritism, it was not until May 1951 that the studios—first Warner Bros., then Columbia and Paramount—clamped down on producers, directors, assistant directors, and others requesting specific extras.

The Motion Picture Extras and Supporting Players Association was not alone in 1933 in its efforts to represent extras. Competing organizations included: the Hollywood Picture Players Association, headed by Buckley Russell; Cinema Players, Inc., headed by Carlton E. Griffin; and Riding Actors, headed by Fred Burns. There was also the Singers Guild, with its membership made up of extras working in chorus parts. Some extras belonged to multiple groups, including both the Screen Actors Guild and the theatrically oriented Actors' Equity. All took dues from the modest paychecks of these "mobites," as *Daily Variety* disparagingly called them.

On May 13, 1941, Harry Mayo, chairman of the Extras Advisory Committee of the Screen Actors Guild, organized a mass meeting, where it was announced that a complaint had been lodged with the American Federation of Labor. The complainants sought an investigation of matters involving extras within the guild. Eleven hundred senior or class "A" guild members dominated the 8,000 class "B" members, denying them a vote or any form of representation. As reported in the *Hollywood Citizen News* (May 14, 1941), Mayo claimed:

> We, the extras, special players and bit players, all members of the Screen Actors Guild, are taxed without representation. We are merely card carriers. We pay dues of $18.00 a year per member, yet have no vote or voice in

> the choice of the president or any other officers or the board of directors or the executive secretary or any of the paid employees of the guild.

Mayo also expressed concern that seniority within the ranks of the extras was never a consideration:

> The old timers should be given seniority rights on all street sets, hotel lobbies, racetracks, football games and all scenes where age does not enter. Yet this is not done. Old time extra players who have given five, 10, 20 or even 30 years of their life in the building up of this great industry are being slowly starved out of it because of lack of consideration by the guild, the producers or the granting of seniority rights.

After 1937, extras needed to be members of the Screen Actors Guild in order to be registered with Central Casting and to be qualified for employment. But that same year, the Screen Actors Guild, recognizing that there were too many extras desperate for work, introduced closed shop conditions and would accept no more extras into its ranks. The guild had already reduced the number of extras on its books from 14,500 to 8,500. "Their aim," it was reported, "is to whittle the extra list down to a point where it will be reasonably certain that no extra will makes less than a minimum yearly salary of fifteen hundred dollars."[8] To add to extras' woes, while all who were members of the Screen Actors Guild might be registered with Central Casting, only those earning a minimum of fifty dollars a day could be represented by an independent agent.[9] In fact, it was impossible for extras to earn such an amount, meaning that only bit players and above could have agent representation.

The film industry was not unconcerned at the manner in which extras were treated. Between 1939 and 1940, working in tandem with the Screen Actors Guild, the Motion Picture Producers and Distributors of America sponsored research into the "extra problem" and how the employment structure for extras might be reorganized. Stewart McKee served as chairman of the standing committee, with William S. Holman representing the producers, Murray Kinnell representing the guild, and W. C. Gerard as secretary. The research was undertaken by Dr. Paul A. Dodd, associate professor of economics at UCLA. The recommendations, as reported in the *Hollywood Citizen News* (October 8, 1940), were divided into four sections:

1. Extras who by past employment experience appear better qualified to be accorded preference in work over extras whose services have resulted in only casual employment. Extras who have received through Central Casting Corp. in excess of 10 days' employment in 1939 be entitled to preferential employment
2. The guild agrees to grant waivers permitting the use of non-guild extras at the guild wage scale when the reduction in guild extras make it impossible to fill a call with guild members.
3. If the requirements of the industry warrant it, the guild admit to probationary membership each year a number of young people who shall be admitted to full membership after one or two years if the employment record indicates qualification
4. Re-registering, re-describing and re-classification of extras who qualify for preferential employment

The recommendations were submitted to the extras' council of the Screen Actors Guild, but no effort appears to have been made to act upon them.

One interesting statistical survey published in the report provides a record of the average annual earnings of extras placed through Central Casting, and the average number of days worked in 1936 through 1939:

1936—Average number of days worked per individual, 11.72; average annual earnings per individual, $105.63

1937—Average number of days worked per individual, 18.46; average annual earnings per individual, $187.40

1938—Average number of days worked per individual, 29.77; average annual earnings per individual, $320.95

1939—Average number of days worked per individual, 28.89; average annual earnings per individual, $317.26

While these statistics might suggest that the lot of the extra was improving, more damaging statistics were provided by Mike Jeffers in *The Extra!*, an eight-page newsletter. Only one issue appears to have been published, on June 7, 1941.[10] In June 1937, the price of a pound of butter was thirty cents, and the daily wage of an extra was $8.25. In June 1938, a pound of butter cost thirty-four cents, and the daily wage of an extra was $8.25. A year later, a pound of butter cost thirty-eight cents, and the daily wage of an extra was still unchanged. In June 1940, the daily wage remained unchanged, and a pound of butter cost forty-two cents. In June 1941, a pound of butter cost forty-eight cents, and the daily wage of an extra was still $8.25.

In April 1940, the Screen Actors Guild announced an investigation into reports that racketeering had entered the extra arena. Reportedly, some extras had been terrorized and beaten by hoodlums, and mobsters from the East Coast were actively involved in forcing veteran extras and bit players out of the industry and replacing them with the mobsters' own people.

The Screen Actors Guild did negotiate a minor workplace change for the extra in October 1941. Pointing out that the same people do not go out every night to the same nightclub, the guild insisted that in a movie with two scenes representing different nights in the same nightclub, extras could not change their clothes, take different seats, and keep working. They had to be replaced by new extras. By analogy, cowboys could not double as Indians or vice versa. It was no longer acceptable to be filmed riding up the hill as Indians, change clothes, and again ride up the hill chasing themselves.

In 1942, the Screen Actors Guild boasted six thousand extras among its membership, a considerable reduction in number, freely admitting that there was respectable employment for 2,500 at most. In October of that year, President James Cagney went even further, supporting the notion that the number of "regular, vocational extra players" be reduced to 1,000 or 1,200, with a guaranteed monthly, living wage of $150.00. Two years earlier, the guild considered a recommendation from one of its committees that two thousand extras be dropped from its ranks. As in 1937, the problem was determining which two thousand that should be.

The officers and board of the Screen Actors Guild must have become increasingly irritated by the problem presented by the extras within their membership. As critic Otis Ferguson wrote in 1941, "Extras are a problem not only to themselves but to the unions set up for their betterment."[11] Ultimately, there would be no solution to the lack of work for these lowly industry employees, and whatever changes were suggested, these would be unacceptable to many. On March 29, 1943, the board of directors of the Screen Actors Guild voted to charter an autonomous local for its member extras, with its own officers, governing board, administrative staff, offices, and with control of its own finances. The extras, reportedly now numbering 4,500, could bargain directly with the producers. If the extras rejected the board's proposals, the guild threatened to dissolve itself and reorganize with membership consisting of actors only. The extras were on their own, free to make any alliances they might desire.

The extras were not happy with the new plan for autonomy, in large part because ultimately it did not give them what it promised. The Screen Actors Guild did not plan to relinquish its jurisdiction. A mass meeting was held on October 3, 1943, at the Hollywood Legion Stadium, attended by approximately one thousand extras, as well as leaders of the Screen Actors Guild, led by President James Cagney. Cagney attacked some of the extras for what he claimed to be a plan to establish a new union, which would be in competition with the Screen Actors Guild. In fact, a new union, the Screen Players Union, formed in 1943, already existed, led by extra Mike Jeffers. Jeffers and his cohorts rejected the planned Motion Picture Extras Association, to be established by the Screen Actors Guild, and which would have jurisdiction over those appearing in motion pictures for atmosphere and background purposes only. If an extra were given even a line of dialogue, he would be required to join the Screen Actors Guild—even if the line was not in the script and only decided upon on the set. As it was explained, "Any dialog spoken other than pursuant to the limitations of the preceding sentence would classify the person speaking it as an actor and would bring him or her within the jurisdiction of the SAG and would take him or her out of the jurisdiction of the MPEA." Further, "no jurisdiction would be granted to the MPEA over stunt performers or stunts except that such jurisdiction would be granted over motion picture extras who, employed as extras and not to do stunt work, but who perform stunts which are incidental only to their work as extras."[12] The Motion Picture Extras Association would have no jurisdiction over extras working in New York.

In general, the extras labeled the new plan "illegal" and "disgusting." Many left before the meeting was over, and James Cagney probably wished he were back fighting law officers at Warner Bros. as a gangster instead of trying to cope with Screen Actors Guild extras. He was later to describe extras who sided with the Screen Players Union against the Screen Actors Guild as "troublemakers" and "incorrigibles," according to the *Hollywood Citizen News* (September 22, 1944). Cagney perceived the Screen Players Union as invading the acting field and designed to compete with the Screen Actors Guild. The Screen Players Union responded:

> Mr. Cagney's closing remark of "You the actors are the Guild" more than ever increases the determination of the extra players to have their own union; without which they would forever be the unwanted stepchildren

> of the fabulous "A's"—a predicament which, in the light of the past seven years experience, has not been relished. The extra player is interested in many reforms . . . all of which spring from one main source—to wit, autonomy, their kind. An autonomy worthy of its name, in being and practice.

What had become an internal dispute between actors and extras within the Screen Actors Guild broadened with the appearance of the rival organization, the Screen Players Union. Its chairman, Harry Mayo, led the charge at a hearing before the National Labor Relations Board in March 1944. The Screen Actors Guild argued that it had made no attempt to limit the potential of extras, while the Screen Players Union produced evidence that extras did everything from skating, dancing, and riding to singing and playing speaking parts. Further, the Screen Players Union claimed that wage adjustments for extras negotiated by the Screen Actors Guild in 1941 had actually led to a reduction in salaries for extras and savings for producers.

The accusations and the vitriol continued, with the Screen Players Union advancing the fight for the rights of extras. The union argued that the Screen Actors Guild classified its extras as apprentices, and that, therefore, they would not be qualified for consideration in any bargaining unit. The union demanded that the three-hundred-mile zone around Los Angeles, in which producers were required to employ union extras, be extended to a three-thousand-mile zone. The union made more demands. Mothers chaperoning their children at the studios should receive payments in their own right. If extras were required to "pantomime," an additional twenty-five dollars should be payable. A union representative should also be present at Central Casting "to insure closer cooperation and protection both for the membership and the employer."[13] Call backs from Central Casting should be posted on studio sets by 3:30 a.m., insuring extras had time to check in with Central Casting if they were not needed. In November 1944, extra Hal Craig, on behalf of himself and four thousand other "B" actors, filed a claim with the Wage and Hour Division of the US Department of Labor in Los Angeles alleging that extras were not being paid time-and-a-half for overtime, as required under the Fair Labor Standards Act of 1938.

In December 1944, extras in the Screen Actors Guild voted 1,451 to 456 for the Screen Players Union to be their collective bargaining agency with the American Federation of Labor. The vote was condemned by the Screen Actors Guild, which refused to abide by the decision. George Murphy, then SAG president, announced, "[The] Screen Actors Guild . . . will continue to represent all actors in the motion-picture industry and will continue to assert exclusive jurisdiction over all acting work in the industry."[14]

From March through July 1944, the National Labor Relations Board held hearings about the choice of a collective bargaining agent for Hollywood extras. The transcript of the hearings was sent to Washington, DC, for review and incorporation into an order. In December 1944, extras voted by an overwhelming majority that they did not wish to stay part of the Screen Actors Guild. A jurisdictional fight developed between organizations when both the Screen Players Union and the newly-established Screen Extras Guild (founded in 1945) applied to the Associated Actors and Artistes of America (AAAA),[15] affiliated with the American Federation of Labor, for recognition and membership. Initially, in January 1945, the National Labor Relations Board granted the Screen Players Union jurisdiction as the bargaining agent for extras, but within two months reversed that decision, in all probability influenced by the AAAA's decision to support the Screen Extras Guild. With the Screen Actors Guild also supporting the Screen Extras Guild—in part because of a desire to destroy the Screen Players Union—only the Screen Extras Guild was admitted to membership in the AAAA in July 1945.

With its offices located at 1526 Las Palmas Avenue in Hollywood, the Screen Extras Guild held its first board of directors meeting on June 14, 1945. Among the original 157 founders of the guild were Jean Acker, Brooks Benedict, Dulcie Day, Franklyn Farnum, Bess Flowers, John Ince, Marjorie "Babe" Kane, and Snub Pollard.[16] One of the guild's first orders of business was to set up various admission committees to oversee the various types of extras who would become members, with such categories as cowboys, dress, veterans, stand-in, and dance (divided into three areas: square, ballet, and general).

As David F. Prindle has written,

> Viewed in isolation, the tussle over extras seems a small and obscure episode. Placed in historical context, however, it becomes crucially important. In the course of fighting what was to them a desperately important battle, the leadership of the Screen Actors Guild came to have strong prejudices about who in Hollywood was a friend and who was a foe. Any person or organization who supported them on the extras question would be a potential ally; anyone who endorsed the Screen Players Union would likely be their enemy. And because this contest became entangled in a much larger and more significant conflict, it had momentous consequences.[17]

The jurisdictional dispute came at a time when the major union confederation, IATSE (the International Alliance of Theatrical Stage Employes [*sic*]) and the Moving Picture Machine Operators of the United States and Canada, was in battle with the militant CSU (Conference of Studio Unions), founded in 1941 by Herb Sorrell. The latter included office workers, publicists, painters, cartoonists, and laboratory technicians, but the producers preferred to deal with the more amenable IATSE, and as a result, a thirty-week strike broke out in the spring of 1945. Eventually, IATSE and CSU came to an agreement, known as the Treaty of Beverly Hills, but ultimately the former, led by Roy Brewer, turned against the CSU, which was branded a communist front organization. Brewer was aided in his anti-CSU stance by the Screen Actors Guild and its new president, Ronald Reagan.

Longtime Screen Extras Guild president, the extremely right-wing Richard H. Gordon, explained:

> A small group of troublemakers had led the extras out of the Screen Actors Guild, and now sought to take them into the group supported by the Commies. That's when the rest of the extra players, the majority woke up. Extras, like actors, are fundamentally conservative. They wanted no part of the Red brethren who sought to shut down the film studios for their own subversive aims.[18]

As with other Hollywood unions, the Screen Extras Guild benefited from its refusal to align itself with the Conference of Studio Unions, receiving one million dollars in back pay from the producing entities, according to the *Los Angeles Times* (December 20, 1947). Not surprisingly, during the McCarthy era, the Screen Extras Guild voted on March 2, 1955, by a margin of twenty-five to one to empower its board of directors to expel any member refusing to testify before a "properly constituted Government body" concerning present or former membership in a "Communist or Fascist organization." Leading the campaign was Screen Extras Guild president Richard H. Gordon,[19] who just happened to be a member of the ultra-rightwing Motion Picture Alliance for the Preservation of American Ideals.

The negotiations and eventual recognition of the Screen Extras Guild brought little relief for the membership, 90 percent of which were reported to be unemployed in January 1948. However, the following year, the guild did negotiate a new five-year contract with the producers, establishing new wage rates in some classifications and providing for a union shop and preference in hiring for extras already registered with casting agencies. In 1952, another new contract—this time for six years—was approved, increasing the daily rate for general extras from $15.56 to $18.50, and for dress extras from $22.23 to twenty-five dollars. Within a year, the Screen Extras Guild was in contention with producers, this time over compensation for work performed in more than one picture per day and for the "reuse" of television films.

The Screen Extras Guild was often involved in controversy, notably in 1968, when executive secretary H. O'Neil Shanks became embroiled in a fight with member Ed Kerr, who claimed that Shanks ran the guild like a private club for the benefit of certain board members. In 1972, Shanks was ordered to repay the guild an estimated twenty thousand dollars in legal fees and twenty-four thousand dollars of his salary. In 1986, the Screen Extras Guild seriously considered a merger with the Teamsters. The following year, its board authorized a strike against the producers, which ended after one week. The strike, the first in the guild's history, had little impact and in hindsight appears to have done more harm than good. In 1990, the story of the Screen Extras Guild came full circle when its membership voted for its jurisdiction to be taken over by the Screen Actors Guild. It was an idea first mooted in 1977, again in 1981, and finally in 1989. It was not until July 1994 that all Screen Extras Guild assets were liquidated.

One extra who had a long and checkered history with the Screen Extras Guild was Mike Jeffers, who spent five years litigating against the organization, claiming that it had libeled him. The action stemmed from a statement in the guild's newsletter of April 5, 1950, which stated that Jeffers "likes us to forget that he was once part of the Commie-influenced Conference of Studio Unions, that pulled two disastrous jurisdictional strikes in 1945–46." Jeffers claimed that he was not a communist and that the guild had held him up to ridicule among members of the profession. After three trials—the first ending in a hung jury, the second in a verdict in Jeffers's favor, and the third finding for the guild—Jeffers was ordered to pay substantial costs and vanished from sight.

The Screen Extras Guild, when not fighting with Jeffers, fought hard for decent pay for extras and substantially widened the classifications of its members. The January 3, 1954 revision of the basic agreement between the guild and the Association of Motion Picture Producers, governing the employment of extra players, provided a minimum 5 percent increase in pay for all, and documented the extraordinary descriptive range now used to classify extras. Amounts listed below constitute the daily wage:

A. Stand-In, $17.85

B. Midget, $19.43

C. General Extra, $19.43

D. Photographic Double, $26.25

E. Dress Extra, $26.25

F. Dancers, Skaters & Swimmers

1. Dancers employed or used for dance routines, $26.25
2. Ballet and/or Toe, $31.50
3. Dance-In, $31.50
4. Ice Skaters employed or used in formation routines, $26.25
5. Dancers and Skaters doing lifts, throws, catches and falls, Graded up ward in accordance with work performed.
6. Swimmers employed or used in aquacade formation swimming routines, $26.25

Diving from platform or springboard

7. Three feet and over but less than four feet $26.25
8. Four feet and over but less than six feet $34.13
9. Six feet and over but less than ten feet $42.000

G. Riders

1. Straight riding, $26.25
2. Riding double, $36.75
3. Riding bareback (no stirrups), $39.38
4. Jockeys (riding race horse in actual race), $52.50
5. Riding on a spirited horse (without handler or groom), $36.75
6. On race horse (when held by groom or handler), $26.25

H. Drivers

1. Driving one or two horses, or handling livestock, $26.25
2. Driving four-up, $36.75
3. Driving six-up, $52.50

Sulky Drivers

(a) Driving spirited horse in race, $52.50

(b) Driving spirited horse, $36.75

(c) Spirited horse (held or led by groom), $26.25

I. Singers (Non-Professional—Hired in groups of eight or less)

1. Rehearsing and /or recording, $36.75
2. Mouthing to playback, $26.25

J. Sports

1. Water Polo (actually playing water polo), $39.38
2. Polo (actually playing and polo riding), $52.50

3. Mounted on a polo pony, stick in hand, $26.25
4. Football (actually playing football), $31.50
5. Basketball (actually playing basketball), $31.50
6. Baseball (actually playing professional, collegiate or other similar type), $31.50

K. Riding camel or elephant, $52.50
L. Leading camel or elephant, $36.75
M. Special Ability Extras (including Practical Dealers), $26.25
N. Inserts and wardrobe tests, $19.43
O. Silent bit, $50.00
P. Amputees, $36.75
Q. Motorcycle Driver, $24.25

The only possible category that seems to be missing is pilot. Such individuals had actually already been covered in a September 30, 1946, agreement between the Screen Actors Guild and the major studios. When pilots were engaged to fly or taxi an aircraft before the camera, they were to be paid seventy-five dollars a day or $250 a week. Location rates ("any airport or airfield") were one hundred dollars a day or $250 a week. Additional amounts were payable for wet work ($3.75), and adjustments were made for body makeup, rubber skull caps, or hair goods affixed with spirit gum ($7.08).[20] Most importantly, though, the agreement extended the Screen Extras Guild's jurisdiction to San Francisco, where a seventy-five-mile zone (compared to a 125-mile-zone in Los Angeles) applied before the employment of non-registered extras was permitted. A minimum of 125 extras in Los Angeles and seventy-five in San Francisco had to be employed on large sets before non-registered extras could be hired.

The Screen Extras Guild's authority eventually extended not only to Los Angeles and San Francisco, but also to Las Vegas, Hawaii, and San Diego. In New York, the extras had their own contract, but they were still required to be members of the Screen Actors Guild. It was the guild that negotiated a new ten-year contract, effective January 1, 1946, with East Coast producers. Atmosphere players in New York were to receive a minimum of $10.50 a day.

With the expansion of television production, the guild secured agreement that the first seventy-five to the first one hundred extras hired (depending upon the length of the show) had to be members of the Screen Extras Guild before waivers were issued. If a large number of a particular type of extra was needed but unavailable, then a waiver would automatically be issued. Those individuals working under a waiver were unlikely ever to

The tent accommodation provided for extras and the entire crew on a typical Hollywood production on location, here *Drums Along the Mohawk* (1939).

be invited to join the Screen Extras Guild, in which membership was always heavily restricted. The Screen Extras Guild also recognized the need for younger members between the ages of eighteen and twenty-five, and in December 1953, the organization agreed to allow in twenty-five new members from that age group. At the same time, it was still relatively easy for producers to request certain favored individuals for extra work. In the mid 1950s, Hal Roach, Jr. would routinely write to the Screen Extras Guild, introducing such persons, and stating, "We would like very much to use [name] in some of our forthcoming pictures and would appreciate your efforts in securing [name] a membership in the Screen Extras Guild."[21]

In 1953, for the first time, a form of residual payments was negotiated for extras. If they were seen in the openings and closings of series or in advertising, over and above their original appearances, they were to receive three times the amount earned on the day of employment—subject to their appearances not exceeding thirteen episodes.

As noted above, "midgets," or little people, came into their own with the institution of a special category at the Screen Extras Guild. Obviously, their opportunities for extra work were somewhat limited, but as a group little people became known on screen for their performances as Munchkins—categorized as both extras and bit players—in the 1939 production of *The Wizard of Oz*.[22]

Lesser known as a showcase for little people—and certainly a lesser production—is *The Terror of Tiny Town*, produced a year before *The Wizard of Oz*. A Western, featuring a cast of sixty "midgets," all members of the Screen Actors Guild, *The Terror of Tiny Town* was the brainchild of low budget independent producer Jed Buell. Legend has it Buell was so parsimonious that

The stars of *The Terror of Tiny Town* (1938). AMPAS.

one of the crew from another of his films commented, "If they cut the budget any more, they'll have to make all the actors midgets." And thus was an idea born. Sets were built to scale, miniature animals, including horses, were hired—only the guns were regulation size. "On the Lazy A ranch at Santa Susana, Calif., producer Buell started filming the first all-midget photoplay ever made. He had troubles. The flaccid little people tumbled off ponies, had trouble handling man-sized six guns, had attacks of temperament and sunburn," reported *Time* magazine (August 1, 1938). The film cost between seventy-five and a hundred thousand dollars to make—"big salaries for little people," proclaimed Buell—and should have become a cult classic.

Starring in *The Terror of Tiny Town* as the hero is Billy Curtis, a four feet, two inch, little person, who had appeared as the city father in *The Wizard of Oz*, and also worked as a wrestler when screen employment was unavailable. Curtis, with an oversize cigar always in his mouth, was something of a character. I can recall his hanging out at the Ontra Cafeteria in Hollywood in the early 1970s, regaling customers with stories about his career and about being married six times, "three times seriously, three not so seriously."

Billy Curtis had entered films, appearing in a short subject, in the early 1930s. As a member of the Screen Extras Guild, he and other little people announced in the summer of 1947 that they planned to hire out as stand-ins for children:

> We stand-in for any kid entitled to a stand-in for any picture . . . The result is fewer kids, fewer kids' mothers on a set. The studio saves money, time and transportation on all three. For instance, children have to knock off every three or four hours by law; we're there right through from early morning till late at night. What's more, when there's a stunt to be done we can do it!
>
> Most of all, we're a set thing; kids aren't. A Shirley Temple moves out and a Margaret O'Brien moves in; Darryl Hickman grows up and Butch Jenkins takes his place. We stay the same. All they have to do is rotate us for size![23]

Curtis doubled for Bobby Driscoll in a thirty-six-foot fall for *The Window* (1949), and he was a stand-in for Jimmy Hunt in *The Mating of Millie* (1947). Around the same time, other little people—including Johnny Banbury, George Havens, and Charlotte Sullvian—were doubling for Peter Miles in *The Red Pony* (1949), and for Butch Jenkins, Margaret O'Brien, and other juveniles. It was pointed out that the cigar which remained steadfastly in Curtis's mouth helped fend off any children who might try to bully them. The 1948 musical *April Showers* features Jack Carson as a vaudevillian who passes off his son, appearing with him onstage, as a "midget." The film contains an incident borrowed from Billy Curtis. Accused of being an underage child working in vaudeville, Curtis confronted his accusers, smoking a cigar and asking, "What do you want?"

In 1970, Billy Curtis led a drive to give "midgets" full membership in the Screen Actors Guild. Two years earlier, he had appeared as a simian child in *Planet of the Apes*. Not only was he not cast as a little person, the production cast him as a non-person. Curtis died in Dayton, Nevada, on November 9, 1988, at the age of seventy-nine.

The best known of little people was undoubtedly Billy Barty (1925–2000), measuring three feet, nine inches. He began is career on screen in 1927, and was best known for his silent, scene-stealing moments in two 1933 Warner Bros. musicals, *Footlight Parade* and *Gold Diggers of 1933*. While he did not appear in *The Wizard of Oz*, in 1981, Barty was hired by Warner Bros. to coordinate the casting of 150 little people in a spoof of the making of the film, titled *Under the Rainbow*. When a star honoring Barty was placed on the Hollywood Boulevard Walk of Fame in 1981, its placement indicated Barty's superior status in the ranks of extras and bit players.

Those little people willing to don blackface and black body makeup were assured jobs as pygmies in a handful of Hollywood films, beginning in 1932 with *Tarzan the Ape Man*, which provided employment for some fifty of them. From Tarzan in 1932, Johnny Weissmuller progressed to Jungle Jim, and his 1950 film, *Pygmy Island*, included sixty-five little people wearing makeup and black wigs portraying islanders. Billy Curtis was there, along with his pal Jerry Maren, who had also appeared in *The Wizard of Oz*, and who had toured with Curtis for the USO during World War II. Other little people in the cast included: Angelo Rossito, who operated a newsstand on Hollywood Boulevard; bookkeeper Marion Nichols; Buster Resmondo, billed as "The World's Smallest Cowboy Fiddler"; Resmondo's wife, Hazel; ranch worker Wayne Johnson; Johnson's wife, Lillie; bookbinder Mary Brown; and Jeanette Fern, a night club dancer billed as "The Miniature Sally Rand."

Chapter Twelve

"EXTRAS, EXTRAS, READ ALL ABOUT 'EM"

"Extras, Extras, Read All about 'Em" is a phrase—often used as the title of an article—that has seemed to crop up a great deal in more recent years. Perhaps the increased frequency of its use indicates a modern approach to the role of the extra. Gone are the stories of sexual harassment and of men and women eking out a pathetic existence against all odds. Gone are the stories of star-struck girls heading to Hollywood and becoming extras on the first step of the ladder to stardom. Instead, the work of the extra, en masse or individually, provides reliable copy when there is nothing else to write about. The truth is that the extras of more recent vintage are not very interesting, despite their continuing desire to vote themselves awards. In 1986, in Chicago, it was the Spark Awards, the "Sparky,"[1] given—incredibly enough—in fourteen categories, including dependability, courage, resilience, and frustration. In 2007, Sweden introduced the Silver Fish Awards, with seven categories, including "most sacrificing" (including head shaving) and "rookie of the year" (for those who moved up from the ranks of extras).

One overlooked element of an extra's life is that there is often a permanent—and very public—record of his or her maturation. Extras themselves might get some satisfaction in watching their colleagues age together on screen. In 1975, Gerald Mast, then a distinguished college professor, recalled his early life in Hollywood as an extra, beginning in 1958:

> I got a start recently while watching *Young Frankenstein* [1974] when, in the scene of Dr. Frankenstein's medical class, I suddenly found myself looking at the familiar faces of extras. Many of them were literally the same faces with whom I had worked 15 years earlier. We had sat together in high school with Tuesday Weld in *Because They're Young*; we had sat together with Tony Perkins in *Tall Story*; we had graduated together with Paula Prentiss and Connie Francis, in *Where the Boys Are*. Now they had made it to medical school. Perhaps Mel Brooks' decision to use ordinary,

old-style extras was part of his film's parodic conception, for those extras are as much a part of the dead movie past as the Frankenstein genre.[2]

As the 1950s drew to a close, extras remained active within the industry, often facing new challenges and demands. Some 250 were hired to appear in the battle scenes for *Spartacus* (1960) and paid $22.05 a day. The highest paid extras in the film were those playing crucified, rebellious slaves, lining the road to Rome; the going rate for crucifixion, it was reported, was two hundred dollars a day.[3] In what surely must be something of an exaggeration, one extra, Karl Brindle, reported hanging on a cross for three months during production. For the screen adaptation of John O'Hara's novel *From the Terrace* (1960), set in the 1940s and shot in New York, eighty-five extras were hired as appropriately-attired pedestrians, and thirty extras who owned 1940s vintage automobiles were also put on the payroll Rather like the dress extras of the golden age, today's extra might be hired not for his or her appearance, but for what he or she owns.

The Naked and the Dead (1958) was shot on location in Panama, standing in for a South Pacific island. Standing in for the usual Hollywood extras who might have been hired for the production were 250 US troops from Fort Kobbe in the Panama Canal Zone. The *New York Times* reported:

> Jumping and scrambling ashore from LST's was good practice in the opinion of their commander, Maj. Gen. Thomas L. Harrold. One vehicle fouled on a reef in an all-too-natural accident. Once ashore, the soldiers moved into a mess and pup tents (circa 1943) in a grove of cocoanut palms just outside of the little Panamanian village of Cameron.
>
> Several G.I.'s graduated to bit roles, as did a Canal Zone civilian who will be seen as a chaplain. From the Army also were recruited about a dozen men, all of Japanese descent, who were born in Hawaii or Guam. They "fought" bravely for the cameras as the "enemy."[4]

New genres could offer new moneymaking opportunities for extras. During filming of the *Planet of the Apes* series, which began in 1968, extras playing apes received a basic wage of fifty-five dollars a day to compensate for an early morning makeup call at 4:30 a.m. With various adjustments for type of work required, a good extra might make as much as $150 a day.

Foreshadowing what extras would have to contend with in the future, in the battle scenes of *Spartacus*, live extras were supplemented with 150 dummies, purchased at a cost of forty-five dollars each. This is one of the earliest

Cowboy extras provide verisimilitude to *The Gallant Legion* (1948), supposedly filmed on location in Texas. The "Hollywoodland" (later "Hollywood") sign gives the lie to this claim.

recorded uses of non-human extras, and it was to set a trend. It quickly became apparent that it was far more cost effective to use dummies and add crowd noises than to employ large numbers of extras. Companies with the improbable names of Crowd in a Box and Inflatable Crowd Co. sold inflatable vinyl torsos, which stood in for the crowds in *Million Dollar Baby* (2004), *Be Cool* (2005), and *Oceans Thirteen* (2007). For *Seabiscuit* (2003), Inflatable Crowd Co. provided some seven thousand inflatable extras, life-size dolls without arms or legs that could easily be attached to seating with the use of Velcro. The *Seabiscuit* dummies were the creation of Joe Biggins of the DreamWorks development department. They might not be able to move or to act, but they could be deflated so that ten thousand could fit in a fifty-foot truck. "Like digital extras and cardboard cutouts, they don't require lunch and bathroom breaks, and they won't snap secret photos of, say, Brad Pitt for *Us* Weekly. They similarly refuse to complain about paltry pay, long hours or cold weather. . . . What's more, each comes with a free patch kit."[5]

One new area that opened up to extras in the 1960s and 1970s was the television soap opera. For CBS's *The Guiding Light*, Betty Ross would interview would-be extras three days a week, with her main concern that new recruits not trip over a cable and sue the network. Generally the same extras routinely worked in soap operas, a practice that meant familiar faces might be spotted in three soap operas airing on the same day. Some extras were lucky to gain recurring roles. For example, on *The Guiding Light*, Tom Kelsey played a court stenographer, Fred Porcelli appeared as a maître d', and Julie Wiener performed the role of an operating room nurse. In the 1980s, extras had an issue with one casting agency, Rich Mar, which operated a closed shop when hiring extras for the major nighttime soap operas *Hotel*, *Knots Landing*, and *Dallas*.

The era of the nighttime soap operas has ended, and the daytime soap opera is in its death throws. Both developments spell a decline in the work available to extras, as one more genre disappears from the scene. It is unfortunate that no one has yet figured out a way for "real" extras to be used in new entertainment media, such as video games.

The increase in violence-directed productions, often falling under the rubric of "biker" or "road" movies, meant an expansion in the need for appropriate-looking extras. In the early 1980s, Dutch Van Dalsem, a former guard at the Correction Training Facility at Soledad, California, founded Rent-a-Gang, providing motorcycle gangs for Sylvester Stallone movies such as *Cobra* (186) and *Over the Top* (1987), as well as *Lost in America* (1985), *Ruthless People* (1986), and various crime-oriented television series, such as *Cagney and Lacey* and *L.A. Law*. "These guys look bad because they *were* bad-ultra-tough ex-cons, assorted outlaws and hoods, bad-ass bikers," noted one reporter.[6]

The Hollywood extra is protected by a union and by contractual obligations. And yet, it seems almost as if all these protections are unnecessary. The new breed of extra is often no longer a professional, but rather a star-struck fan hoping to work her or his way up through the ranks. Hollywood extras are frequently housewives earning a little extra money on the side—much as in the 1910s—or workers looking for a second job with flexible hours.

By the 1970s, many producers were advertising for unpaid extras through flyers and leaflets posted on telephone poles and the like throughout Los Angeles. When a large number of extras was needed to fill the Los Angeles Coliseum for *Two Minute Warning* (1976), the first 125 were members of the Screen Extras Guild, but the remaining 475 came off the street, interested in a day's pay, a free lunch, and the opportunity to watch a football game. Shooting at a prison facility for *Harry and Walter Go to New York* (1975), Columbia decided simply to hire sixty-five of the inmates at the Ohio State Reformatory in Mansfield, Ohio, as extras. The inmates were not paid, but the studio was required to contribute to a state-run fund and to provide a television and some newly released films free of charge for the entertainment of the prisoners.

The lure of free food has always been a factor in employment as an extra. As one individual pointed out, upon arrival on the set in the morning, "the first thing I do is look for the coffee and doughnuts and the bagels and cream cheese."[7] It was cold MacDonald's hamburgers and checks for thirty dollars that the producer had on offer for the junkies and the homeless of Harlem who were willing to work in *Who's the Man?* (1993). Maybe not in Harlem, but the lure of stardom is another motivator—although now it is not the potential to become a star, but rather the possibility of sitting down with the stars to share the same food from the catering truck. The realization that stars today do not eat with lesser mortals—and generally do not even eat in the studio commissary—has not trickled down to the extra level. And such opportunities may be few and far between, working on location can be a most attractive proposition if the location is somewhere warm and close to a beach. For many extras, location work amounts to a free vacation.

When recession hit, many out-of-work residents of Los Angeles signed on with Central Casting. Now operating out of a warehouse in Burbank, the organization would register anyone over eighteen with proof of citizenship or legal residency and twenty-five dollars to spare. A reported three hundred a week where signing on in 2009. As a spokesperson explained, "Whenever there's a downturn in the economy, we see an increase in the number of people applying for background work."[8] Unfortunately, the downturn also applied to the film studios and the television networks, resulting in a decrease in need for extras.

Aside from Central Casting, a new venue for extras to register is Hollywood OS, with its online service, ExtraCastingGuild.com, founded by Angela Bertolino. Extras are registered on line, and casting directors can search the site free of charge. The same claim could not be made by other casting agencies. As the recession hit in 2010 and 2011, the Screen Actors Guild reported that of the twenty-three thousand members classified as "background artists" (extras), only eleven hundred earned enough—a minimum of $14,800 a year—to qualify for the guild's health plan. As income diminished, extras were often forced to pay casting companies (sometimes multiple entities) or online services, which posted photographs and provided access to casting information. California law forbade talent agencies from charging a fee just to apply for work, and as a result, in May 2011, the Los Angeles city attorney sent cease-and-desist letters to some fourteen casting companies, including Entertainment Partners, the owner of Central Casting, which was charging $25 for photographic/electronic image processing.

The new breed of extras is generally less expectant of stardom. As one writer put it, "Extras don't become actors, actors become extras!"[9] Or as Otis Pembroke, an extra since the 1940s, remarked, "A star can say he's been in thirty, maybe forty pictures. I've been in two thousand."[10] They might not want to be stars, but extras welcome the opportunity to say a line or to have what is described as a "silent bit." The latter is a means by which producers can save money and avoid hiring Screen Actors Guild members. A player can ask an extra a question on camera, and the extra can respond, with a gesture. The gesture, the "silent bit," could earn the extra as much as eighty-five dollars more than his base pay in the 1970s. If a director should decide a spoken line was necessary, the extra would be paid off in the former capacity and rehired at the SAG minimum—providing, of course, he was a member of the guild. (In the early 1970s, it was reported that 80 percent of extras belonged to the Screen Actors Guild, a percentage that is steadily decreasing.) Non-union members assigned speaking roles, or special parts, would be given vouchers by the assistant directors. Once an extra had three such vouchers, he would be eligible to apply for membership in SAG. Assistant directors were often "courted" by extras in an effort to obtain these highly desirable vouchers. At the same time, the extra had to decide if it was financially viable for him to join the union. Was he better off working in non-union productions? Could he afford the initiation fee and first-year membership? The "omnie" or ordinary extra of recent years is always watching for parts that demand something beyond the normal requirements—the "whammy," as it is called.

"Extras! Extras! Read All about Them," headlined The [London] *Times* in 2004. The story revolved around a new BBC/HBO comedy series from Ricky Gervais and Stephen Merchant. *Extras*, which first aired on the BBC in September 2005, featured Gervais as Andy Millman, a disposable scene-filler supported by Ashley Jensen as Maggie. The latter was more at peace with her role in life as an extra, whereas Andy was desperate for a line of dialogue. Over the two seasons it ran, *Extras* became a depressingly realistic sitcom. The series, which featured a star cameo in each episode and concerned the "banal dreams of extras,"[11] won both a BAFTA and an Emmy for its star and co-creator.

Thanks to *Extras*, the viewing public gained a different perspective on the lives and careers of these purveyors of atmosphere. Extras ceased to be tragic, desperate, or even hard working, and became instead not merely figures of fun, but endearing personages (in Gervais's peculiar way), with dreams and enthusiasm. It might even be argued that with *Extras*, the extra became the star—on BBC and HBO, if not on the studio lots and locations of Hollywood.

In the beginning, the work of the extra might be depicted as both a fascinating experience and a tragic one. Today, thanks to *Extras* and a drastic change in public perception, there is no glamor associated with the profession, neither is there any genuine sorrow. Working as an extra is nothing more than an irrelevant job for an irrelevant minority.

NOTES

EPIGRAPH

First published in *Photoplay*, March 1925, p. 125.

INTRODUCTION

1. Beulah Bondi conversation with Anthony Slide, October 23, 1976.
2. Milton Sills in Joseph P. Kennedy, ed., *The Story of the Film*, p. 177.
3. John Scott, "Hindu Caste System Has Parallel among Actors," p. B13.
4. Michelle Morgan contract dated July 29, 1942; *Passage to Marseilles* picture file in Warner Bros. Archives at University of Southern California.
5. Amy S. Jennings, "An Extra in Hollywood," p. 653.
6. Rob Wagner, *Film Folks*, p. 211.
7. Fred W. Beetson, "The Operation of a Central Casting Bureau," pp. 82–83.
8. John Hanlon, "The Town of Types," p. 73.
9. Jack Lait, "The Hollywood As Iz," p. 3.
10. Vachel Lindsay, *The Art of the Moving Picture*, p. 47.
11. Quoted in Rudy Behlmer, *America's Favorite Movies: Behind the Scenes*, p. 80.
12. This story has been told many times with slightly different dialogue. As far as I can ascertain, the earliest report appears in the September 15, 1940, issue of the *Chicago Sunday Tribune*. The extra may have called DeMille something other, and worse, than a baboon, and DeMille's response may have been simply a one-word command: "Lunch."
13. "Cleopatra's Director," p. X2.
14. Myrtle Gebhart, "Why One Hundred Thousand Failed," p. 61.
15. Margaret Reid, "Looking On with an Extra Girl," *Picture-Play*, April 1925, p. 98.
16. Pauline Wagner interview with Anthony Slide, February 16, 2010.
17. Kevin Thomas to Anthony Slide, May 12, 2011.
18. Nathan S. Dyches, "Hollywood's 'Four Hundred,'" p. 38.
19. "Another Work Army—It's in Hollywood," p. 1.
20. In fact, based on a report that the stuntmen working on *Gunga Din* on location at Lone Pine earned a total of $85,353.97, the figure is probably correct. The price paid was deserved in that "RKO Radio Pictures gained a group of persons who knew how to do their work well," *Bulletin of the Screen Actors Guild*, November 1938, p. 5.
21. Quoted in Heidi Kanaga, "Making the 'Studio Girl': The Hollywood Studio Club and Industry Regulation of Female Labour," p. 134. However, in contradiction, *Motion*

Picture Magazine in 1917 claimed that "Sex relationships may be regarded with less prurient curiosity and intolerance than distinguish those employed in less aesthetic occupations, but in no other vocation is clean living more necessary to secure, much less to keep work." H. Sheridan Bickers, "Extra Ladies and Gentlemen," p. 80.

22. Corinne Lowe, "The Hope That Springs," p. 39.
23. Otis Ferguson, "Hollywood Footnote," p. 670.
24. H. Sheridan-Bickers, "Extra Ladies and Gentlemen," p. 85.
25. Joseph Henabery, *Before, In and After Hollywood*, p. 123.
26. "Former Extras Graduate," p. 61.
27. "Real Mertons of Movies a Problem at Hollywood," p. XX9.
28. Bennie Zeidman, "The Extra Girl," p. 45.
29. Georges Sadoul, "Louis Lumière: The Last Interview," *Sight and Sound*, Summer 1948, pp. 68–70.
30. Helen G. Smith, "The Extra Girl Is Handed a Few Snickers," p. 108.

CHAPTER 1

1. The "supers" were also at times designated "thinking parts," in which actors were not required to speak, but presumably needed to think what they were doing.
2. H. Sheridan-Bickers, "Extra Ladies and Gentlemen," *Motion Picture Magazine*, September 1917, p. 80.
3. Corinne Low, "The Hope That Springs," p. 112.
4. Information from Harry Carr, "Wild Extras I Have Known."
5. "Movie 'Extras' Whose Lives Rival Screen Romance," p. 69.
6. Information from Helen Carlisle, "Odd Folks of Hollywood."
7. H. Sheridan-Bickers, "Extra Ladies and Gentlemen," *Motion Picture Magazine*, September 1917, p. 81.
8. Helen Carlisle, "Odd Folks of Hollywood," p. 30.
9. H. Sheridan-Bickers, "Extra Ladies and Gentlemen," *Motion Picture Magazine*, August 1917, p.95.
10. Thomas H. Ince, "The Type Actor," p. 234.
11. Rob Wagner, *Film Folks*, p. 214.
12. Ibid.
13. Ibid, p. 235.
14. Ibid, p. 236.
15. For more information, see Ted Breton, "Mobilizing an Army for Moving Pictures."
16. Katharine Anne Porter telephone conversation with Anthony Slide, September 29, 1975.
17. Horace A. Fuld, "The Fakes and Frauds in Motion Pictures," p. 112.
18. Rob Wagner, "Supes and Supermen," p. 33.
19. Joseph E. Henabery, *Before, In and After Hollywood*, p. 124.
20. "Men Who Refuse to Work Before the Camera in Nude for One Dollar per Day in Hot Sun, Meet, Organize and Pass Resolution," *The Citizen*, March 24, 1916, p. II1.
21. Alfred A. Cohn, "What Every Girl Wants to Know," p. 28.
22. At least according to Billy Bitzer's remembrance in *His Story: The Autobiography of D. W. Griffith's Master Cameraman*, New York: Farrar Straus and Giroux, 1973, pp. 136–37.
23. Karl Brown, *Adventures with D. W. Griffith*, New York: Farrar, Straus and Giroux, p. 34.
24. Bennie Zeidman, "The Extra Girl," p. 48.
25. Quoted in H. Sheridan-Bickers, "Extra Ladies and Gentlemen," *Motion Picture Magazine*, August 1917, p. 96.

26. Robert E. McIntyre is believed to have joined Goldwyn in 1917, after moving from his hometown of Philadelphia. He died in Los Angeles in June 1952 at the age of sixty-nine.
27. Robert O. McIntyre, "The Still Hunt for New Faces," *Photoplay*, May 1922, p. 41.
28. Ruth Waterbury, "The Truth about Breaking into the Movies," *Photoplay*, January 1927, pp.106–7.
29. Priscilla Bonner interview with Anthony Slide, Spring 1972.
30. "Fineman Planning to Solve Extra Problem," p. A7.
31. Frances Denton, "Ride, Swim and Dance," p. 97.
32. Alfred A. Cohn, "What Every Girl Wants to Know," p. 31.
33. Frances Denton, "Ride, Swim and Dance," p. 97.
34. Samuel F. Kingston, "Casting for Pictures," p. 427.
35. Marilynn Conners, *What Chance Have I in Hollywood: The Mystery of the Movies*, p. 10.
36. Fred Datig to Anthony Slide, April 20, 2009.
37. Quoted in Laurence A. Hughes, ed., *The Truth about the Movies by the Stars*, p. 285.
38. Paul Bradley interview with Anthony Slide, June 3, 1994.
39. Some of the later films in which Bradley recalled appearing are *The Honeymoon Machine* (1961), *A Global Affair* (1964), *How to Murder Your Wife* (965), *Our Man Flint* (1966), and *In Cold Blood* (1967). He may also be seen in *4 for Texas* (1963), not in person but as the subject of an oil painting on the wall.
40. Joseph F. Poland, "Storming the Studio," p. 101.
41. Named for Famous Players-Lasky/Paramount producer, Jesse L. Lasky
42. Cedric Belfrage, *Promised Land: Notes for a History*, p. 120.

CHAPTER 2

1. "Hollywood Warns Film-Struck Extras," p. 23.
2. Ibid.
3. Thomson Burtis was to become a prominent author of juvenile novels with flying themes, including the Russ Farrell series from 1924–29 and the Rex Lee series from 1928–32. He also authored *Daredevils of the Air* (1932) and worked as an occasional Hollywood writer.
4. Dorothea Knox, "What Every Extra Knows," *Picture-Play*, October 1922, p. 58.
5. Ibid, p. 59
6. Dorothea Knox, "What Every Extra Knows," *Picture-Play*, November 1922, p. 68.
7. Myrtle Gebhart, "Why One Hundred Thousand Failed," p. 60.
8. Ibid, p. 61.
9. Ibid, p. 67.
10. "Drilling the Picture 'Mobs,'" p. X4.
11. Otis Ferguson, "Hollywood Footnote," p. 670.
12. "Griffith Forced to Re-Take Scenes in 'Mother and Law,'" *Variety*, April 7, 1916, p. 3.
13. Souvenir program for *Noah's Ark*, p. 15.
14. "Facts from the Studio about *Noah's Ark*," souvenir program, pp. 6–7.
15. Souvenir program for *Noah's Ark*, p. 14.
16. There is no contemporary documentation on what actually happened. The *New York Times*, March 10, 1929, p. X8, provides information as to the quantity of water used.
17. Loretto Coffield Clarke "What It Means to Be an 'Extra,'" pp. 38–39.
18. Frederick F. Isaac, "Working in a Hollywood Mob," p. 6.
19. Hal G. Evarts, "Movie Extras Win Plaudits," p. B17.
20. "Real Mertons of Movies a Problem at Hollywood," p. XX9.

21. Mignon Rittenhouse, "The Pleasures of Poverty Row," p. 69.
22. Ibid, p. 118.
23. An extra girl, "On the Set with Valentino," p. 64.
24. Pauline Wagner interview with Anthony Slide, February 16, 2010.
25. Quoted in Brian Taves, *Robert Florey: The French Expressionist*, pp. 89–90.
26. Benjamin B. Hampton, *A History of the Movies*, pp. 210–11.

CHAPTER 3

1. " After Office Hours," p. 33.
2. Alfred A. Cohn, "What Every Girl Wants to Know," p. 31.
3. Myrtle Gebhart, "The Studio Club Grows Up," p. 84.
4. Ruth Waterbury, "The Truth about Breaking into the Movies," *Photoplay*, January 1927, p. 38.
5. T. Howard Kelly, "Fund Raised to Create Home for Horde of Screen-Struck Girls Invading Hollywood," p. 4.
6. Quoted in Heidi Kenaga, "Making the 'Studio Girl': The Hollywood Studio Club and Industry Regulation of Female Labour," p. 137.
7. Waterbury, Ruth, "The Truth about Breaking into the Movies," *Photoplay*, December 1926, p. 32.
8. Elizabeth McGaffey, "The Studio Club," p. 87.
9. Erskine Johnson, "A Port in a Storm for Movie-Struck Girls," p. SM2
10. "Hollywood Better Says Girls' Adviser," p. E19.
11. Jean Muir, "Boarding House of Broken Hearts," p. 135.
12. Evelyn Keyes, *Scarlett O'Hara's Younger Sister: My Lively Life in and out of Hollywood*, p. 26.
13. Philip K. Scheuer, "Lonely Girls Find Home at Studio Club," p. C3.
14. Leon Surmelian, "Part of the Show," p. 66.
15. Winfrid Kay Thackrey, *Member of the Crew*, p. 204.
16. Doris Nolan interview with Anthony Slide, October 1996.
17. Lynn Simross, "Studio Club Closes Doors on Memories," p. 1.
18. Quoted in Kirk Crivello, "The Hollywood Studio Club," p. 29.

CHAPTER 4

1. Murray Ross, "Hollywood Extras," p. 223.
2. It is not clear if this is a successor to the Screen Service Bureau, opened in 1917.
3. Quoted in Heidi Kenaga, "Making the 'Studio Girl': The Hollywood Studio Club and Industry Regulation of Female Labour," p. 132.
4. "Mob of Extras," p. 23.
5. "Coast Meeting over Extras Conditions," p. 29.
6. "Regulating 'Extras,'" p. 29.
7. *The Problem of the Extra Player*, original manuscript, pp. 148–49.
8. "Hays Begins Clean-Up of Hollywood Today," *New York Times*, January 25, 1926, p. 22.
9. "Hays Lauds Film Bureau," p. I3.
10. Jack Harrower, "Scientific Casting," p. 5.
11. No. 5 in the series, with the girl now called Judy Keene, *Photoplay*, June 1927.
12. "New Deal for Central," p. 7.

13. In the spring of 1933, plans were announced for an artists' service bureau, which would register unemployed directors, writers, and players, and operate on a cooperative basis. The idea was that once a contract expired, the worker could only obtain future employment through the bureau. Nothing seems to have come of the notion, which was obviously highly flawed.
14. "Hollywood Bay Window Is Watched," p. MR7.
15. Ibid.
16. "Bureau Gateway to Pictures," p. A8.
17. Susan Squire, "The Road to Extradom," p. 24.
18. "Central at Work," p. 12.
19. Undated Warner Bros. press release from Ken Whitmore.
20. Ruth Waterbury, "The Mother Confessor of Hollywood," p. 94.
21. Douglas W. Churchill, "A Casting Machine for Hollywood's Hopefuls," p. X4.
22. Ibid.
23. "Central Casting Corporation," unpaged.
24. Ruth Waterbury, "The Truth about Breaking into the Movies," *Photoplay*, December 1926, p. 92.
25. Jack Harrower, "Scientific Casting," p. 5.
26. *The Problem of the Extra Player*, original manuscript, p. 117.
27. Ruth Waterbury, "Don't Go to Hollywood!," p. 126.
28. "Central Casting," unpaged.
29. "Casting Figures Out," p. A7.
30. *Daily Variety*, September 6, 1933, p. 11.
31. "Ask Committee to Supervise All Casting Offices," p. 4.
32. Sara Hamilton, "The Tragedy of 15,000 Extras," p. 94.
33. "Glamour at $8.97 a Week," p. X4.
34. "Central Casting Will Reopen Interviews," p. 8.
35. Will Hays in Joseph Kennedy, ed., *The Story of the Films*, pp. 41–42.
36. Information from "Central Casting," unpaged.
37. Murray Ross, *Stars and Strikes: Unionization of Hollywood*, pp. 83, 84.
38. Kenneth Macgowan, *Behind the Screen*, p. 304.
39. Murray Ross, "Hollywood Extras," p. 222.

CHAPTER 5

1. Adela Rogers St. Johns had earlier written a novel, *The Skyrocket*, in which the principal character, Sharon Kimm, begin her Hollywood career as a bathing beauty and extra.
2. Adela Rogers St. Johns, "The Port of Missing Girls," *Photoplay*, March 1927, p. 29.
3. Ibid, p. 141.
4. Ibid, p. 28.
5. John Parris Springer, *Hollywood Fictions: The Dream Factory in American Popular Culture*, p. 142.
6. Ibid, p. 147.
7. Other "Hollywood Novels" dealing in whole or in part with extras are Florenz Branch, *The Fleshpots* (1944); Robert Carson, *The Bride Saw Red* (1943) and *Love Affair* (1958); Phyllis Gordon Demarest, *Hollywood Gold*; Sandra Hochman, *Happiness Is Too Much Trouble* (1976); E. Nils Holstius, *Hollywood Through the Back Door* (1937); Wayne

Karlin, *The Extras* (1989); James D. O'Hanlon, *Murder at Malibu* (1937), *Murder at 300 to 1* (1938), *Murder at Coney Island* (1939), *As Good as Murdered* (1940), and *Murder at Horsethief* (1941), all featuring Hollywood extras turned amateur sleuths, Jason and Pat Cordry; Carol Snyder, *Ike & Mama and the Once-in-a-Lifetime Movie* (1981); Charles E. Van Loan, *Buck Parvin at the Movies* (1919), in which one of the stories, "The Extra Man and the Milkfed Lion," as its title suggests, features an extra.

8. *Merton of the Movies* was filmed in 1924, 1932 (as *Make Me a Star*), and 1947. The 1932 Harold Lloyd vehicle *Movie Crazy* obviously owes something to *Merton of the Movies*.
9. Reported in *Newsweek*, August 1, 1975.
10. Ruth Waterbury, "The Truth about Breaking into the Movies," January 1927, p. 39.
11. Ibid, p. 108.
12. Ibid, p. 108.
13. Ruth Waterbury, "Don't Go to Hollywood!," p. 125.
14. Theodore Dreiser, "Hollywood: Its Morals and Manners," February 1922, p. 66.
15. Marilyn Conners, *What Chance Have I in Hollywood: The Mystery of the Movies*, p. 10.
16. Ibid, p. 12.
17. Jack Lait, "The Hollywood As Iz," p. 3.
18. Gladys Hall, "Confessions of an Extra Girl," p. 83.
19. There are at least two modern, book-length volumes in which the central character is an extra. The first is a novel in verse about an Australian farm boy of German descent whose career includes that of a Hollywood extra, appearing in *All Quiet on the Western Front*. The other, *The Girl in Alfred Hitchcock's Shower*, by Robert Graysmith (Berkley, 2010) is basically the story of the author's fixation on Marli Renfro, who, among other things, was Janet Leigh's body double in the shower scene from *Psycho*. Reference should perhaps also be made to *The Extra* by Elizabeth Sims (Minotaur Books, 2009), in which the central character becomes an extra in order to raise money, dons a police uniform for a low-budget film, and becomes embroiled in an attack.
20. As far as I can ascertain, there was only one recorded murder of a Hollywood extra in the 1920s and 1930s. On April 27, 1927, Tom Kerrick, who worked as a cowboy extra, was shot and killed by his wife in the climax to a wild Hollywood party. Sarah Kerrick was found guilty of manslaughter, but released after serving only a six-month sentence. For more information, see the *New York Times*, April 28, 1927, p. 25, and the *Los Angeles Times*, November 8, 1927, p. A2.
21. Norman Lloyd conversation with Anthony Slide, January 19, 2011.
22. Page 163.
23. Page 312.
24. Page 317.
25. David Stenn, "It Happened One Night . . . at MGM," p. 298.
26. Clara Weatherwax, "Ain't Hollywood Romantic?," p. 17.
27. Ibid.
28. Fred Datig to Anthony Slide, April 20, 2009.
29. Robert Young, Jr., *Roscoe "Fatty" Arbuckle: A Bio-Bibliography*, p. 71.
30. Pauline Wagner interview with Anthony Slide, February 16, 2010.
31. *The Problem of the Extra Player*, original manuscript, p. 121.
32. Margaret Reid, "Looking on with an Extra Girl," *Picture-Play*, March 192, p. 18.
33. The film industry itself did not necessarily present the life of the extra in negative terms. The 1926 Paramount feature, *Miss Brewster's Millions*, stars Bebe Daniels as an impoverished Hollywood extra, Polly Brewster, who inherits one million dollars. Forced to invest rather than spend the money, she buys into a film company

and makes a handsome profit. The story is, of course, a feminized version of the 1905 George Barr McCutcheon novel, *Brewster's Millions*.

34. "Confessions of an Extra Girl," *Modern Screen*, January 1936, p. 79.

CHAPTER 6

1. Murray Ross, *Stars and Strikes: Unionization of Hollywood*, p. 86.
2. Katherine Albert, "The Passing of the Extra Girl," p. 30.
3. Ibid, p. 122.
4. Ibid.
5. Roland Francis, "The New Extra Girl," p. 122.
6. Elena Boland, "Chorus Ranks Luring Extras," p. B9.
7. Ibid, p. B10.
8. Ibid.
9. Ibid.
10. "Casting Audible Pictures," p. X3.
11. Leon Surmelian, "Part of the Show," p. 68.
12. James O. Spearing, "The 'Chorus Lady' Fades into the Past," p. SM16.
13. Ibid, p. 67.
14. "Hollywood Extras Are Hit by Talkies," p. I4.
15. "Extra Voices Needed Now," p. MR6.
16. Ibid, p. 45.
17. *Daily Variety*, April 13, 1934, pp. 1,2.
18. Jules Garrison, "How I Crashed the Movies," p. 70.
19. "Dying Is Profitable to Hollywood Extras," p. 47.
20. Idwal Jones, "Memoirs of an Extra Girl," p. X4.
21. Diana Serra Cary, *The Hollywood Posse: The Story of a Gallant Band of Horsemen Who Made Movie History*, pp. 160–61.
22. Sara Hamilton, "The Tragedy of 15,000 Extras," p. 28.
23. Sean P. Holmes, "The Hollywood Star System and the Regulation of Actors' Labour, 1916–1934," p. 100.
24. John Scott, "Talkies 'Shock Troops' Get Plenty of Shooting," p. B13.
25. Others were Bob Milash, P. J. Mazutis, Constantine Romanoff, Martin Cichy, Fred Behrle, Dick Alexander, Abe Lane, John Northpole, Harry Tenbrook, Larry Fisher, Jimmy Dime, Tony Stabenaux, William Keeler, E. A. Laidlaw, Karl Morse, Mike Tellegan, Don Peterson, Bill Martin, Bob Page, T. C. Jacks, Pat Harmon, and Joe and Jack Herrick.
26. John Scott, "Talkies 'Shock Troops' Get Plenty of Shooting," p. B13.
27. Ibid.
28. Isobel Silden, "Two of the Faces in the Crowd," p. SM11.
29. Fritz Goodwin, "His Face Is His Fortune," p. 62.
30. Richard von Opel was in the news under very different circumstances when, on Christmas Day, 1938, his automobile accidentally hit and killed a pedestrian in Hollywood.
31. Kay Campbell, "Spectacular Hollywood Means 'Extra' Groceries," p. C1.
32. Henry K. Silversmith, "Central Casting Bureau Performs a Comprehensive Service," p. I28
33. John Scott, "Hindu Caste System Has Parallel Among Actors," p. B13.
34. Paul Bradley interview with Anthony Slide, June 3, 1994.

35. Ibid.
36. Jimmie Fidler, "Jimmie Fidler in Hollywood," syndicated column.
37. Murray Ross, *Stars and Strikes: Unionization of Hollywood*, p. 78.
38. "Prods May Close Cent. Casting," p. 12.
39. As reported in *The Official Bulletin of the Screen Actors Guild*, p. 7.
40. "Three Steps to Raise Pay of Vocational Extra Player," pp. 12, 13.
41. Undated Warner Bros. press release from Ken Whitmore.

CHAPTER 7

1. Charles Ray, *Hollywood Shorts*, p. 37.
2. Blanche Sweet to Anthony Slide, November 17, 1974.
3. "Your First Guess Is Wrong!," *Photoplay*, July 1919, p. 96.
4. "Not a Single Double!," *Photoplay*, July 1919, p. 86.
5. Grover Jones, "Star Shadows," p. 46.
6. Lois Shirley, "The Girl Who Played Garbo," p. 29.
7. Wikipedia entry on Hal Le Seuer; there is no cited source for the Crawford quote.
8. Dan Mainwaring, "Hollywood Nobodies," p. 41.
9. Ibid, pp. 41, 134.
10. Ibid, p. 137.
11. Information taken from Grover Jones, "Star Shadows" and other sources.
12. Ed Churchill, "True Story of Cary Grant's Stand-In," p. 76.
13. Frank Dougherty, "Back Talk from a Stand-In," p. X4.
14. Lowell E. Redelings, "Men Behind the Scenes," p. 6.
15. Dan Thomas, "Pay Cuts Raise Hopes of Picture Stand-In."
16. Information from "Me and My Shadow . . . ," p. 22.
17. "'Stand-Ins' for Stars," p. 35.
18. David O. Selznick memorandum to Messrs. Lambert, Plunkett, and Richards, dated March 13, 1939, Wilber G. Kurtz Collection, Margaret Herrick Library of the Academy of Motion Picture Arts and Sciences, file f.29.
19. "Jimmie Fidler in Hollywood," syndicated column, June 23, 1939.
20. Jules Garrison, "How I Crashed the Movies," p. 20.
21. Gladys Hall, "Honest Confessions of an Extra Girl," p. 83.
22. Ed Sullivan, "Exploding the Stand-In Myth!," p. 41.
23. Ed Churchill, "True Story of Cary Grant's Stand-In," p. 31.
24. Ed Sullivan, "Exploding the Stand-In Myth!," p. 41.
25. Ibid, p. 66.
26. Jean Harlow had begun her career in the 1920s as an extra, with her best-known and most famous appearance being in the 1928 Laurel and Hardy short, *Double Whoopee*.
27. Herbert Biberman, *Salt of the Earth: The Story of a Film*, p. 93.
28. Helen Klumph, "Bust 'Em, Cowgirl!," p. 17.
29. Helen Klumph, "Bust 'Em, Cowgirl!," p. 16.
30. James Bell Smith, "Would You Break Your Neck to Get into the Movies?," p. 25.
31. Lila Finn interview with Anthony Slide, April 15, 1994.
32. Angela Allen in conversation at the Cinema Museum, London, November 4, 2010.
33. Pauline Wagner interview with Anthony Slide, February 16, 2010.
34. Ibid.
35. For more information, see Amy Kaufman, "A Stand-Up Guy for Jeff Bridges," *Los Angeles Times*, February 21, 2010, p. D6.

CHAPTER 8

1. Jan Muenchener, "Super the Great," p. 67.
2. Ibid.
3. August 1929, p. 116.
4. Helen Carlisle, "Odd Folks of Hollywood," p. 31.
5. "Jannings and 'Extras,'" p. X7.
6. "Among the Extras," p. X5.
7. Ibid.
8. Elinor Glyn, "Fate or Chance?"
9. "Archduke Leopold Now a Movie Actor," p. 16.
10. Helen Klumph, "Poor Little Rich Boy!," p. 112.
11. David Niven, *The Moon's a Balloon*, pp. 193–94.
12. Jerome Beatty, "A Movie Star Nobody Knows," p. 106.
13. Gwen Zetter, p. 52.
14. "Actors Find Clothes Make Them Money," p. A2.
15. Bess Flowers interview with Anthony Slide, date unknown.
16. Ibid.

CHAPTER 9

1. "Execs as Extras, Real Barometer of Picture Biz," p. 1.
2. Franklyn Farnum, who died in July 1961 at the age of eighty-three, was not related to the more famous silent screen stars, William and Dustin Farnum.
3. For the record, the other thirty-four extras, whose names, sadly, will never mean anything to the film going public, are Eugene Beday, Jeanne H. Beeks, C. Bishop, Nora Bush, Ben Corbett, Jane Crowley, Jack Deery, Fanny Drabin, Charles Dunbar, Billy Engle, Harry H. Evans, Adolph Faylauer, Curt Furberg, Anna Giles, Albert Godderis, Bessie Gordon, Silver Harr, John Impolito, Sugar Willie Keeler, Jack H. Kenney, William J. Kolberg, Art LaForest, A. B. Lane, Michael Macy, George McDonald, Karl E. Miller, Charles Nickum, William H. O'Brien, Millie Schottland, Bill Schroff, Lucille M. Sewell, Paul Stathes, Albano Valerio, and Eleanore Vogel.
4. Margaret Reid, "Looking on with an Extra Girl," *Picture-Play*, March 1925, p.94.
5. Anthony Slide, *The Big V: A History of the Vitagraph Company*, p. 43.
6. Ann Cummings, "The Tragedy of Costello," p. 78.
7. Marquis Busby, "The Port of Missing Girls," p. 139.
8. Marquis Busby, "The Port of Missing Stars," p. 40.
9. Ibid, p. 140.
10. "Among the Extras," p. X5.
11. Earl Theisen, "The Old Timer," p. 12.
12. Ibid, p. 27
13. "Pioneers of Screen Given Preference in Casting *San Francisco*," MGM pressbook for *San Francisco*.
14. "Renewed Vogue for Old-Time Film Personalities: Still Fresh in Memory, They Have Definite B.O.," p. 2.
15. In later years, Baggot would spell his name Baggott.
16. Fred Datig interview with Anthony Slide, April 20, 2009.
17. Ibid.
18. Quoted in DeWitt Bodeen, "May McAvoy," p. 494.

19. Kevin Thomas to Anthony Slide, May 12, 2011.
20. I recall in the mid-1970s there was a dispute as to who was the real Monte Blue. Was it (correctly) the man whose widow was Betty Blue of Beverly Hills, or was it the husband of Ellen Blue of Lancaster, California, who would come into the Margaret Herrick Library of the Academy of Motion Picture Arts and Sciences, insisting that its files be appropriately amended? Gossip columnist James Bacon even wrote a December 5, 1976, story about the dispute.
21. Paul Panzer file, Warner Bros. Archives, University of Southern California.
22. For his brother, Francis Ford appeared in *Seas Beneath* (1931), *Airmail* (1932), *Pilgrimage* (1933), *The Lost Patrol* (1934), *The World Moves On* (1934), *Judge Priest* (1934), *The Informer* (1935), *Steamboat 'round the Bend* (1935), *The Whole Town's Talking* (1935), *The Prisoner of Shark Island* (1936), *Stagecoach* (1939), *Young Mr. Lincoln* (1939), *Drums along the Mohawk* (1939), *The Grapes of Wrath* (1940), *Tobacco Road* (1941), *My Darling Clementine* (1946), *Fort Apache* (1948), *Three Godfathers* (1948), *She Wore a Yellow Ribbon* (1949), *Wagonmaster* (1950), *The Quiet Man* (1952), and *The Sun Shines Bright* (1953).
23. John Ford maintained a company of stock players, including Ruth Clifford and Mae Marsh from the silent era, but it seems inappropriate to label them as extras even if, at times, their parts were extremely small (though never minor).
24. Kevin Thomas to Anthony Slide, May 12, 2011.
25. Kevin Thomas to Anthony Slide, May 12, 2011.
26. Original document in the author's possession.
27. "New Faces for Old," p. 15.
28. "Three Steps to Raise Pay of Vocational Extra Player," p. 12.
29. Aline Mosby, United Press syndicated stories, May 11 and May 15, 1951.

CHAPTER 10

1. H. Sheridan-Bickers, "Extra Ladies and Gentlemen," *Motion Picture Magazine*, August 1917, p. 91.
2. Rob Wagner, *Film Folk*, p. 217.
3. Ibid, p. 224.
4. Thomas H. Ince, "Troubles of a Motion Picture Producer," p. 115.
5. Luis Reyes and Peter Rubie, *Hispanics in Hollywood: A Celebration of 100 Years in Film and Television*, pp. 9–10.
6. Clara Weatherwax, "Ain't Hollywood Romantic?," p. 17.
7. *The Silent Spirit* by Margaret Coel (New York: Berkley Prime Crime, 2009) is a mystery novel involving one of the Indian extras who came to Hollywood and vanished, and whose disappearance is investigated by a great-grandson who is subsequently murdered.
8. "Indian Actors Bury the Hatchet in Hollywood 'War Paint Club,'" p. 5A.
9. "Notes from the Cinema Gold Coast," p. X4.
10. Neil Diamond, "Keeping It Reel," p. 27.
11. "Drilling the Picture Mobs," p. X4.
12. "Gilda Gray's 'Extras,'" p. X3
13. Anthony Slide interview with Satini Puailoa, May 30, 1994.
14. Thomas H. Ince, "Troubles of a Motion Picture Producer," p. 114.
15. Ibid.
16. Emma Lindsay Squier, "Mr. Wang of Chinatown," p. 102.

17. Gordon Gassaway, "John Chinaman—Actor," p. 31.
18. Helen Carlisle, "Odd Folks of Hollywood," p. 31.
19. A. L. Wooldridge, "Our Chinese Movie Actors," p. 83.
20. Ibid, pp. 83–84.
21. Madame Sul-Te-Wan's quotes here are taken from an interview with Raymond Lee, which was at one time in the author's possession. The interview served as the basis for an article by Lee titled "A Walk in the Silents," published in a periodical titled *Offbeat*, which I do not believe is the New Orleans magazine of that name. Neither do I believe, as at least one academic has claimed, that the interview dates from 1948; it took place much later.
22. Rob Wagner, "Supes and Supermen," p. 16.
23. Donald Bogle, *Bright Boulevards, Bold Dreams: The Story of Black Hollywood*, p. 63.
24. Loretto Coffield Clarke, "What It Means to Be an 'Extra,'" p. 37.
25. Charlene Regester, "African American Extras in Hollywood during the 1920s and 1930s," p. 98. I am indebted to this essay for some of my information on African American extras in Hollywood.
26. Quoted in Donald Bogle, *Bright Boulevards, Bold Dreams: The Story of Black Hollywood*, p. 62.
27. Fred W. Beetson, "The Operation of a Central Casting Bureau," p. 85.
28. "Central Casting Will Reopen Interviews," p. 9.
29. "To Hear Appeal Against Central Casting Bureau," *New York Amsterdam News*, June 2, 1962, p. 27.
30. Maurice Dancer, "Stage Facts: Colored Movie Extras," p. 1.
31. Thomas Cripps, "Walter's Thing," p. 118.
32. Harry Levette, "Don't Look Now, Walter White, But Hollywood Extras Are Back," p. 17.
33. *Daily Variety*, July 26, 1935, p.5.
34. Floyd G. Snelson, "The 'Low-Down' on the Negro in Hollywood: Snelson Reveals 'Inside' Story of Noted Movie City," p. 6.
35. The only non-ethnic strike by extras that I have come across took place at Corona Del Mar Beach, in Southern California, on May 7, 1941, during the filming of the Dorothy Lamour vehicle, *Aloma of the South Seas*. A group of extras, led by Dave Robel, who usually worked as a dancer, participated in a sit-down strike claiming they had been promised $16.50 a day to paddle a canoe, but were receiving only eleven dollars. Producer Paramount threatened to take the names of all extras refusing to work, and the latter quickly decided to end the dispute. Paramount Production Records, Margaret Herrick Library of the Academy of Motion Picture Arts and Sciences, file f.90.
36. Minutes of the Screen Extras Guild annual meeting, Los Angeles, May 20, 1951, p. 85.
37. As far as I can ascertain, this organization had no connection with the Negro Actors Guild of America, founded in 1937 by actress Fredi Washington, actor Leigh Whipper, and entertainer Noble Sissle, among others. The guild sought to eliminate stereotyping and argued for realistic roles for African Americans. While it served both the theatre and film communities, it appears primarily to have been focused on the former.
38. Larry Glenn, "Hollywood Change," p. I23.
39. Ibid.

CHAPTER 11

1. Reported in the *Los Angeles Daily News*, May 30, 1938.
2. "Movie Guild Opens Doors to Extras," p. 22.

3. David F. Prindle, *The Politics of Glamour: Ideology and Democracy in the Screen Actors Guild*, p. 20.
4. John Scott, "Ten Thousand Extras Doomed," p. C1.
5. *Screen Guild Magazine*, March 1938, p. 34.
6. Garcia was a favorite of Charlie Chaplin, appearing for the comedian in *The Idle Class* (1921), *Pay Day* (1922), *The Gold Rush* (1925), *The Circus* (1928), *City Lights* (1931), and *Modern Times* (1936).
7. W. B. Francis, "Academy-Equity Clash Marks Film Code Hearing," p. 5.
8. James Bowles Fisher, "Hollywood Doesn't Want You," p. 90.
9. *Daily Variety*, March 23, 1944, p. 1.
10. Some modern sources claim that there was a publication for extras titled *Hollywood Megaphone*, but I can find no record of a periodical of that name.
11. Otis Ferguson, "Hollywood Footnote," p. 670.
12. "Boos at Autonomy Meeting," *Daily Variety*, p. 7.
13. "Xtras Want 300-Mile Zone Raised to 3000," *Daily Variety*, p. 1.
14. "Film Extras Vote to Break from Screen Actors' Guild," p. A1. Extras might be on the attack, but they could also be self-destructive. In November 1944, the California Department of Unemployment accused some extras of claiming unemployment insurance when Central Casting had work for them, but had been unable to contact them. Some extras, it was said, worked enough hours to qualify for unemployment insurance and then took vacations.
15. The Associated Actors and Artistes of America was known as the Four A's (AAAA) because it consisted of the Screen Actors Guild, the American Federation of Radio Artists, the American Guild of Variety Artists, and Actors Equity.
16. The records of the Screen Extras Guild list the 157 founding members by number, but it must be noted that no names appear against nine of the numbers.
17. David F. Prindle, *The Politics of Glamour: Ideology and Democracy in the Screen Actors Guild*, p. 39.
18. Richard H. Gordon, "Extra! Extra!," p. 22.
19. Richard H. Gordon had joined SAG in 1933 and had been on its board of directors. He became first vice-president of the Screen Extras Guild in 1945 and its president in May 1948. He died in September 1956 at the age of sixty-three, while still president of the Screen Extras Guild.
20. A typical requisition for extra talent (from Warner Bros.) had boxes that could be ticked: work around fire or smoke; work around animals; hazardous work; have hair added; sing to playback; hair applied to face; sing in unison; work in rain; shoot guns; carry props; work in water; dance; body makeup. From Warner Bros. Archives, University of Southern California.
21. Letters in the Hal Roach Collection, housed in the Cinema Library at the University of Southern California.
22. Many in the film had previously worked in vaudeville as members of [Leo] Singer's Midgets act, and some were non- professionals. Just about all of the 124 signed by the studio caused havoc at the Culver City Hotel, where they were housed, with accusations ranging from alcoholism to participation in sex orgies. One writer described them as "The most deformed, unpleasant bunch of adults imaginable." Hugh Fordin, quoted in Aljean Harmetz, *The Making of the Wizard of Oz*, p. 188.
23. Philip K. Scheuer, "Screen Tot Stand-In New Job for Midgets," p. 1.

CHAPTER 12

1. In 1954, an award of the same name had been introduced (more logically) by the National Fire Protection Association.
2. Gerald Mast, "In Memoriam: Central Casting," p. 27
3. Ibid.
4. Olive Brooks, "Canal Zone Campaign," p. X7.
5. John Horn, "Films' Inflatable Extras Create Cast of Thousands," p. A10.
6. "The Wild Bunch," p. 63.
7. Selby Dessner, "A Day in the Life," p. 27.
8. John Burke, "Extra Extras," p. D4.
9. Robert Bobrow, "Extras Should Be Seen, Not Heard," p. 28.
10. William Murphy, "The Atmosphere People," p. 90.
11. Mickey Rapkin, "Leaving the Office Behind," p. 140.

BIBLIOGRAPHY

Abernathy, Basil, "Hollywood Extra's Day," *New York Times*, July 1, 1928, p. 98.

Abrams, Rachel. "Casting Firms Warned," *Daily Variety*, May 19, 2011, p. 3.

"Actors and Producers Agree to New Deal for Hollywood 'Extras,'" *Christian Science Monitor*, February 1, 1935, p. 6.

"Actors Find Clothes Make Them Money," *Los Angeles Times*, February 7, 1938, pp. A1, A2.

"After Office Hours in Hollywood," *Photoplay*, June 1919, pp. 32–33.

Albert, Katherine, "The Passing of the Extra Girl," *Photoplay*, August 1929, pp. 30–31, 122.

"Allen Starts His Defense on Tues.," *Daily Variety*, July 17, 1934, p. 2.

"Among the Extras," *New York Times*, March 20, 1932, p. X5.

Amoroso, Frank, "Lila Finn: Hollywood's Underwater Stuntwoman," *Underwater USA*, November 1985, p. 35.

"Another Work Army—It's in Hollywood," *Los Angeles Times* Rotogravure Section, April 23, 1933, p. 1.

"Archduke Leopold Now a Movie Actor," *New York Times*, July 22, 1927, p. 16.

Arechiga, Brenda, "Location, Location, Location," *Los Angeles Times Magazine*, June 27, 2004, pp. 18–19, 27–28.

"Ask Committee to Supervise All Casting Offices," *Academy of Motion Picture Arts & Sciences Bulletin*, September 5, 1933, pp. 1, 4.

Beach, Barbara, "A Haven for Hopefuls," *New York Times*, January 2, 1944, p. 3X.

Beatty, Jerome, "A Movie Star Nobody Knows," *American Magazine*, July 30, 1930, pp. 30–32, 100–8.

———, "Your Chance in the Movies," *American Magazine*, May 1938, pp. 30–32, 132–36.

"Beef on Bits for Extras," *Daily Variety*, September 21, 1944, pp. 1, 9.

Beetson, Fred W., "The Operation of a Central Casting Bureau," *Transactions of the S.M.P.E.*, vol. XII, No. 33, 1928, pp. 81–85.

Behlmer, Rudy. *America's Favorite Movies: Behind the Scenes*. New York: Frederick Ungar, 1982.

Bell, Arthur, "Hollywood Tells Bell," *Village Voice*, February 25, 1961, p. 55.

Berrey, Lester V., and Melvin Van Den Bark. *The American Thesaurus of Slang*. New York: Thomas Y. Crowell, 1942.

Biberman, Herbert. *Salt of the Earth: The Story of a Film*. Boston: Beacon Press, 1965.

Bigelow, Joe, "New, Old and Out Stars," *Variety*, June 23, 1931, pp. 1, 10.

"Blanche Sweet's Double," *Photoplay*, August 1918, p.95.

Bobrow, Robert, "Extras Should Be Seen, Not Heard," *Westways*, July 1970, pp. 27–28, 47.

Bodeen, DeWitt, "May McAvoy," *Films in Review*, October 1968, pp. 482–98.

Boland, Elena, "Chorus Ranks Luring Extras," *Los Angeles Times*, August 25, 1929, p. B9, B10.

"Boon for Girl Film Workers," *Los Angeles Times*, July 20, 1919, p. II7.

"Boos at Autonomy Meeting," *Daily Variety*, October 4, 1943, pp. 1, 7.
"Breaking into the Game," *Photoplay*, August 1914, p. 131–35.
Breton, Ted, "Mobilizing an Army for Moving Pictures," *Motion Picture Magazine*, April 1915, pp. 77–82.
Brezina, Jim, "Howard Hill's Archery Feats Legendary," *Los Angeles Herald-Examiner*, March 9, 1975, p. B8.
Brooks, Olive, "Canal Zone Campaign," *New York Times*, February 2, 1958, p. X7.
Brown, Kelly R. *Florence Lawrence, The Biograph Girl: America's First Movie Star*. Jefferson, NC: McFarland, 1999.
"Bureau Gateway to Pictures," *Los Angeles Times*, October 6, 1931, p. A8.
Burke, John, "Extra Extras," *Los Angeles Times*, April 5, 2009, p. D1, D4–D5.
Burroughs, Edgar Rice. *The Girl from Hollywood*. New York: Macaulay, 1923.
Busby, Marquis, "The Port of Missing Stars," *Photoplay*, November 1930, pp. 40–41, 138–40.
Cagney, James, "What Shall We Do about the Problem of the B Player?," *Screen Actor*, October 1944, pp. 3–6.
Campbell, Kay, "Spectacular Hollywood Means 'Extra' Goodness," *Los Angeles Times*, September 25, 1938, pp. C1, C4.
Cantarini, Martha Crawford, and Christopher J. Spicer. *Fall Girl: My Life as a Western Stunt Double*. Jefferson, NC: McFarland, 2010.
Carlisle, Helen, "Odd Folks of Hollywood," *Photoplay*, July 1923, pp. 29–31.
———, "Quite the Ritz This Studio Club," *Motion Picture Magazine*, August 1927, pp. 28–29, 107, 111.
Carr, Harry, "Wild Extras I Have Known," *Motion Picture Classic*, pp. 46–47, 91–92, 94.
Cary, Diana Serra. *The Hollywood Posse: The Story of a Gallant Band of Horsemen Who Made Movie History*. Boston: Houghton Mifflin, 1975.
"Casting Audible Pictures," *New York Times*, June 9, 1929, p. X3.
"Casting Figures Given Out," *Los Angeles Times*, July 12, 1926, p. A7.
"Central at Work," *Screen Actor*, May 1940, pp. 11–12.
"Central Caster," *Good Housekeeping*, October 1957, p. 13.
"Central Casting," *Los Angeles Times*, April 8, 1934, p. F8.
"Central Casting," *Los Angeles Times*, January 29, 1939, p. H3.
"Central Casting," *It's Happening in Hollywood: Weekly News of Picures in Production*, March 27, 1939, unpaged.
"Central Casting Corporation," *What's Happening in Hollywood*, November 30, 1946, unpaged.
"Central Casting Opens Door to Picture Extras," *The Actor*, May 1940, p. 5.
"Central Casting Will Reopen Interviews," *Bulletin of the Screen Actors Guild*, July 1938, pp. 8–9.
"Central Casting Will Rotate Employment Among Directors," *Los Angeles Times*, February 4, 1941, p. 26.
Churchill, Douglas W., "Glamour at $8.97 a Week," *New York Times*, September 22, 1935, p. X4.
———, "A Casting Machine for Hollywood's Hopefuls," *New York Times*, October 13, 1935, p. X4.
———, "Extra Trouble in the Hollywood Paradise," *New York Times*, August 30, 1936, p. X3.
———, "The Hollywood Illusion," *New York Times*, April 11, 1937, p. 175.
———, "Hollywood Scorns the Alter Ego," *New York Times*, June 6, 1937, p. 185.
Churchill, Ed, "True Story of Cary Grant's Stand-In," *Silver Screen*, September 1936, pp. 30–31, 73–76.

Churchill, Edward, "True Story of a Stand-In," *Silver Screen*, April 1938, pp. 18–19, 79–80.

Clarke, Loretto Coffield, "What It Means to Be an 'Extra,'" *Motion Picture Classic*, March 1916, pp. 35–39.

"Climbing the Mary Pickford Ladder," *Photoplay*, October 1923, pp. 31–33.

Cline, William Hamilton, "Lost Hosts of the Footlights," *Los Angeles Times*, March 11, 1934, pp. G8, G14.

"Coast Meeting Over Extras Conditions," *Variety*, November 25, 1925, p. 29.

Cohn, Alfred A., "What Every Girl Wants to Know," *Photoplay*, June 1919, pp. 2831.

Collings, Ellsworth, in collaboration with Alma Miller England. *The 101 Ranch*. Norman: University of Oklahoma Press, 1971.

Condon, Frank, "Hollywood," *Photoplay*, January 1923, pp. 39–43, 107–11.

"Confessions of an Extra Girl," *Modern Screen*, August 1935, pp. 30–31, 87–77; September 1935, pp. 38–39, 64; October 1935, pp. 46, 73–75; November 1935, pp. 46, 78–79, December 1935, pp. 46, 79–80; January 1936, pp. 46, 79.

Conners, Marilynn. *What Chance Have I in Hollywood: The Mystery of the Movies*. Hollywood: Famous Authors Imprint, 1924.

Cox, Stephen. *The Munchkins of Oz*. Nashville, TN: Cumberland House, 2002.

Cripps, Thomas, "Walter's Thing," *Journal of Popular Film & Television*, Summer 2005, pp. 116–25.

Crivello, Kirk, "The Hollywood Studio Club," *Film Fan Monthly*, January 1972, pp. 25–29.

———, "Hollywood's Most Beautiful Extra Girls," *Hollywood Studio*, May 1973, p. 34.

Cummings, Ann, "The Tragedy of Costello," *Motion Picture Classic*, January 1928, pp. 18–19, 78.

Dancer, Maurice, "Stage Facts: Colored Movie Extras," *Pittsburgh Courier*, February 2, 1929, p. 1.

"Dangerous Odds in Hollywood," *Literary Digest*, August 23, 1924, pp. 30–31.

Daugherty, Frank, "Back Talk from a Stand-In," *New York Times*, June 14, 1942, p. X4.

Denton, Frances, "Hollywood's Hermit," *Photoplay*, July 1925, pp. 88, 120.

———, "Ride, Swim and Dance," *Photoplay*, May 1921, pp. 55–56, 97.

Dessner, Selby, "A Day in the Life," *Los Angeles*, March 1984, p. 27.

Diamond, Neil, "Keeping It Real," *This Week from Indian Country Today*, January 19, 2011, p. 27.

"Don't Look Now, Walter White, But Hollywood Extras Are Back," *Chicago Defender*, April 20, 1946, p. 17.

Drake, Ross, "Acting Lesson No. 1: Don't Trip over the Cables," *TV Guide*, April 21, 1973, pp. 21–23.

Draper, Maurice, "Stage Facts: Colored Movie Extras," *Pittsburgh Courier*, February 2, 1929, p. 1.

Dreiser, Theodore, "Hollywood: Its Morals and Manners," *Shadowland*, November 1921, pp. 37, 62–63

———, "The Commonplace Tale with a Thousand Endings," *Shadowland*, December 1921, pp. 51, 61.

———, "The Beginner's Thousand-to-One Chance," *Shadowland*, January 1922, pp. 43, 67.

———, "The Extra's Right to Exist," *Shadowland*, February 1922, pp. 53, 66.

"Drilling the Picture 'Mobs,'" *New York Times*, September 2, 1923, p. X4.

Dumaux, Sally A. *King Baggot: A Biography and Filmography of the First King of the Movies*. Jefferson, NC: McFarland, 2002.

Dyches, Nathan S., "Holywood's 'Four Hundred,'" *Photoplay*, July 1925, pp. 38–39, 111.

"Dying Is Profitable to Hollywood Extras," *Baltimore Sun*, November 17, 1935, p. 47.

Ellis, Rick, "Extras! Extras! A Guide to 'Stardom,'" *Chicago Tribune*, March 14, 1986, p. 3.
Evarts, Hal G., "Movie Extras Win Plaudits," *Los Angeles Times*, July 27, 1930, p. B9, B17.
Evelove, Alex, "Ladies of the Ensemble," *New York Times*, December 13, 1936, p. X6.
"Execs as Extras, Real Barometer of Picture Biz," *Variety*, June 23, 1931, p. 1.
An Extra Girl, "On the Set with Valentino," *Picture-Play*, October 1924, pp. 63–65, 111.
"Extra! Extra!," *Photoplay*, January 1924, pp. 52–53.
"'Extra' Potential Star," *Los Angeles Times*, June 3, 1923, p. III28.
"Extra Problem to Be Tough Nut for Rosenblatt," *Daily Variety*, January 22, 1934, p. 3.
"Extra Voices Needed Now," *Baltimore Sun*, July 1, 1928, p. MR6.
"Extras! Extras! Read All About Them . . . ," [London] *Times*, November 25, 2004, p. 15.
"Extras Give Full Autonomy," *Daily Variety*, March 30, 1943, pp. 1, 3.
"Extras Win NLRB Point," *Daily Variety*, March 8, 1944, pp. 1, 11.
Facts about Extra Work. Hollywood: Central Casting Corporation, August 1, 1936.
Ferguson, Otis, "Hollywood Footnote," *The New Republic*, November 17, 1941, p. 670.
Fidler, Jimmie, "Jimmie Fidler in Hollywood," syndicated column, June 1, 1939.
"Film Bureau Fights Gangs," *Los Angeles Times*, April 30, 1940, p. 6.
"Film Extras Vote to Break from Screen Actors' Guild," *Los Angeles Times*, December 18, 1944, p. A1.
"Film Girls Ask New Home," *Los Angeles Times*, February 10, 1923, p. III6.
"Fineman Planning to Solve Extra Problem," *Los Angeles Times*, March 30, 1925, p. A7.
Fisher, James Bowles, "Hollywood Doesn't Want You!," *Screenland*, September 1938, pp. 30–32, 90–91.
"Former Extras Graduate," *Motion Picture News*, January 7, 1928, p. 61.
Fox, Hazel Hitchcock, "My First Job as a Hollywood Extra," *Christian Science Monitor*, June 29, 1962, p. 15.
Fox, Jordan, "Central Casting," *American Film*, December 1983, pp. 13–14.
Francis, Roland, "The New Extra Girl," *Photoplay*, December 1929, pp. 44–45, 122.
Francis, W. B., "Academy-Equity Clash Marks Film Code Hearing," *Los Angeles Times*, September 13, 1933, pp. 1, 5.
Fuld, Horace A., "The Fakes and Frauds in Motion Pictures: 'Posing' for the Movies," *Motion Picture Magazine*, November 1915, pp. 111–12.
Garrison, Jules, "How I Crashed the Movies," *Movie Mirror*, August 1938, pp. 20–21, 69–70.
Gassaway, Gordon, "John Chinaman—Screen Actor," *Picture-Play*, July 1920, pp. 31–33.
Gebhart, Myrtle, "Why One Hundred Thousand Failed," *Picture-Play*, November 1924, pp. 60–61, 93.
———, "The Studio Club Grows Up," *Picture-Play*, January 1927, pp. 83–84, 105, 109.
Gibson, Helen, "In Very Early Days," *Films in Review*, January 1968, pp. 28–34.
Gillespie, Dennis, "I Was an Extra in *Love Story*," *Glamour*, December 1970, pp. 92–93, 148, 150, 152.
"Glamour at $8.97 a Week," *New York Times*, September 22, 1935, p. X4.
Glenn, Larry, "Hollywood Change," *New York Times*, September 22, 1963, p. I23.
Glyn, Elinor, "Fate or Chance?," *Photoplay*, October 1928, pp. 39, 104.
Goldberg, Robert, "Extras, Extras: A Few Seconds in the Limelight," *Wall Street Journal*, March 6, 1984, p. 32.
Goodman, Ezra, "Stars of Yesteryear," *New York Times*, April 25, 1943, p. X5.ss
Goodwin, Fritz, "His Face Is His Fortune," *Collier's*, March 15, 1952, pp. 26–27, 62.
Gordon, James, "3 in a Crowd," *American Magazine*, July 1944, pp. 28–29.
Gordon, Richard H., "Extra! Extra!," *The American Federationist*, August 1951, pp. 21–23.

Gordon, Robert, "Tom Mix's Stand-In Looks Back," *New York Times*, August 22, 1976, p. 289.
Gould, Helen, "Mapping the Moves of the Movie Muppet," *New York Times*, July 23, 1950, p. X5.
Gray, Lois S., and Ronald L. Seeber, ed. *Under the Stars: Essays on Labor Relations in Arts and Entertainment*. Ithaca, NY: Cornell University Press, 1996.
"Guild Gets Increases for New York Extras," *Screen Actor*, January 1946, p. 15.
Hall, Gladys, "Honest Confessions of an Extra Girl," *Screenland*, September 1939, pp. 26–27, 80–83.
Hamilton, Sara, "The Tragedy of 15,000 Extras," *Photoplay*, November 1934, pp. 26–27, 93–94.
Hampton, Benjamin B. *A History of the Movies*. New York: Covici, Friede, 1931.
Hanlon, John, "The Town of Types," *Photoplay*, April 1927, pp. 72–73, 149–51.
Hanson, Patricia King, ed. *The American Film Institute Catalog of Motion Pictures Produced in the United States: Feature Films, 1911–1920*. Berkeley: University of California Press, 1988.
———. *The American Film Institute Catalog of Motion Pictures Produced in the United States: Feature Films, 1931–1940*. Berkeley: University of California Press, 1993.
———. *The American Film Institute Catalog of Motion Pictures Produced in the United States: Feature Films, 1941–1950*. Berkeley: University of California Press, 1999.
Harmetz, Aljean. *The Making of the Wizard of Oz*. New York: Alfred A. Knopf, 1977.
Harrower, Jack, "Scientific Casting," *The Film Daily*, May 16, 1926, p. 5.
"'Has Beens' Can't Come Back," *Variety*, June 8, 1927, pp. 1, 2.
"Hays Begins Clean-Up of Hollywood Today," *New York Times*, January 25, 1926, p. 22.
"Hays Lauds Film Bureau," *Los Angeles Times*, January 24, 1926, p. I3.
Heffernan, Harold, "Hollywood's Studio Club Headquarters for Hope," *Hartford Courant*, May 22, 1938, p. A13.
———, "A Hollywood Extra Demands More Money for Kissing Hedy Lamarr," *Atlanta Constitution*, December 29, 1941, p. 12.
Henabery, Joseph E. *Before, In and After Hollywood*. Lanham, MD: Scarecrow Press, 1997.
Herzberg, Bob. *Savages and Saints: The Changing Image of American Indians in Westerns*. Jefferson, NC: McFarland, 2008.
"Hiring at Hollywood," *American Review of Reviews*, July-December 1926, pp. 658–59.
"Hollywood Bay Window Is Watched," *Baltimore Sun*, May 20, 1928, p. MR.
"Hollywood Better Says Girls' Advisor," *New York Times*, October 10, 1926, p. E19.
"Hollywood Extras," *Look*, February 18, 1947, pp. 28–31.
"Hollywood Extras Are Hit by Talkies," *Washington Post*, December 26, 1930, p. 14.
"Hollywood Extras Bar Doubling Up in Movie Scenes," *Washington Post*, October 26, 1941, p. L3.
"Hollywood Extras Have Own 'Grapevine' Telegraph," *Hartford Courant*, December 6, 1931, p. 15.
"Hollywood Facts Sought," *Los Angeles Times*, April 8, 1927, p. A2.
"Hollywood Has Haven for Girls Seeking Fame," *Los Angeles Times*, January 25, 1948, p. A1.
"Hollywood Warns Film-Struck Extras," *New York Times*, December 4, 1923, p. 23.
Holmes, Sean P., "The Hollywood Star System and the Regulation of Actors' Labour, 1916–1934," *Film History*, vol. XII, no. 1, 2000, pp. 97–114.
Horn, John, "Films' Inflatable Extras Create Cast of Thousands," *Los Angeles Times*, August 14, 2003, pp. A1, A10.
Horne, Gerald. *Class Struggle in Hollywood, 1930–1950s: Moguls, Mobsters, Stars, Reds & Trade Unionists*. Austin: University of Texas Press, 2001.
Hughes, Kathleen A., "Hollywood Beckons, and Our Reporter Reaches for Stardom," *Wall Street Journal*, December 6, 1988, pp. A1, A14.

Hughes, Laurence A. *The Truth About the Movies by the Stars*. Hollywood: Hollywood Publishers, 1924.
Hunt, Donald J., "Hollywood Stereotypes of Villainous Bikers," *Los Angeles Times*, February 28, 1987, p. A2.
Hurst, Harry, III, "A Day in the Life of an Extra, Er, Background Artist," *New York Times*, February 10, 2007, p. C5.
Hylan, Dick, "Risking Life and Limb for $25," *Photoplay*, November 1927, pp. 30–33, 122–23.
Ince, Thomas H., "Troubles of a Motion Picture Producer," *Motion Picture Magazine*, May 1915, pp. 113–15.
———, "The Type Actor," *Picture-Play Magazine*, February 1918, pp. 231–36.
"Indian Actors Bury the Hatchet in Hollywood 'War Paint Club,'" *Christian Science Monitor*, November 24, 1926, p. 5A.
Isaac, Frederick F., "Working in a Hollywood Mob," *New York Times*, January 13, 1929, Part II, p. 6.
Jacobs, Lewis, "Avant-Garde Production in America," in Roger Manvell, ed. *Experiment in Film*. London: The Grey Walls Press, 1949, pp. 113–52.
"Jannings and 'Extras,'" *New York Times*, November 6, 1927, p. X7.
Jennings, Amy S., "An Extra in Hollywood," *Atlantic Monthly*, November 1927, pp. 649–55.
"Jobs Found for Models," *Los Angeles Times*, January 17, 1935, p. A8.
Johnson, Erskine, "Pay Scale High for Child Film Actors; But Here's the Rub; They Seldom Work," syndicated column, March 15, 1935.
———, "A Port in a Storm for Movie-Struck Girls," *Washington Post*, June 30, 1935, p. SM2.
Johnson, Malcolm, "The Man Who Comes to Breakfast," *Hartford Courant*, October 9, 1966, p. 2F.
Jones, Grover, "Star Shadows," *Collier's*, April 30, 1938, pp. 18, 44–46.
Jones, Idwal, "Memoirs of an Extra Girl," *New York Times*, May 10, 1936, p. X4.
Kaufman, Amy, "A Stand-Up Guy for Jeff Bridges," *Los Angeles Times*, February 21, 2010, p. D6.
Kelly, T. Howard, "Fund Raised to Create Home for Horde of Screen-Struck Girls Invading Hollywood," *Movie Weekly*, August 11, 1923, pp. 4–5.
Kenaga, Heidi, "Making the 'Studio Girl': The Hollywood Studio Club and Industry Regulation of Female Labour," *Film History*, vol. 18, 2006, pp. 129–39.
Keyes, Evelyn. *Scarlett O'Hara's Younger Sister: My Lively Life in and out of Hollywood*. Secaucus, NJ: Lyle Stuart, 1977.
Kimball, Rhea Irene, "The Extra Girls of the Essanay Company—Girls, Girls, Girls!," *Motion Picture Magazine*, September 1915, pp. 97–100.
Kingsley, Grace, "How Famous Film Stars Have Been Discovered," *Los Angeles Times*, October 18, 1914, P. III2.
———, "Extra Girls Who Became Stars," *Photoplay*, April 1917, pp. 67–70, 145–46.
———, "A Debutante in Starland," *Los Angeles Times*, June 29, 1919, p. III1.
Kingston, Samuel F., "Casting for Pictures," *Moving Picture World*, July 21, 1917, p. 427.
Klumph, Helen, "Bust 'Em, Cowgirl!," *Picture-Play*, January 1925, pp. 16–17, 96.
———, "Poor Little Rich Boy!," *Picture Play*, December 1927, pp. 23, 112.
Knepper, Max. *Sodom and Gomorrah: The Story of Hollywood*. Los Angeles: End Poverty League/Max Knepper, 1935.
Knox, Dorothea, "What Every Extra Knows," *Picture-Play*, October 1922, pp. 58–60; November 1922, pp. 67–71, 88; December 1922, pp. 51–55, 101; February 1923, pp. 66–68, 100–1.
Koury, Phil, "Rationed Violence," *New York Times*, October 9, 1949, p. X5.
"Ladies of the Ensemble," *New York Times*, March 10, 1935, p. X3.

Lait, Jack, "The Hollywood As Iz," *Variety*, January 12, 1927, p. 3.
Lane, Rose Wilder, "How I Became a Great Actress; Ten Minutes in a Barroom with Doug Fairbanks, the Optimist," *Sunset*, April 1918, pp. 35–38.
Lawless, Jill, "UK Spies Sought German Movie Extra and Nazi Agent," Associated Press, August 26, 2011.
Lee, Raymond, "A Walk in the Silents," *Offbeat*, vol. I, no. 6 (date undetermined), pp. 20–23.
Levette, Harry, "Don't Look Now, Walter White, But Hollywood Extras Are Back," *Chicago Defender*, April 20, 1946, p. 17.
Lewis, Carl, "Has Anybody Here Seen Connie?," *Motion Picture*, August 1928, pp. 49, 93.
Lindsay, Vachel. *The Art of the Moving Picture*. New York: Macmillan, 1916.
Little, B. M., "It Pays to Be Extra," *Los Angeles Times*, September 2, 1934, p. H7, H13.
Louvish, Simon, "Burning Crosses," *Sight and Sound*, September 2000, pp. 12–13.
Lowe, Corinne, "The Hope That Springs," *Photoplay*, August 1920, pp. 36–39, 112.
McClay, Howard, "'Bravo' 200th Role for Him," *Los Angeles Daily News*, November 20, 1953, pp. 38, 39.
McCormick, Anne O'Hare, "Hollywood Weird Factory of Mob Art," *New York Times*, December 6, 1931, p. SM3, SM5, SM71.
McCoy, Horace. *The Shoot Horses, Don't They?* New York: Simon and Schuster, 1935.
———. *I Should Have Stayed Home*. New York: Alfred A. Knopf, 1938.
McGaffey, Elizabeth, "The Studio Club," *Photoplay*, September 1917, pp. 83–87.
MacGowan, Kenneth. *Behind the Screen: The History and Technique of the Motion Picture*. New York: Delacorte Press, 1965.
McIntyre, Robert E., "The Still Hunt for New Faces," *Photoplay*, May 1922, pp. 40–41.
McKenna, Denise, "The Photoplay or the Pickaxe: Extras, Gender, and Labour in Early Hollywood," *Film History*, vol. XXIII, no. 1, 2011, pp. 5–19.
MacPherson, Harry, "Mug Colony," *Los Angeles Times*, June 2, 1940, p. H7, H10.
Mainwaring, Dan, "Hollywood Nobodies," *Good Housekeeping*, April 1938, pp. 40–41, 134, 137–38, 140, 142.
Martin, Pete, "A Day as a Dress Extra," *Saturday Evening Post*, February 19, 1944, pp. 37, 101.
Mast, Gerald, "In Memoriam: Central Casting," *New Republic*, December 27, 1975, pp. 25–27.
"Me and My Shadow . . . ," *Modern Screen*, June 1936, p. 22.
"Me and My Shadow," *Modern Screen*, June 1938, pp. 60–61.
"Mob of Extras," *Variety*, March 22, 1923, p. 23.
Montoya, Carina Monica. *Filipinos in Hollywood*. Charleston, SC: Arcadia Publishing, 2008.
"Movie Extras Whose Lives Rival Screen Romance," *Literary Digest*, September 25, 1920, pp. 69–70.
"Movie Guild Opens Doors to Extras," *New York Times*, October 27, 1933, p. 22.
"Movie Tempest: Screen Extras Drive for Own Union," *Business Week*, July 29, 1944, p. 104.
"Movie Stand-Ins for Hollywood's Most Glamorous Stars," *Life*, June 27 1944, pp. 49–51.
Muenchener, Jan, "Super the Great," *Photoplay*, October 1916, p. 67.
Muir, Jean, "Boardinghouse of Broken Hearts," *Saturday Evening Post*, September 19, 1953, pp. 41–42, 135–36.
Mullett, Mary, "Thousands Want to Be 'Extras' in the Movies," *American Magazine*, July 1926, pp. 50–52.
Munden, Kenneth W., ed. *The American Film Institute Catalog of Motion Pictures Produced in the United States: Feature Films, 1921–1930*. New York: R.R. Bowker, 1971.
Murray, William, "The Atmosphere People," *Playboy*, August 1974, pp. 75, 78, 90, 148, 150.
N.R.A. Motion Picture Code Provisions. Hollywood: Central Casting Corp., 1934.
Naughton, John, "That's Me, That Is," *Empire*, August 1997, pp. 96–104.

Neuman, Johanna, "The Effort Behind Being Just Faces in the Crowd," *Los Angeles Times*, August 17, 2005, p. E9.
"New Casting Chief Named," *Los Angeles Times*, September 12, 1934, p. A2.
"'New Deal' for Central," *Official Bulletin of the Screen Actors Guild*, April 1940, pp. 1, 7.
Nicholson, Jacquelyn, "Casting Couch: The Real Hollywood Sex Scandal," *Playgirl*, February 1977, pp. 33–35, 110.
Niven, David, *The Moon's a Balloon*. New York: G. P. Putnam's Sons, 1972.
"Notes from the Cinema Gold Coast," *New York Times*, October 14, 1934, p. X4.
"One Hundred Career Girls Find Home at Hollywood Studio Club," *Los Angeles Times*, August 3, 1941, p. F3.
"Pair Held in Asserted Film Plot," *Los Angeles Times*, August 31, 1926, p. A3.
"Pearl's Big Moment," *Life*, July 3, 1950, pp. 71–75.
Perry, George, "Hays Organization Gets Race Casting Manager," *Pittsburgh Courier*, October 15, 1927, p. 2.
Perry, Stella. *Extra-Girl*. New York: Frederick A. Stokes, 1929.
"Pictures Boom in Hollywood; Extras on Job," *Washington Post*, September 11, 1933, p. 12.
Poland, Joseph F., "Storming the Studio," *Motion Picture Magazine*, January 1917, pp. 99–101.
Prindle, David F. *The Politics of Glamour: Ideology and Democracy in the Screen Actors Guild*. Madison: University of Wisconsin Press, 1988.
The Problem of the Extra Player: First Recommendation of the Standing Committee of the Motion Picture Producers and of Screen Actors Guild, Inc. Unpaged [twelve-page] published report, dated October 1940.
The Problem of the Extra Player. 554-page manuscript, dated June 6, 1940, which was distilled into the item above.
"Prods. May Close Cent. Casting," *Hollywood Reporter*, December 4, 1939, pp. 1, 12.
Pryor, Thomas M., "Film Extras Get Wage Rise of 5%," *New York Times*, January 4, 1954, p. 23.
Rapkin, Mickey, "Leaving the Office Behind," *GQ*, October 2005, p. 140.
Ray, Charles. *Hollywood Shorts: Compiled from Incidents in the Everyday Life of Men and Women Who Entertain in Pictures*. Los Angeles: California Graphic Press, 1935.
"Real Mertons of the Movies a Problem at Hollywood," *New York Times*, July 29, 1923, p. XX9.
Redelings, Lowell E., "Men Behind the Scenes" *Hollywood Citizen-News*, February 10, 1947, p. 6.
Reece, Cornelius H., "The Army of Extras," *New York Today*, September 12, 1936, pp. 16–17, 28.
Regester, Charlene, "African American Extras in Hollywood during the 1920s and 1930s," *Film History*, vol. 9, 1997, pp. 95–115.
"Regulating 'Extras,'" *Variety*, January 20, 1926, p. 29.
Reid, Margaret, "Looking on with an Extra Girl," *Picture-Play*, January 1925, pp. 18–22; March 1925, pp. 47–49, 94; April 1925, pp. 25–27, 98, 106; June 1925, pp. 32–34, 98; July 1925, pp. 24–26, 98; September 1925, pp. 51–53, 108; October 1925, pp. 62–64, 96.
——, "Star for a Day," *Picture-Play*, May 1925, pp. 88–90, 106–7.
"Renewed Vogue for Old-Time Film Personalities; Still Fresh in Memory, They Have Definite B.O.," *Variety*, April 3, 1936, p. 2.
Reyes, Luis, and Peter Rubie. *Hispanics in Hollywood: A Celebration of 100 Years in Film and Television*. Hollywood: Lone Eagle Publishing Company, 2000.
Riley, John, "A Face in the Crowd," *Los Angeles Times*, January 19, 1986, p. AJ22B.
Rittenhouse, Mignon, "The Pleasures of Poverty Row," *Motion Picture*, November 1928, pp. 68–69, 118.
Rivlin, Michael, "Casting: Couches to Computers," *Millimeter*, December 1977, pp. 62, 64, 66–68.

Romero, Ramon, "Prisoners of Heart-Break Town," *The New Movie Magazine*, September 1933, pp. 26–27, 96–101.

Roseman, Ethel, "The Extra Girl Plays Atmosphere for the World War," *Motion Picture Classic*, September 1918, pp. 39–42, 72.

"Rosenblatt Meets with Two Groups," *Los Angeles Times*, January 26, 1934, pp. A1, A2.

Ross, Murray. *Stars and Strikes: Unionization of Hollywood*. New York: Columbia University Press, 1941.

———, "Hollywood Extras," in *The Movies in Our Midst: Documents in the Cultural History of Film in America*, ed. Gerald Mast. Chicago: University of Chicago Press, 1982, pp. 222–28. [Despite its appearance, this is not a full reprint of the original piece.]

"SAG Promises It'll Give Autonomy to B Players," *Daily Variety*, September 11, 1944, pp. 1, 12.

"Safecracking Suspect Adept with Cards," *Los Angeles Times*, August 6, 1946, p. A1.

St. Johns, Adela Rogers, "Stunting into Stardom," *Photoplay*, December 1922, pp. 39, 89.

———. *The Skyrocket*. New York: Cosmopolitan, 1925.

Sampson, Henry T. *Blacks in Black and White: A Source Book on Black Films*. Metuchen, NJ: Scarecrow Press, 1995.

Sangster, Margaret E., "The Stars That Never Were," *Photoplay*, August 1928, pp. 52–54, 116–17; September 1928, pp. 46–47, 84, 127; October 1928, pp. 50–51, 134–35; November 1928, pp. 46–47, 135–36; December 1928, pp. 44–45, 108–9.

Scheuer, Philip K., "Lonely Girls Find Home at Studio Club," *Los Angeles Times*, March 13, 1938, p. C3.

———, "Hollywood's Extras Live in Own World," *Los Angeles Times*, March 2, 1962, p. C17.

Schuessler, Fred, "Present-Day Casting Methods," *Moving Picture World*, March 26, 1927, p. 409.

Scott, John, "Talkies 'Shock Troops' Get Plenty of Shooting," *Los Angeles Times*, November 15, 1931, pp. B11, B13.

———, "Hindu Caste System Has Parallel among Actors," *Los Angeles Times*, February 28, 1932, pp. B13, B14.

———, "Central Casting Bureau Extras' Only Hope for That Long-Awaited 'Break,'" *Los Angeles Times*, April 8, 1934, p. A1.

———, "Ten Thousand Extras Doomed," *Los Angeles Times*, May 23, 1937, p. C1.

Scott, John L., "Little People Have Big Time in Films," *Los Angeles Times*, April 26, 1968, Part IV, pp. 1, 12.

"Screen Director Asks for Extras: Gets Office Wrecked," *Chicago Defender*, December 31, 1932, p. 6.

"Screen Extras' Plea Assailed," *Los Angeles Times*, August 31, 1933, p. A5.

"Screen Extras Win," *Business Week*, December 23, 1944, p. 106.

Shane, Bob, "The Movie Extra—Just Another Face in the Crowd," *Los Angeles Times* Calendar, September 24, 1967, p. 11.

Sheridan-Bickers, H., "Extra Ladies and Gentlemen," *Motion Picture Magazine*, July 1917, pp. 65–70; August 1917, pp. 91–96; September 1917, pp. 80–85.

Sherward, David, "Do's and Don'ts of Working as an Extra," *Back Stage*, June 23, 1989, pp. 22, 24.

Shirley, Lois, "The Girl Who Played Greta Garbo," *Photoplay*, August 1929, pp. 29, 108.

Silden, Isobel, "Two of the Faces in the Crowd," *Baltimore Sun*, January 14, 1973, p. SM11, SM14.

———, "Faces in the Crowd," *Southland Sunday*, June 3, 1973, pp. 14–18.

Silverman, Henry K., "Central Casting Performs a Comprehensive Service," *Los Angeles Times*, December 4, 1931, p. I28.

Simross, Lynn, "Studio Club Closes Doors on Memories," *Los Angeles Times*, February 9, 1975, Part X, pp. 1, 18–20.
Slide, Anthony. *The Big V: A History of the Vitagraph Company*. Metuchen, NJ: Scarecrow Press, 1987.
———, "The Character Player," *Films in Review*, March 1990, pp. 130–38; April 1990, pp. 204–11.
———. *They Also Wrote for the Fan Magazines: Film Articles by Literary Giants from E. E. Cummings to Eleanor Roosevelt, 1920–1939*. Jefferson, NC: McFarland, 1992.
———. *The Hollywood Novel: A Critical Gide to Over 1200 Works*. Jefferson, NC: McFarland, 1995.
———. *Silent Players: A Biographical and Autobiographical Study of 100 Silent Film Actors and Actresses*. Lexington: University Press of Kentucky, 2002.
Smith, Helen G., "The Extra Girl Is Handed a Few Snickers," *Photoplay*, March 1920, pp. 107–8.
Smith, James Bell, "Would You Break Your Neck to Get into the Movies?," *So This Is Paris and Hollywood*, September 1925, pp. 18–20.
Snelson, Floyd G., "The 'Low-Down' on the Negro in Hollywood: Snelson Reveals 'Inside' Story of Noted Movie City," *Pittsburgh Courier*, September 24, 1932, p. 6.
Spearing, James O., "The 'Chorus Lady' Fades into the Past," *New York Times*, August 7, 1926, pp. SM16, SM18.
Springer, John Parris. *Hollywood Fictions: The Dream Factory in American Popular Culture*. Norman: University of Oklahoma Press, 2000.
Squier, Emma Lindsay, "Mr. Wang of Chinatown," *Picture-Play Magazine*, April 1922, pp. 72, 102.
Squire, Susan, "The Road to Extradom," *New York Times* Sunday Magazine, March 22, 1981, pp. 21–24.
Standard Casting Directory. Hollywood: The Standard/Standard Casting Directory, 1922–37.
"Stand-Ins Belong to an Exclusive Profession," *Life*, November 1, 1937, pp. 98–99.
"Stand-Ins for Stars," *Literary Digest*, November 4, 1933, p. 35.
"A Stand-In Speaks on 'Nepotism' in Casting Extras," *Los Angeles Herald Examiner*, December 5, 1983, p. A10.
"Stars Assume Humble Parts," *Los Angeles Times*, February 4, 1923, Part III, p. 33.
Stenn, David. *Bombshell: The Life and Death of Jean Harlow*. New York: Doubleday, 1993.
———, "It Happened One Night . . . at MGM," *Vanity Fair*, April 2003, pp. 282–98.
Sterling, Anna Kate, ed. *The Best of Shadowland*. Metuchen, NJ: Scarecrow Press, 1987.
Steward, Robert W., "Bad Actors," *Los Angles Times*, Metro Section, February 15, 1987, pp. 1, 3.
The Story of the Screen Actors Guild. Los Angeles: Screen Actors Guild, 1982.
Strong, Ralph, "One Extra Girl," *Picture-Play Magazine*, April 1916, pp. 54–64.
"Studio Club Dedicates New Home," *Los Angeles Times*, May 8, 1926, p. A1.
Sullivan, Ed, "Exploding the Stand-In Myth!," *Silver Screen*, August 1939, pp. 40–41, 66.
Surmelian, Leon, "Part of the Show," *Silver Screen*, April 1938, pp. 52–53, 66–68.
Taves, Brian. *Robert Florey: The French Expressionist*. Metuchen, NJ: Scarecrow Press, 1987.
Tensing, Helen, "I Am an Extra," *Los Angeles Times* Magazine, May 23, 1937, pp. 11, 27.
Thackrey, Winfrid Kay. *Member of the Crew*. Lanham, MD: Scarecrow Press, 2001.
Theisen, Earl, "The Old Timer," *International Photographer*, April 1935, pp. 12, 27.
———, "Eyes toward Hollywood," *International Photographer*, September 1935, pp.21–22.
"They Also Serve in Realm of Motion Pictures Who Only Stand In and Wait," *Los Angeles Times*, March 21, 1938, p. 24.

Thibodeaux, Cressandra, "Extra! Extra!," *Back Stage West*, October 3, 2002, pp. 14–16.
Thomas, Dan, "A New Deal for Hollywood's Extra Girls," December 17, 1934, syndicated column.
———, "Pay Cuts Raise Hopes of Picture Stand-Ins," January 31, 1935, syndicated column.
Thompson, Howard, "Movie 'Terrace' under Local Construction," *New York Times*, January 3, 1960, p. X7.
"Three Steps to Raise Pay of Vocational Extra Player," *Screen Actor*, November 1940, pp. 11–14.
Tracy, Virginia, "Acting for the Camera: Experiences of a Woman in the Motion Picture Studios," *Century Magazine*, September 1917, pp. 641–56.
Van Dyke, Clayton, "They Also Serve," *Picture Play*, August 1936, pp. 48–49, 63.
Vaught, Steve, "Hollywood Studio Club," *Architectural Digest*, November 2008, pp. 118–23.
Vazzana, Eugene Michael. *Silent Film Necrology*. Jefferson, NC: McFarland, 2001.
Verrier, Richard, "Extras Star in Real-Life Drama," *Los Angeles Times*, June 10, 21011, pp. B1, B5.
Waddell, Al G., "With the Photoplayers," *Los Angeles Times*, March 12, 1913, p. III4.
Wagner, Rob, "Supes and Supermen," *Saturday Evening Post*, March 31, 1917, pp. 15–17, 33–34, 37–38.
———. *Film Folk: "Close-Ups" of the Men, Women, and Children Who Make the "Movies."* New York: The Century Co., 1918.
Wallace, Inez, "Robin Hood's Double," *Collier's*, August 6, 1938, pp. 17, 42.
Waterbury, Ruth, "The Truth about Breaking into the Movies," *Photoplay*, December 1926, pp. 32–34, 92; January 1927, pp. 38–39, 106–8; February 1927, pp. 40–41, 130–33.
———, "Don't Go to Hollywood," *Photoplay*, March 1927, pp. 50–51, 125–28.
———, "The Mother Confessor of Hollywood," *Photoplay*, October 1927, pp. 40–41, 94.
———, "The Underworld of Hollywood," *Photoplay*, August 1928, pp. 28–29, 113–14.
Watkins, Mel. *Stepin Fetchit: The Life and Times of Lincoln Perry*. New York: Pantheon Books, 2005.
Weatherwax, Clara, "Ain't Hollywood Romantic?," *New Theatre*, June 1936, pp. 16–17.
Weaver, John V.A., "The Extra Man," *Vanity Fair*, February 1930, p. 61.
Webb, Ken. *Extras! in the Movies*. Allentown, PA: The Author, 2004.
Weinert, Laura, "Atmosphere Report," *Back Stage West*, October 4, 2001, pp. 10–11.
Welkos, Robert W., "Extras! Extras! Read All about 'Em," *Los Angeles Times*, December 31, 1991, pp. F1, F10–F11.
"The Wild Bunch," *L.A. Weekly*, February 27, 1987, pp. 61, 63.
Wilson, Harry Leon. *Merton of the Movies*. Garden City, NY: Doubleday, Page, 1922.
Wolfe, Ron, "From Stillwater to Hollywood and Back," *Tulsa Tribune*, August 1, 1986, pp. C1, C6.
Wooldridge, A. L., "Our Chinese Movie Actors," *Picture-Play Magazine*, September 1926, pp. 83–85, 104.
"Xtras Want 300-Mile Zone Raised to 3000," *Daily Variety*, June 20, 1944, p. 1, 9.
"You Call Us," *Newsweek*, May 18, 1959, p. 118.
Young, Robert, Jr. *Roscoe "Fatty" Arbuckle: A Bio-Bibliography*. Westport, CT: Greenwood Press, 1994.
"Zanuck Resigns from Warners," *Los Angeles Times*, April 15, 1933, p. A1.
Zeidman, Bennie, "The Extra Girl," *Motion Picture Magazine*, December 1916, pp. 45–48.
Zetter, Gwen, "Hollywood's Most Successful Extra," *The New Movie Magazine*, May 1935, pp. 18, 52–53.

INDEX

Academy of Motion Picture Arts and Sciences, 73, 140, 209
Acker, Jean, 11, 165, 175, 181, 215
Actors Agency Directory, 67
Actors Equity, 209
Adair, Virginia, 46
Adventures of Robin Hood, The, 125
African American Extras, 195–204
Ai-Li-Ling, 195
Airplane Pilots as Extras, 219
Alice in Wonderland, 127
All about Eve, 153
Allen, Angela, 138
Allen, Dave, 65–66, 70, 108
Allen, Irene, 198
Alvarado, Don, 119
American Federation of Labor, 214, 215
Anderson, Claire, 118
Anderson, Eddie "Rochester," 204
Andre, Carl, 12
Animal Noise Imitation, 99, 102
Anti-Semitism, 39–40, 66, 89
Apfel, Oscar, 169, 171–72
"Appetite Bill," 20
Applause, 100–101
Arbuckle, Roscoe "Fatty," 95, 194
Arden, Jane 151
Arizona, 115
Arlen, Richard, 123
Arnold, Edward, 123, 135
Arnow, Max, 130
Arthur, Jean, 128
Artist, The, 140
Artists and Models Club, 103
Associated Actors and Artistes of America, 215
Astaire, Fred, 136
Astor, Gertrude, 166, 177–79, 181, 186
Atherton, Jane, 20
Auber, Brigitte, 138
Ayres, Lew, 123

Baby Face, 203
"Baby LeRoy," 127
"Baby Peggy," 107
Baer, Lillian, 120
Baggott, King, 165, 166
Bailey, Lynn, 103
Baird, Leah, 167
Baker, Carroll, 138
Bakewell, William, 13
Ball, Lucille, 129
Ballerino, Mel, 81
Banbury, Johnny, 222
Barham, Gene, 46
Barnett, Vince, 147–48
Barry, Fern, 121
Barrymore, John, 4, 135
Barrymore, Lionel, 123
Barthelmess, Richard, 123
Barty, Billy, 222
Battle, The, 6
Bauchens, Anne, 52
Baxter, Warner, 123
"Beach Pete," 20
Beal, Frank, 160
"Beards," 78
Beauchamp, Joan, 135
Beban, George, 6
Bedford, Barbara, 175
Beery, Noah, 38
Beery, Wallace, 93, 96, 124
Beetson, Fred W., 5, 66, 197
Belfrage, Cedric, 33, 89, 92

Benedict, Brooks, 215
Bergman, Ingrid, 128
Berkeley, Busby, 101–2
Berry, Art, Jr., 123
Bertolino, Angela, 228
Bevan, Billy, 162–63
Big Broadcast of 1935, 201
Big Country, The, 138
Big Trail, The, 43–44
Biggins, Joe, 226
Biker Gang Extras, 227
Birth of a Nation, The, 6, 25, 37, 195, 196
Blagol, Lieutenant George, 144
Blake, Roland, 32
Blondell, Joan, 117
Bloom, Phil, 108
Blue, Monte, 161, 167, 181, 185
Blythe, Betty, 176–77, 183
Boardway, William, 152
Bogart, Humphrey, 128
Bohn, John, 135
Bohnen, Elissa, 103
Bondi, Beulah, 3
Bonner, Priscilla, 28
Boob, The, 44
Boren, Charles, 198
Borgani, Nick, 123
Bowman, Sid, 43
Boyea, Samuel A., 198
Boyer, Charles, 126, 128, 134
Bracken, Eddie, 126
Bradley, Paul, 32, 112–13, 120
Brent, Evelyn, 13, 169
Brent, George, 123, 125
Breton, "General" Ted, 24
Brewer, Roy, 216
Brewster, Lucille, 128
Bridges, Jeff, 140
Brill, Marty, 146
Brindle, Karl, 81, 225
Broken Blossoms, 193
Bronson, Arthur S., 66
Bronson, Betty, 46, 53
"Bronze Boys," 78
Brooks, Betty, 128
Brooks, Louise, 169
Brown, Frank, 135
Brown, Joe E., 123, 135, 136
Brown, Lucille, 27, 196
Brown, Winna/Winnie, 137
Bruce, Howard, 135
Buccaneer, The, 8
Buchanan, Arch, 43
Buell, Jed, 220
"Bumpers," 78
Bunny, George, 162
Bupp, Moyer "Sonny," 152
Bupp, Tommy, 152
Burns, Edward, 169
Burns, Fred D., 209
Burroughs, Edgar Rice, 87
Burtis, Thomson, 35
Bushman, Francis X., 168, 169, 183
Butler, Charles, 197, 198
Butterworth, Charles, 124

Cabanne, Christy, 161
Cagney, James, 135, 137, 207, 212, 213
California Department of Industrial Relations, 63
California Free Employment Bureau, 67–68
California Industrial Welfare Commission, 63, 64, 70, 74, 94
California Light Horse Regiment, 112
California National Guard, 111
Call Bureau, 67
Calm, Alan, 135
Cameron, Gene, 46
Campbell, Agatha, 60
Campbell, Barbara, 127
Campbell, Eva, 24
"Cannibals," 78
Cantlon, Wanda, 129
Cantor, Eddie, 126, 136, 208
Cantway, Maxine, 99
Capra, Frank, 135, 205
Carmen, Jewel, 27
Carmona, Pedro, 188
Carol, Sue, 13
Carr, Harry, 19
Carter, Ben, 200
Casablanca, 128, 147
Castle, William, 182
Catlett, Lloyd, 140
Cavalcade, 11
Cavitt, Jane, 58
Caylor, Roy, 45

Ceballos, Larry, 99, 101
Central Casting, 12, 13, 62–81, 89, 102, 104, 108, 110, 112, 115, 116, 150, 151, 152, 181, 190, 197, 198, 199, 200, 202, 205, 210, 214
Chadwick, Helene, 165
Chamur, Boris, 124
Chan, George, 195
Chan, Jim, 195
Chan, Luke 195
Chan, Spencer, 195, 201
Chan Lee, 194
Chaplin, Charlie, 48, 90, 132, 135, 153, 161
Charge of the Light Brigade, The, 111
Charlot, André, 170
Chasing thru Europe, 154-55
Chautard, Emile, 173
Chew, Frank, 195
Chick, Dude, 109
Childers, Naomi, 165
Children as Extras, 22, 71–72, 80–81, 127, 152, 195, 221–22
Chinese Extras, 193–95, 201
Chirva, Alex, 144
Chorus Girls, 98–103, 105
Christie, Al, 29
Churchill, Randolph, 106
Cinema Auxiliary, 197
Cinema Players, Inc., 209
Cinema Troop, 111
Citizen Kane, 147
Civilization, 12
Clark, Bert, 120
Clark, Charles, 135, 136
Clark, Gordon, 128
Clarke, Mae, 163, 186
Clayton, Ethel, 160, 181
Cleopatra, 7, 61, 161, 198, 199
Clifford, Ruth, 169
Coffey, Walter, 123
Cohen, Irving "Big Gangi," 110
Colbert, Claudette, 121, 131, 136
Coleman, Beatrice, 136
Collins, C. B., 68
Collins, Neil, 128, 135
Colman, Ronald, 119, 120, 126
Compson, Betty, 169
Condon, Frank, 84
Conference of Studio Unions, 216
Conklin, Chester, 161, 163-64, 168, 181
Conklin, Heinie, 184
Conley, James, 196
Conley, Nellie. *See* Sul-Te-Wan, Madame
Conley, Onest, 196
Conley, Otto, 196
Conners, Marilynn, 87–88
Conniff, Vincent, 93
Constance, Al, 136, 137
Conte, Richard, 182
Conti, Albert, 169
Cook, Clyde, 162–63, 185
Cook, Paul, 206
Cooper, Edna Mae, 26
Cooper, Gary, 13, 124, 169
Cooper, Miriam, 119
Corey, Eugene. *See* Corrado, Gino
Corey, Wendell, 126
Cornell, Jimmy, 128
Corrado, Gino, 147
Corsaro, Franco, 96
Costello, Delmar, 123
Costello, Helene and Dolores, 15
Costello, Maurice, 158–59, 169
Covan, Will, 201
Covered Wagon, The, 189
Coxen, Ed, 160
Craig, Hal, 214
Crawford, Joan, 13, 119, 121, 124, 131
Crawford, Mildred, 123
Cripple Creek Bar-Room Scene, 16
Crosby, Bing, 123, 126, 131, 135, 136, 191
Cross, Oliver, 152
Crowd, The, 50–51
Crowd in a Box, 226
Crowd Pictures, 6, 10, 38, 40, 104, 205–6, 227
Crucifixion of Extras, 225
Cruze, James, 189
Cukor, George, 11, 90, 178
Cunard, Grace, 175
Curtis, Billy, 221–22
Curtiz, Michael, 6, 40

Daddy's Gone a-Hunting, 157
Dakin, Douglas, 202
Dancing Pirates, 189
D'Arcy, Roy, 169
Dare, Frances, 46
Dark Cloud, William, 119, 189
"Dash," 140

Datig, Fred, 30, 31, 37, 95, 102, 104, 163, 166
Daumery, Carrie Ysave, 144
Davidoff, Lieutenant Colonel Alexis, 144
Davidson, Max, 161
Davies, Marion, 47, 157
Davis, Bette, 122, 131
Davis, Lieutenant Cedric B., 145
D'Avril, Yola, 181
Daw, Marjorie, 53
Day, Dulcie, 54, 215
"Day Checks," 25
De Brulier, Nigel, 38, 176
De Foe, Annette, 119
De Havilland, Olivia, 130
de Lanti, Stella, 46
De Long, June 65–66
De Vorak, Geraldine, 121
De Witt, Daisy, 121
Dearborn, Dr. W. W., 124, 135
DeBeaver, Charles "Jumpy," 125
deCoy, Bob, 202
Dee, Aileen, 45
Dees, Mary, 132–33, 134
DeKay, Jean, 118
Del Rio, Dolores, 119
DeMille, Cecil B., 6–8, 9, 27, 39–40, 61, 84, 138, 145, 161, 172
Denny, Reginald, 166
Desmond, William, 169
DeVerdi, Eugene, 135
Devil Dancer, The, 191
Dieterle, William, 113
Dietrich, Betty, 136, 137
Dietrich, Carol, 136, 137
Dietrich, Marlene, 136, 137
"Dinge," 203
Dive Bomber, 206
Divine Lady, The, 42
Dix, Richard, 123, 135, 189
Dixon, Jeannette, 105
Dodd, Father Neil, 147–50
Dodd, Paul A., 210
Dolan, Rose Marie, 65
Donat, Robert, 126
Doner, Ted, 160
Dooley, Billy, 160
Doubles, 135–40
Douglas, Laurie, 58
Douglas, Patricia, 92–94
Downey, Jane, 121
Downing, Della, 126
Doyle, Mimi, 120
Doyle, Patricia, 120–21
Dr. Jekyll and Mr. Hyde, 146
Dragon Seed, 195
Dreiser, Theodore, 6, 86–87
Drendell, Paula, 152
"Dress Extras," 79, 137, 151, 152, 153–54, 217
Driscoll, Bobby, 222
"Drugstore Cowboys," 11
Dry White Season, A, 202
DuBrey, Claire, 159–60, 161
"Dude," 140
Dummies Replacing Extras, 226
Dunne, Irene, 121, 136, 137
Duprez, June, 128
Durbin, Deanna, 120
Durfee, Minta, 8
Dvorak, Ann, 119, 129
Dying on Camera, 106

Eagle Eye, Charles, 189
East Indian Extras, 191
Eaton, Pearl, 101
Eddy, Don, 136
Eddy, Helen Jerome, 53
Edison, Thomas, 16
Edward, Prince of Wales, 154
Edwards, Mary, 59
Efron, Nadja, 144
Eilers, Sally, 13
Elder, Jack, 146
Elderly Extras, 23, 141–42
Elinor, Carli, 186
"Ella, the Extra Girl," 36
"Ella Cinders," 13
Elliott, Maurice, 135
Ellis, Patricia, 121
Elmer Awards, 132
Essanay Studios, 24
Ethnic Extras, 187–204
Evarts, Hal G., 44
Extra, The, 45
Extra!, The, 211
ExtraCastingGuild.com, 228
Extra-Girl, 83
Extras, 229–30
Extras Advisory Committee, 209
Extras in Fiction, 82–97

Fair, Elinor, 181
Fairbanks, Douglas, Jr., 128
Fairbanks, Douglas, Sr., 138, 190
Farnum, Franklyn, 156, 160, 161, 215
Farnum, William, 161, 183, 184
Farr, Frank E., 136, 137
Farrell, Charles, 46
Farrell, Major John, 11, 145
"Father Dodd's Boys," 150
Faye, Alice, 121
Faye, Julia, 26, 181, 183
Fazenda, Louise, 13
Felix, Seymour, 101
Ferguson, Otis, 12, 39, 212
Fern, Jeanette, 223
Fields, W. C., 135, 137
Filipino Extras, 192
Finch, Flora, 165
Fineman, B. P., 29
Finn, Lila, 138
Fisher, Gloria, 127
Fitzgerald, Barry, 124, 128
Fitzgerald, Byron, 135
Fleming, James, 125
Fleming, Victor, 146
Florey, Robert, 48, 119, 162, 167–68
Flowers, Bess, 153–54, 215
Flynn, Errol, 125, 191
Fonda, Henry, 129
Fong, William, 195
Football Matches, Extras in, 146
Ford, Mme. Elizabeth, 200
Ford, Francis, 174–75, 191
Ford, John, 174, 191
Forrester, Mel, 11
Foster, Richard, 117, 124
Foster, Susanna, 132
Fox Movietone Follies of 1929, 99–100
"Frenchie," 96
Friganza, Trixie, 160
From Here to Eternity, 225
Fung, Willie, 194, 195

Gable, Clark, 13, 132, 191
Gabriel, Guy, 123
Gan, Chester, 195
Gangster Films, 108–10
Garbo, Greta, 13, 97, 121, 136
Garcia, Allan, 74, 209
Gardner, Ava, 138
Gardner, Jack, 109
Garnetz, Max, 38
Garon, Pauline, 183
Garrison, Harold (Slickem), 200
Garrison, Jules, 129
Garthwaite, Dr. J. S., 19
Gaynor, Janet, 121
Gebhart, Myrtle, 53, 54
George, Voya, 48
Gerard, W. C., 210
Gervais, Ricky, 229, 230
Ghosal, Profulla Kumar, 191
Gibson, Helen, 183, 185
Gibson, Hoot, 166
Giesler, Jerry, 66
Gilbert, Althea, 35
Gilman, Mat, 124
Girl from Hollywood, The, 87
Girl 27, 93
Gish, Lillian, 119
Glass, Carter, 123
Glass, Gaston, 11
Gleason, Adda, 175
Gleason, James, 124
Glyn, Elinor, 144–45
Goddard, Frank, 108, 146
Goddard, Paulette, 138
Golden Bed, The, 7–8
Goldwyn, Samuel, 28, 191, 206
Golitzin, Princess Natalie, 144–45
Gomez, Angela, 188
Gone with the Wind, 110, 128, 129, 147
Good Earth, The, 195
Goodbye, Mr. Chips, 155
Goodrich, Jack, 123
Goodstadt, Louis M., 20, 26
Gordon, Richard H., 216
Gould, Gypsy, 179–80
Grace, Martin, 139–40
Grace, Meyer, 146
Graham, Herschel, 152, 153
Graham, Julia, 57
Granas, Marilyn, 127
Grant, Cary, 123, 131–32
Gray, Margaret, 152
Gray, Marion, 38
Great Dictator, The, 161
Great Gabbo, The, 101

Great Train Robbery, The, 16
Green, Myron C. "Babe," 151
Green Goddess, The, 191
Greenberger, Lillian, 119
Gregory, Bob, 109
Grey, Arnold, 123
Griffin, Carlton E., 209
Griffith, D. W., 6, 25, 27, 37, 119, 189, 193, 195, 196
Griffith, Gertrude, 52
Groves, Scotty, 69
Gubbins, Tom, 194
Guiding Light, The, 226–27
Gullivan, Tim, 23
Gung Ho, 132
Gunga Din, 10, 112
Gunn, Fronzi, 46

Haar, Silver, 189
Haddon, Earl, 136
Hale, Creighton, 169, 184, 185
Half Shot at Sunrise, 145
Hall, Betty, 123
Hall, Eddie, 123
Hall, Ella, 160
Hall, Gladys, 89
Hall, Jon, 138
Hall, Stuart, 151
Hall, Ted, 123
Hallellujah, 197, 198, 200
Halliday, John, 169
Hamblem, Alberta, 107
Hamilton, George, 13
Hamilton, Guy, 138
Hamilton, Mahlon, 165, 166, 181
Hampton, Benjamin B., 51
Hampton, Burt, 72
Hankin, Katherine, 105
Harding, Ann, 119, 123
Hargreaves, Bryan, 125
Harlan, Kenneth, 176
Harlow, Jean 132–33
Harman, Doris, 103
Haro, Daro, 195
Haroldi, Kasha, 121
Harris, Edna, 53
Harris, Mildred, 53, 161, 181
Harris, Theresa, 203–4
Harron, Robert, 6
Harry and Walter Go to New York, 227
Hart, Neil, 160
Hatton, Raymond, 181
Havens, George, 222
Haydon, Julie, 119
Hayes, Helen, 121
Hays, Will, 55, 62, 65, 80
Hayworth, Rita, 128
Hearn, Edward, 160
Hearts in Dixie, 198
Hello, Dolly!, 11, 179
Henabery, Joseph, 12, 25
Henderson, Del, 160, 165
Henderson, Mae, 202
Henie, Sonja, 120
Henkel, Alice, 24
Henry, Charlotte, 127
Hepburn, Katharine, 120
Herbert, Hugh, 123, 125
Here Comes the Groom, 135
Higgins, V., 20
Hill, Howard, 125
Hinds, Joe, 124
Hindu Extras, 191, 193
Hogan, Hap, 108
Holden, William, 128
Holl, Karl, 119
Holloway, Carol, 160
"Hollywood," 84–85
Hollywood Boulevard, 48
Hollywood Extra Theatrical Cold Cream, 17
Hollywood Hotel, 132
Hollywood OS, 228
Hollywood Picture Players Association, 209
Hollywood Standin Players, Inc., 132
Hollywood Stand-Ins Guild, 132
Hollywood Story, 182–84, 185
Hollywood Studio Club, the, 52–61
Holman, William S., 210
Holmes, Helen, 160
Holmes, Helene, 121
Holmes, Stuart, 183, 185
Hoover, Bill, 123
Hope, Bob, 128, 131
Hopkins, Una M., 209
Hopper, DeWolf, 191
Horton, Clara, 176

Horton, Edward Everett, 123
Howard, Leslie, 117, 126, 128
Howard, Peter, 142
Howell, John Holmes, 19
Huff, Louise, 52
Hughes, Shirley, 131
Hunchback of Notre Dame, The, 37–38, 113, 119
Hurricane, The, 138, 191
Hussey, Ruth, 128

I Should Have Stayed Home, 91
IATSE, 216
Ickioka, Mia, 195
If I Were King, 112
Ikonikoff, General Alexander, 144
Imitation of Life, 199
Ince, John, 173, 215
Ince, Ralph, 173
Ince, Thomas H., 12, 20, 22, 173, 188, 189, 193
Indian War Council, 16
Inflatable Crowd Co., 226
Ingraham, Lloyd, 171
Intermezzo, 128
International Union of Photoplayers of America, 25–26
Intolerance, 12, 25, 27, 37, 119, 150, 189
Irving, Dorothy, 104
Irving, Mary Jane, 107, 121
Isleib, Mary Lou, 127
It Happened in Hollywood, 135–36
It's a Wonderful Life, 138
Italian, The, 6
Ivano, Paul, 48
Izumioa, Lois, 195

Jackson, Peaches, 107
Jackson, Robert M. Parrington, 147
Jake, Yukon, 109
Jannes, Maris, 30
Jannings, Emil, 143–44, 145
Japanese Extras, 193, 195
Jazz Singer, The, 98
Jeffers, Mike, 211, 213, 217
Jenkins, Buth, 222
Jensen, Ashley, 229
Jensen, Dayle, 121
Jewish Extras, 39–40
Jezebel, 123
Joan of Arc, 11
Johnson, Lillie, 223
Johnson, Noble, 196–97
Johnson, Wayne, 223
Johnston, Julanne, 53, 161
Johnstone, Frances, 104
Jones, Chester, 198, 202
Jones, Mrs. Eleanor, 52
Joy, Billy, 21
Joy, Carl, 68
Joy, Leatrice, 68, 194
Judith of Bethulia, 141, 142
Jue Fong, 195
Junior Screen Actors Guild, 208
Jurado, Elena, 194

Kalo, 194
Kam Tang, 195
Kane, Marjorie "Babe," 183, 215
Kearns, Madge, 24
Keaton, Buster, 182
Kellogg, Sue, 127
Kelly, Dan, 86
Kelsey, Tom, 227
Kennedy, Bert, 123
Kennedy, Madge, 90
Kentucky, 199
Keyes, Evelyn, 57, 90
Keys of the Kingdom, The, 195
Kilgannon, James, 152
Kimbrough, Betty, 152
King, Anita, 27
King Hou Chang, 195
King Kong, 119, 138
King of Kings, 27, 39, 145
Kingsley, Grace, 36
Kingston, Samuel F., 30–31
Kinnell, Murray, 210
Kinney, Mabel E., 94
Kirkwood, James, 181, 185
Knepper, Max, 89
Kobliansky, Nicholas, 144
Kolovaloss, Major Nicholai, 144
Komai, Tetsu, 195
Kraft, Henry, 123

La Cava, Gregory, 57, 58
La Plante, Laura, 46
La Rocque, Rod, 168

La Rue, Carmen, 119
Ladd, Alan, 13, 128
Lait, Jack, 87
Lake, Alice, 169, 181
Lamarr, Hedy, 124, 146
Lamarr, Sylvia, 124
Lamour, Dorothy, 138
Lamphier, Fay, 160
Lane, Rosemary, 132
Lanoe, J. Jiquel, 141, 142
L'argent, 15
L'arroseur arosé, 15
LaRue, Jack, 129
Lasky Home Guard, 33
Last Command, The, 143, 145
Laughton, Charles, 123
Lawrence, Florence, 165, 169
Le Saint, Edward, 160
Le Seuer, Hal, 121–22
Lee, Eddie, 195
Lee, Fred, 152
Lee, Jennie, 6
Lee, Sammy, 101
Leeman, Jack, 123
Leigh, Leona, 45
Leigh, Vivian, 128
Leisen, Mitchell, 105
Leong, James B., 195
Leopold of Austria, Archduke, 145
Lewis, Vera, 191
L'Herbier, Marcel, 15
Life and Death of 9413—a Hollywood Extra, The, 48–49
Limelight, 162
Lincoln, Elmo, 183, 184
Lincoln Motion Picture Company, 197
Lindsay, Earl, 101
Lindsay, Margaret, 121
Lindsay, Vachel, 6
Little People, 220–23
Liu, Maurice, 195
Llewellyn, Russ, 128
Lloyd, Harold, 125, 169
Lloyd, Norman, 90
Location Filming, 42–44, 225
Lodijensky, Theodore, 144
Loff, Jeanette, 13
Loller, George, 123
Lombard, Karen, 123
London, Jean "Babe," 164
Lonely Party, The, 15
Loo, Bessie, 190
Loo, Richard, 195
Loo Loy, 195
Lorre, Peter, 123
Lost Horizon, 120
Lotus Long, 195
Louie, Yasha, 11
Love Me Tender, 138
Loy, Myrna, 13, 131
Lubou, Haynes, 84
Lucas, Wilfred, 160, 161, 168
Lumière Brothers, 15
Luther, Ann, 181
Lynch, Richmond, 128, 134–35
Lynn, Leo, 123
Lyons, Cliff, 125
Lyons, Red, 109

Mabry, Anna, 201, 202
MacCulloch, Campbell, 66, 70, 72, 78, 89
MacDonald, Allan, 72
MacDonald, Marie, 24
Mack, Berna, 136
Mack, Eric, 38
MacLaren, Mary, 161, 176, 185
MacMurray, Fred, 123
Mailes, Charles Hill, 175–76
Malone, Pat, 124
Mamoulian, Rouben, 100
Mann, Hank, 163, 168, 183, 185
Mann, Leonard, 126
Manon, Marcia, 26
Many Treaties, Chief, 190, 201
March, Fredric 123
Maren, Jerry, 223
Marlow, Pat, 135
Marsh, Adriane, 48
Marsh, Gloria, 65–66
Marsh, Mae, 13, 169, 185, 186
Marshall, Herbert, 123
Martin, Chris-Pin, 188
Marvin, Lee, 13
Mason, Sarah Y., 53
Mast, Gerald, 224
May, James, 135, 137
Mayer, Louis B., 164, 165, 166
Mayo, Frank, 169, 191

Mayo, Harry, 209, 210, 214
McAvoy, May, 166
McChessey, Alice, 24
McClure, Reverend A. W., 150
McConnell, Mary, 20
McCoy, Horace, 89, 91
McCoy, Tim, 188, 189
McCrea, Joel, 47, 123
McDowell, Claire, 161, 175, 181
McGill, Barney, 42
McGuirk, LeRoy, 109
McIntyre, Robert E., 26, 28
McKee, Stewart, 210
McKenzie, Jack, 108
McKim, Josephine, 146
McLaglen, Arthur, 135, 137
McLaglen, Victor, 112, 135, 137
McNarre, Lucille, 51
Meader, Bill, 123
Meeker, Chris Marie, 121
Meet John Doe, 205, 206
Mel, Marian L., 71, 98–99, 102, 151
Melford, George, 161, 173, 185
Menjou, Adolphe, 123, 126
Merchant, Stephen, 229
Merrihugh, Malcolm, 123, 131–32
Merton of the Movies, 85
Metro-Goldwyn-Mayer, 165
Mexican Extras, 187–89, 201
Miatleva, Nina, 144
"Midgets." *See* Little People
Midsummer Night's Dream, The, 130
Miles, Peter, 222
Military Extras, 111–12, 143–45, 147
Milland, Ray, 123
Miller, Mozelle, 128
Miller, Pearl, 128, 135
Miller Bros. 101 Ranch, 189
Miner, Mary, 136, 137
Mix, Tom, 119
Mob Scenes, 38–39
Models, 103–4
Modern Times, 161
Mogul, Gale, 126
Mohr, Hal, 42
Money, 15
Monroe, Marilyn, 57, 90
Monsieur Beaucaire, 45–46
Monsieur Verdoux, 161
Montgomery, Jack, 119
Montt, Christina, 46
Moore, Colleen, 13, 86
Moore, Matt, 185
Moore, Victor, 135
Moraine, Lyle, 128, 135
More the Merrier, The, 128
Morgan, Julia, 55
Morgan, Michelle, 4
Mori, Tochia, 195
Morita, Mike, 195
Morley, Karen, 123
Morris, Clara, 46
Morris, Raphael, 45
Morse, Holly, 69
Motion Picture Extras and Supporting Players Association, 66, 208–9, 213
Motion Picture Producers and Distributors of America, 35, 55, 62, 63, 64, 66, 210
Motion Picture Relief Fund, 170, 171
Mouster, John, 142
Moving Picture Machine Operators of the United States and Canada, 216
Moy Ming, 195
Muir, Jean, 121
Mulhall, Jack, 161, 168, 169
Mulligan, Betty, 46
Muni, Paul, 123
Murder at the Vanities, 105
Murphy, George, 214
Murray, James, 13, 50–51
Mussolini, Benito, 154
My Official Wife, 155
Myers, Harry, 169, 181

NAACP, 200
Naish, J. Carroll, 128
Naked and the Dead, The, 225
Napier Raikes, Brigadier General R. D., 119, 120
Napp, Natalie, 104
National Labor Relations Board, 215
National Recovery Administration, 73, 74, 209
Native American Extras, 188, 189–91, 201
Nazarian, Mike, 109
Negri, Pola, 117–18, 137
Negro Actors Associated, 202
Neilan, Marshall, 186

Newton, "Fig," 128
Nichols, Marion, 223
Night and Day, 198
Nilsson, Anna Q., 181, 182, 185, 191
Niven, David, 150–51
Noah's Ark, 37–38, 40–42
Noison, Pluma, 121
Nolan, Doris, 58
Nolan, Lloyd, 128
Noonan, Tommy, 123
North West Mounted Police, 7
Norton, Barry, 161, 185
Novak, Jane, 169
Novinsky, Alexander, 144
Noyer, Edna Eckert, 121
"Number 1 Boys," 78

Oberle, Florence, 108
Oberon, Merle, 128
O'Brien, Margaret, 127, 222
O'Brien, Pat, 123
Odin, Jack, 20
O'Donnell, Spec, 183
Oie Chan, 195
O'Keefe, Robert, 135, 137
Oland, Warner, 144
Olcott, Sidney, 38, 191
Oliver, Ted, 74
Olson, Nancy, 128
Opel, Richard von, 111
Orlando, Tony, 129
Orth, Paul, 109
Osborne, Marie, 119–20, 183
O'Shea, Pat, 123
Otto, Henry, 181
Owen, Seena, 13
Ownby, Violet, 103

Pagan, The, 193
Paget, Debra, 138
Pandora and the Flying Dutchman, 138
Panter, Dorothy, 119
Paramount Pictures, 181, 200
Parker, Jack, 132
Parnell, 106
Parsons, Louella, 24
Partie d'ecarté, 15
Passage to Marseilles, 4
Passion Play at Oberammergau, 16
Patriot, The, 144
Patten, Thomas, 62
Pay of Extras, 4, 24, 25, 74–77, 105, 106, 211, 217, 218–19, 225
Pembroke, Otto, 229
Perry, Jack, 108
Perry, Stella G. S., 83
Peter the Hermit, 142–43
Peters, House, 185
Phantom of the Opera, The, 37
Phelps, Lee, 209
Philbin, Mary, 46
Philbrick, Howard, 66
Phillips, Dorothy, 119
Pickford, Mary, 14, 15, 34
"Pinkies," 78
Pitts, ZaSu, 53
Plack, Werner, 155
Planet of the Apes, 222, 225
Plastic Age, The, 13
Poliseno, Anthony. *See* Bradley, Paul
Pollard, Harry "Snub," 157, 162, 163, 215
Polo, Eddie, 175, 183
Polonsky, George, 144
Polynesian Extras, 191–92
Poppem Young, Sir and Lady, 19
Porcelli, Fred, 227
"Port of Missing Girls, The," 82
Porter, Katherine Anne, 24–25
Potel, Victor, 164
Poverty Row Bugler, The, 45
Powell, Dick, 123, 126
Powell, William, 123, 135, 143, 145
Power, Tyrone, 123
Prentice, Eva, 179
Pretty, Arline, 183
Preview Murder Mystery, The, 168
Pride of the Yankees, 206
Pringle, Aileen, 180, 191
Prisoner of Zenda, The, 111
Private Worlds, 126
Production Payments, Inc., 81
Professional Sweethearts, 203
Promised Land: Notes for a History, 92
Puailoa, Satini, 131, 191
Purdy, "Old Pop," 20
Purdy, "Pop," 196
Purviance, Edna, 162

Quirk, James R., 85

Rae, Connie, 117
Raft, George, 123, 128, 136, 137
Ralston, Esther, 168, 169
Rambova, Natacha, 45
Ramona, 190
Rand, Ayn, 60, 61
Rappe, Virginia, 55, 94, 95
Rasch, Albertina, 101
Raucourt, Jules, 48
Rawlinson, Herbert, 169, 176, 183, 185
Ray, Charles, 168, 169, 174
Raye, Martha, 121
Real Glory, The, 193
Reap the Wild Wind, 138, 161
Reckless Hollywood, 84
Red Lantern, The, 193
Reed, Carol, 138
Reed, Donna, 138
Reicher, Frank, 161, 173
Reid, Margaret, 97
Reid, Wallace, 200
Rendell, Virginia, 136
Rent-a-Gang, 227
Resmondo, Buster, 223
Resmondo, Hazel, 223
Revueltas, Rosaura, 134
Richardson, Helen, 86
"Richmond Lynch and His Stand-Ins of Hollywood," 135
Ricketts, Thomas, 171
Ridgley, Cleo, 183
Riding Actors, 209
Riffraff, 93–94
Right to Happiness, The, 119
Road to Mandalay, The, 198
Robbins, Jack, 128
Roberts, Marguerite, 168
Robertson, Clifford, 28
Robinson, Ann, 129–30
Robinson, Bill, 201
Robinson, Edward G., 125
Robson, May, 121, 136
Rockne, Rose, 147
Rockwell, Norman, 83
Roderick, Frank, 66
Rogers, Ginger, 119, 131, 136, 138, 147
Rogers, Will, 22, 123
Rollins, David, 13
Romero, Caesar, 123
Rooney, Big Pat, 108
Roosevelt, Buddy, 120
Rose, Blanche, 179
Rosen, Al, 109–10
Ross, Betty, 226
Ross, David, 93
Ross, Shirley, 123
Rossito, Angelo, 223
Royce, Riza, 186
Rudy, Jeanette, 121
Russell, Buckley, 209
Russell, J. B., 209
Russell, Rosalind, 123
Russell Sage Foundation, 62
Russian Extras, 38, 143–45
Ryan, James, 109

Sackville West, Lady, 19
Sage, Sally, 122–23, 131
Salt of the Earth, 133–34
Sam Tang, 195
Sangster, Margaret E., 82
Saratoga, 132–33, 134
Satan Met a Lady, 12
Saunders, Mrs. Bernice, 81
Saunders, Carol Ann, 127
Saunders, Mary Jane, 126
Savitsky, Viacheslav, 144
Sawtelle Veterans Hospital, 23
Sawyer, Frances, 120
Schildkraut, Joseph, 137
Schnell, Ida, 146
Scott, Kenneth, 110
Scott, Randolph, 132
Screen Actors Guild, 66, 79, 113, 115, 132, 138, 181, 191, 205–16, 222, 228, 229
Screen Extras Guild, 80, 138, 154, 156, 157, 201, 202, 215–20, 221, 227
Screen Players Union, 213, 214, 215
Screen Service Bureau, 36
Seabiscuit, 226
Seale, Jean, 103
Sebastian, Dorothy, 161, 181
Selznick, David O., 129
Sennett, Mack, 29–30, 163, 183
Sergeant York, 206
Service Bureau, 62

Sexual Harassment, 11, 28, 83, 84, 85–86, 87, 89, 92–94
Shanks, H. O'Neil, 217
Sharkey, Sailor, 108
Shearer, Norma, 13
Sherrill, Dorothy, 120
Sherwood, George, 25
Short, Antrim, 205
Show of Shows, The, 98
Siegmann, George, 6
Silent Stars as Extras, 156–86
Sills, Milton, 3
Silver Fish Awards, 224
Simmons, Jean, 138
Simon, S. S., 21
Singers Guild, 209
Singin' in the Rain, 103, 154, 163
Skonnikov, General Alexander, 144
Sleers, Larry, 209
Smalley, Phillips, 161, 168, 172–73
Smaney, June, 128
Smith, Al, 66
Smith, C. Aubrey, 119, 120
Smith, Jimmie, 197
Smith, Oscar (Cutie Pie), 200
Smith, Ronald, 127
Snowden, Melba, 124
So Red the Rose, 201
Soap Operas, 226–27
"Society Types," 19, 37, 146
Sodom and Gomorrah: The Story of Hollywood, 89
Song of Love, The, 137
Soo Hoo, Betty, 195
Soo Hoo, Eunice, 195
Souls at Sea, 124
"Soup and Fish," 78
Spark Awards, 224
Spartacus, 225
Splane, Bert, 123
Sportsmen as Extras, 146
St. Albans, Harry, 36
St. John, Al, 163
St. Johns, Adela Rogers, 65, 82, 83
Stader, Paul, 138
Stage Door, 57–59
Stand-In, 117
Stand-Ins, 117–40
Stanley, Kathryn/Kay, 121
Stanwyck, Barbara, 121, 203
Star Is Born, A, 147, 160, 186
Starke, Pauline, 27
Stedman, Myrtle, 167
Steele, Bob, 146
Stenn, David, 92, 93
Stephenson, Henry, 124
Stephenson, Robert Louis, 146
Stevens, Charles, 190
Stevens, Lila, 119
Stewart, Ray, 123
Stock Companies, 14
Stokes, Sylvanus, Jr., 146
Stone, Fred, 124
Stonehouse, Ruth, 13
Storm, Jerome, 174
Stuart, Gloria, 121
"Studio Mothers," 27, 35
Stunt Doubles, 137–40
Suan Yee, 195
Suez, 10, 112
Sullivan, Charlie, 108
Sullivan, Charlotte, 222
Sullivan, Ed, 132
Sul-Te-Wan, Madame, 195–96
Summers, Tommy, 128, 135
Supernumeraries/Supers, 18
Swanson, Gloria, 96, 181
Sweet, Blanche, 118
Swenski, John, 109
Sylvia Scarlet, 11

Talbot, Lyle, 208
Talbot, Slim, 24
Tale of Two Cities, A, 13
Talent & Residuals, 81
Tallon, Gus, 124
Talmadge, Constance, 119, 137
Talmadge, Norma, 13, 137
Talmadge, Richard, 136, 138
Tamiroff, Akim, 124
Tapley, Rose, 160
Tarzan Escapes, 201
Tate, Cullen, 84, 154
Taylor, Beth, 11
Taylor, "Dad," 142
Taylor, Joan, 120
Taylor, Leonard, 123
Tearle, Conway, 166, 168

Teitelbaum, Lily, 156–57
Temple, Shirley, 127
Ten Commandments, The, 39–40
Tennant, Barbara, 157
Tension at Table Rock, 11
Terror of Tiny Town, The, 220–21
Testing of Mildred Vane, The, 29
Thackrey, Winfrid, 58
Thaw, Benjamin, 95
Theby, Rosemary, 160, 166, 169, 181
Theisen, Earl, 164
They Died with Their Boots On, 191
They Shoot Horses, Don't They?, 89–91
Third Man, The, 138
This Is the Life, 132
Thomas, Jameson, 170
Thomas, Kevin, 178
Thompson, Ken, 207
"Three Dollar Stiffs," 78
Thunder Afloat, 113
Tilbury, Zeffie, 136
To Catch a Thief, 138
Tolstoy, Count Ilya, 143
Too Hot to Handle, 201
Tortilla Flat, 146
"Tough Guy" Extras, 108–10, 227
Tours, Lillian, 136
Tovey, Arthur, 128
Tracy, Spencer, 134, 146
Trail of '98, The, 42–43
Trebaol Family, 21–22
"Tripe," 78
Trotsky, Leon, 155
Troupers, the, 45
True, Jimmy, 45
"Truth about Breaking into the Movies, The," 85–86
Turner, Don, 125
Turner, Florence, 157–58
Turner, Lana, 13
Turner, Martin, 198
Twinkletoes, 86
Two Minute Warning, 227

"Uggie," 140
Uncle Tom's Cabin, 196, 197
Unconquered, 138
Universal City, 78

"Vags," 78
Vale, Vola, 160
Valentino, 173
Valentino, Rudolph, 13, 14, 45, 119
Van, Frankie, 125
Van Dalsem, Dutch, 227
Van den Ecker, Lieutenant Louis, 145
Van Dyke, W.S., 8
Van Kleek, Mary, 62
Van Syckle, Dale, 146
Vanderveer, Ellinor, 152
Varela, Trini, 201
Variety Girl, 59
Veher, Lieutenant Nicholas, 144
Vernon, Bobby, 163
Vernon, Jean, 128
Viault, Max-Anne, 146
Vidor, Florence, 13
Vidor, King, 50, 197, 198, 201
Vincent, "Sailor," 108
Viva Villa, 188–89
Vogues of 1938, 103
Voltaire, 10
Vorkapich, Slavko, 48

Wadsworth, Jessie, 104
Wagner, Pauline, 8, 47–48, 96, 138, 207
Wagner, Rob, 5, 25, 187, 196
Wagoner, Kid, 108
Wahlberg, General Robert, 38
Waite, Malcolm, 37
Waldron, Phil, 135, 137
Waln-Morgan Draper, Colonel T., 141–42
Walsh, George, 13, 161
Walthall, Henry B., 166
Wang, James, 193
Wang, Jimmie, 193
Wanger, Walter, 103
War Paint Club, 189
War Veterans, 23, 111
Wardrobe, 36
Warner, H. B., 182
Warner, Jack L., 41, 167
Warner Bros., 167
Warren, Mae, 121
Washburn, Bryant, 161, 168, 169, 175
Waterbury, Ruth, 54, 72, 85–86
Waterer Watered, The, 15
"Weary Annies," 78

Webb, Fay, 47
Weber, Anita, 132
Wedding March, The, 198
Weed, Marion H., 60
Weidler, Virginia, 22, 127
Weidler Family, 22
Welch, Niles, 175
Welles, Orson, 138
West, Mae, 121, 136
Westover, Winifred, 27
What Chance Have I in Hollywood: The Mystery of the Movies, 87–88
White, Walter, 200
White Bird, 189
Whitus, Marjorie, 46
Who's the Man, 228
Wicks, Mrs., 151
Wiener, Julie, 227
Williams, Florence, 60
Williams, Fred, 74
Williams, Horace, 20
Williams, Marjorie, 55, 56, 57, 60
Williams, Zach, 200
Willis, Ouida, 104
Wilson, Ben, 160
Wilson, Harry, 110
Wilson, Harry Leon, 85
Wilson, Lois, 13, 97
Wilson, Ruby, 121
Windsor, Claire, 13
Windsor, Marie, 121
Windsor, Mary, 122
Winning of Barbara Worth, The, 119
Wise, Henry, 123
Withers, Jane, 127
Wizard of Oz, The, 220, 221, 222
Woloshin, Lieutenant Alexander, 144
Woman of Paris, A, 153
Wong, Anna May, 194, 195
Wong, James, 195
Wong, Victor, 195
Wong Chung, 195
Wood, Sally, 132
Woods, Donald, 125
Workers Leaving the Lumière Factory, 15
World and the Flesh, The, 144
Wormser, Margaret, 135, 137
Wray, Fay, 138
Wyatt, Ginger, 93
Wyler, William, 122
Wyman, Jane, 135
Wyman, O. C., 67, 70

Yamaoka, Iris, 195
Yamaoka, Josephine, 195
Yamaoka, Otto, 195
Yates, Phyllis, 123
Young, Clara Kimball, 155, 174, 176
Young, Loretta, 135, 136
Young, Olive, 195
Young Frankenstein, 224
Yuen Tsung Sze, 195
YWCA, 52, 55, 56, 61

Zetter, Gwen, 152
Zimina, Valentina, 30
Zimmer, Norma, 163
"Zombres," 203